AUTHENTIC
Sardinia

TOURING CLUB
OF ITALY

Touring Club Italiano
President and Chairman: *Roberto Ruozi*
General Manager: *Guido Venturini*

Touring Editore
Managing Director: *Alfieri Lorenzon*
Editorial Director: *Michele D'Innella*

International Department
Fabio Pittella
fabio.pittella@touringclub.it

Senior Editor: *Paola Pandiani*
Editor: *Monica Maraschi*
Writer and Researcher: *Vittoria Majocchi,*
with Banca Dati Turistica for Practical info
Translation: *Timothy Dass, Judith Mundell,*
Elisabeth Poore, Studio Queens
Maps: *Touring Club Italiano*
Design and layout: *Studio Gatelli, Milano*
Cover photo: *The 17th-century Chia tower,*
gulf of Cagliari (P. Sanna)

Advertising Manager: *Claudio Bettinelli*
Local Advertising: *Progetto*
www.progettosrl.it - info@progettosrl.it

Typesetting and Color Separations:
Emmegi Multimedia, Milano
Printing and Binding: *CPM, Casarile*

Distribution
USA/CAN – *Publishers Group West*
UK/Ireland – *Portfolio Books*

Touring Club Italiano, corso Italia 10, 20122 Milano
www.touringclub.it
© 2006 Touring Editore, Milan

Code K8P
ISBN-13: 978 – 88365 – 3768 – 6
ISBN-10: 88 – 365 – 3768 – 5

Printed in January 2006

SUMMARY

WHAT IS THE TOURING CLUB OF ITALY?

Long Tradition, Great Prestige

For over 110 years, the Touring Club of Italy (TCI) has offered travelers the most detailed and comprehensive source of travel information available on Italy. The Touring Club of Italy was founded in 1894 with the aim of developing the social and cultural values of tourism and promoting the conservation and enjoyment of the country's national heritage, landscape and environment.

Advantages of Membership

Today, TCI offers a wide rage of travel services to assist and support members with the highest level of convenience and quality. Now you can discover the unique charms of Italy with a distinct insider's advantage.

Enjoy exclusive money saving offers with a TCI membership. Use your membership card for discounts in thousands of restaurants, hotels, spas, campgrounds, museums, shops and markets.

These Hotel Chains offer preferred rates and discounts to TCI members!

How to Join

It's quick and easy to join.
Apply for your membership online at
www.touringclub.it
Your membership card will arrive within
three weeks and is valid for discounts
across Italy for the entire year.
Get your card before you go and start
saving as soon as you arrive.
Euro 25 annual membership fee
includes priority mail postage for
membership card and materials.
Just one use of the card will more than
cover the cost of membership.

Benefits

• Exclusive car rental rates with Hertz
• Discounts at select Esso gas stations
• 20% discount on TCI guidebooks
and maps purchased in TCI bookstores
or directly online at
www.touringclub.com
• Preferred rates and discounts available
at thousands of locations in Italy: Hotels -
B&B's - Villa Rentals - Campgrounds -TCI
Resorts - Spas - Restaurants - Wineries -
Museums - Cinemas - Theaters - Music
Festivals - Shops - Craft Markets - Ferries -
Cruises - Theme Parks - Botanical Gardens

VILLAGGIO VACANZE TCI

At Punta Cannone, 5 km north of La Maddalena
tel. +39 02 8526746 (for information
and reservations), www.touringclub.it
★ Special TCI Rates

The photo shows the splendid setting of the
Touring Club of Italy's Holiday Village, open
from May till September, in the Arcipelago
della Maddalena. Situated on a quiet bay
in an idyllic setting of stunning natural
landscape, this green corner off north-east
Sardinia, with its beaches of golden sand
and crystal-clear water, is the perfect place
for a truly relaxing holiday.

ITALY: INSTRUCTIONS FOR USE

Italy is known throughout the world for the quantity and quality of its art treasures and for its natural beauty, but it is also famous for its inimitable lifestyle and fabulous cuisine and wines. Although it is a relatively small country, Italy boasts an extremely varied culture and multifarious traditions and customs. The information and suggestions in this brief section will help foreign tourists not only to understand certain aspects of Italian life, but also to solve the everyday difficulties and the problems of a practical nature that inevitably crop up during any trip.

This practical information is included in brief descriptions of various topics: public transport and how to purchase tickets; suggestions on how to drive in this country; the different types of rooms and accommodation in hotels; hints on how to use mobile phones and communication in general. This is followed by useful advice on how to meet your everyday needs and on shopping, as well as information concerning the cultural differences in the various regions. Lastly, there is a section describing the vast range of restaurants, bars, wine bars and pizza parlors.

TRANSPORTATION

From the airport to the city
Public transportation in major cities is easily accessible and simple to use. Both Malpensa Airport in Milan and Fiumicino Airport in Rome have trains and buses linking them to the city centers. At Malpensa, you can take a bus to the main train station or a train to Cadorna train station and subway stop.

Subways, buses, and trams
Access to the subways, buses, and trams requires a ticket (tickets are not sold on board but can be purchased at most newsstands and tobacco shops). The ticket is good for one ride and sometimes has a time limit (in the case of buses and trams). When you board a bus or tram, you are required to stamp your previously-acquired ticket in the time-stamping machine. Occasionally, a conductor will board the bus or tram and check everyone's ticket. If you haven't got one, or if it has not been time-stamped, you will have to pay a steep fine.

Trains
The Ferrovie dello Stato (Italian Railways) is among the best and most modern railway systems in Europe. Timetables and routes can be consulted and reservations can be made online at www.trenitalia.com. Many travel agents can also dispense tickets and help you plan your journey. Hard-copy schedules can be purchased at all newsstands and most bookstores.

Automated ticket machines, which include easy-to-use instructions in English, are available in nearly all stations. They can be used to check schedules, makes reservations, and purchase tickets.
There are different types of train, according to the requirements:
Eurostar Italia Trains *ES★* : Fast connections between Italy's most important cities. The ticket includes seat booking charge;
Intercity *IC* and **Espresso** *E* Trains: Local connections among Italy's towns and cities. Sometimes *IC* and *E* trains require seat booking. You can book your seat up to 3 hours before the train departure. The seat booking charge is of 3 euro.
Interregionale Trains *iR* move beyond regional boundaries. Among the combined local-transport services, the *iR* Trains are the fastest ones with the fewest number of stops. No seat booking available.
Diretto *D* and **Regionale** *R* Trains can circulate both within the regions and their bordering regions. No seat booking available.

DO NOT FORGET: You can only board trains in Italy with a valid ticket, which must be time-stamped before boarding; there are numerous time-stamping machines in every station. You cannot buy or stamp tickets on board.

If you don't have a ticket - or did not stamp before boarding - you will be liable to pay the full ticket price plus a 25 euro fine. If you produce a ticket that is not valid for the train or service you're using (i.e. one issued for a different train category at a different price, etc.) you will be asked to pay the difference with respect to the full ticket price, plus an 8 euro surcharge.

Taxis

Taxis are a convenient but expensive way to travel in Italian cities. There are taxi stands scattered throughout major cities. You cannot hail taxis on the street in Italy, but you can reserve taxis, in advance or immediately, by phone: consult the yellow pages for the number or ask your hotel reception desk or maitre d'hotel to call for you.

Taxi drivers have the right to charge you a supplementary fee for every piece of luggage they transport, as well as evening surcharges.

Driving

Especially when staying in the countryside, driving is a safe and convenient way to travel through Italy and its major cities. And while it is best avoided for obvious reasons, driving in the cities is not as difficult as it may seem or may have been reported to be. It is important to be aware of street signs and speed limits, and many cities have zones where only limited traffic is allowed in order to accommodate pedestrians. Although an international driver's license is not required in Italy, it is advisable. ACI and similar associations provide this service to members.

The fuel distribution network is reasonably distributed all over the territory. All service stations have unleaded gasoline ("benzina verde") and diesel fuel ("gasolio"). Opening time is 7am to12:30 and 15 to 19:30; on motorways the service is 24 hours a day.

Type of roads in Italy: The *Autostrada* (for example A14) is the main highway system in Italy and is similar to the Interstate highway system in the US and the motorway system in the UK. Shown on our Touring Club Italiano 1:200,000 road maps as black. The Autostrada are toll highways; you pay to use them. The *Strada Statale* (for example SS54) is a fast moving road that may have one or more lanes in each direction. Shown on our Touring Club Italiano 1:200,000 road maps as red. *Strada Provinciale* (for example SP358) can be narrow, slow and winding roads. They are usually one lane in each direction. Shown on our Touring Club Italiano 1:200,000 road maps as yellow. *Strada Comunale* (for example SC652) is a local road connecting the main town with its sorrounding. Note: In our guide you will sometime find an address of a place in the countryside listed, for example, as "SS54 Km 25". This means that the you have to drive along the Strada Statale 54 until you reach the 25-km road sign.
Speed limits: 130 kmph on the

Autostrada, 110 kmph on main highways, 90 kmph outside of towns, 50 kmph in towns.

The town streets are patrolled by the Polizia Municipale while the roads outside cities and the Autostrada are patrolled by the Carabinieri or the Polizia Stradale. They may set up road blocks where they may ask you to stop by holding out a small red sign.

Do not forget:

- Wear your seat belt at all times;
- Do not use the cellular phone while driving;
- Have your headlights on at all times when driving outside of cities;
- The drunk driving laws are strict - do not drink and drive;
- In case of an accident you are not allowed to get out of your car unless you are wearing a special, high-visibility, reflective jacket.

ACCOMMODATION

Hotels

In Italy it is common practice for the reception desk to register your passport, and only registered guests are allowed to use the rooms. This is mere routine, done for security reasons, and there is no need for concern.

All hotels use the official star classification system, from 5-star luxury hotel to 1 star accommodation.

Room rates are based on whether they are for single ("camera singola") or double ("camera doppia") occupancy. In every room you will find a list of the hotel rates (generally on the back of the door). While 4- and 5-star hotels have double beds, most hotels have only single beds. Should you want a double bed, you have to ask for a "letto matrimoniale". All hotels have rooms with bathrooms; only 1-star establishments usually have only shared bathrooms.

Most hotel rates include breakfast ("prima colazione"), but you can request to do without it, thus reducing the rate. Breakfast is generally served in a communal room and comprises a buffet with pastries, bread with butter and jam, cold cereals, fruit, yoghurt, coffee, and fruit juice. Some hotels regularly frequented by foreign tourists will also serve other items such as eggs for their American and British guests.

The hotels for families and in tourist localities also offer "mezza pensione", or half board, in which breakfast and dinner are included in the price.

It's always a good idea to check when a hotel's annual closing period is, especially if you are planning a holiday by the sea.

Farm stays

Located only in the countryside, and generally on a farm, "agriturismo" – a network of farm holiday establishments – is part of a growing trend in Italy to honor local gastronomic and wine traditions, as well as countryside traditions. These farms offer meals prepared with ingredients cultivated exclusively on site: garden-grown vegetables, homemade cheese and local recipes. Many of these places also provide lodging, one of the best ways to experience the "genuine" Italian lifestyle.

Bed & Breakfast

This form of accommodation provides bed and breakfast in a private house, and in the last few years has become much more widespread in Italy. There are over 5,000 b&bs, classified in 3 categories, and situated both in historic town centers, as well as in the outskirts and the countryside. Rooms for guests are always well-furnished, but not all of them have en suite bathrooms.

It is well-recommended to check the closing of the open-all-year accommodation services and restaurants, because they could have a short break during the year (usually no longer than a fortnight).

COMMUNICATIONS

Nearly everyone in Italy owns a cellular phone. Although public phones are still available, they seem to be ever fewer and farther between. If you wish to use public phones, you will find them in subway stops, bars, along the street, and phone centers generally located in the city center. Phone cards and pre-paid phone cards can be purchased at most newsstands and tobacco shops, and can also be acquired at automated tellers. For European travelers, activating personal cellular coverage is relatively simple, as it is in most cases for American and Australian travelers as well. Contact your mobile service provider for details. Cellular phones can also be rented in Italy from TIM, the Italian national phone company. For information, visit its website at www.tim.it. When traveling by car through the countryside, a cellular phone can really come in handy.

Note that when dialing in Italy, you must always dial the prefix (e.g., 02 for Milan, 06 for Rome) even when making a local call. For cellular phones, however, the initial zero is always dropped.

Freephone numbers always start with "800". For calls abroad from Italy, it's a good idea to buy a special pre-paid international phone card, which is used with a PIN code.

Internet access

Cyber cafés have sprung up all over Italy and today you can find one on nearly every city block. The Italian national phone company, TIM, has also begun providing internet access at many of its public phone centers.

EATING AND DRINKING

The bar

The Italian "bar" is a multi-faceted, all-purpose establishment for drinking, eating and socializing, where you can order an espresso, have breakfast, and enjoy a quick sandwich for lunch or even a hot meal. You can often buy various items here (sometimes even stamps, cigarettes, phone cards, etc.). Bear in mind that table service ("servizio a tavola") includes a surcharge. At most bars, if you choose to sit, a waiter will take your order. Every bar should have a list of prices posted behind or near the counter; if the bar offers table service, the price list should also include the extra fee for this.

Lunch at bars will include, but is not limited to, "panini," sandwiches with crusty bread, usually with cured meats such as "prosciutto" (salt-cured ham), "prosciutto cotto" (cooked ham), and cheeses such as mozzarella topped with tomato and basil. Then there are "tramezzini" (finger sandwiches) with tuna, cheese, or vegetables, etc. Often the "panini" and other savory sandwiches (like stuffed flatbread or "focaccia") are heated before being served. Naturally, the menu at bars varies according to the region: in Bologna you will find "piadine" (flatbread similar to pita) with Swiss chard; in Palermo there are "arancini" (fried rice balls stuffed

with ground meat); in Genoa you will find that even the most unassuming bar serves some of the best "focaccia" in all Italy. Some bars also include a "tavola calda". If you see this sign in a bar window, it means that hot dishes like pasta and even entrées are served.

A brief comment on coffee and cappuccino: Italians never serve coffee with savory dishes or sandwiches, and they seldom drink cappuccino outside of breakfast (although they are happy to serve it at any time).

While English- and Irish-type pubs are frequented by beer lovers and young people in Italy, there are also American bars where long drinks and American cocktails are served.

Breakfast at the bar

Breakfast in Italy generally consists of some type of pastry, most commonly a "brioche" – a croissant either filled with cream or jam, or plain – and a cappuccino or espresso. Although most bars do not offer American coffee, you can ask for a "caffè lungo" or "caffè americano", both of which resemble the American coffee preferred by the British and Americans. Most bars have a juicer to make a "spremuta", freshly squeezed orange or grapefruit juice.

Lunch and Dinner

As with all daily rituals in Italy, food is prepared and meals are served according to local customs (e.g., in the North they prefer rice and butter, in South and Central Italy they favor pasta and olive oil).

Wine is generally served at mealtime, and while finer restaurants have excellent wine lists (some including vintage wines), ordering the house table wine generally brings good results (a house Chianti to accompany your Florentine steak in Tuscany, a sparkling

Prosecco paired with your creamed stockfish and polenta in Venice, a dry white wine with pasta dressed with sardines and wild fennel fronds in Sicily). Mineral water is also commonly served at meals and can be "gassata" (sparkling) or "naturale" (still).

The most sublime culinary experience in Italy is achieved by matching the local foods with the appropriate local wines: wisdom dictates that a friendly waiter will be flattered by your request for his recommendation on what to eat and drink. Whether at an "osteria" (a tavern), a "trattoria" (a home-style restaurant), or a "ristorante" (a proper restaurant), the service of lunch and dinner generally consists of – but is not limited to – the following: "antipasti" or appetizers; "primo piatto" or first course, i.e., pasta, rice, or soup; "secondo piatto" or main course, i.e., meat or seafood; "contorno" or side-dish, served with the main course, i.e., vegetables or salad; "formaggi", "frutta", and "dolci", i.e., cheeses, fruit, and dessert; caffè or espresso coffee, perhaps spiked with a shot of grappa.

The pizzeria

The pizzeria is in general one of the most economical, democratic, and satisfying culinary experiences in Italy. Everyone eats at the pizzeria: young people, families, couples, locals and tourists alike. Generally, each person orders her/his own pizza, and while the styles of crust and toppings will vary from region to region (some of the best pizzas are served in Naples and Rome), the acid test of any pizzeria is the Margherita, topped simply with cheese and tomato sauce. Beer, sparkling or still water, and Coca Cola are the beverages commonly served with pizza. Some restaurants include a pizza menu, but most establishments do not serve pizza at lunchtime.

The wine bar (enoteca)

More than one English-speaking tourist in Italy has wondered why the wine bar is called an enoteca in other countries and the English term is used in Italy: the answer lies somewhere in the mutual fondness that Italians and English speakers have for one another. Wine bars have become popular in recent years in the major cities (especially in Rome, where you can find some of the best). The wine bar is a great place to sample different local wines and eat a light, tapas-style dinner.

CULTURAL DIVERSITY

Whenever you travel, not only are you a guest of your host country, but you are also a representative of your home country. As a general rule, courtesy, consideration, and respect are always appreciated by guests and their hosts alike. Italians are famous for their hospitality and experience will verify this felicitous stereotype: perhaps nowhere else in Europe are tourists and visitors received more warmly. Italy is a relatively "new" country. Its borders, as we know them today, were established only in 1861 when it became a monarchy under the House of Savoy. After WWII, Italy became a Republic and now it is one of the member states of the European Union. One of the most fascinating aspects of Italian culture is that, even as a unified country, local tradition still prevails over a universally Italian national identity. Some jokingly say that the only time that Venetians, Milanese, Florentines, Neapolitans, and Sicilians feel like Italians is when the national football team plays in international competitions. From their highly localized dialects to the foods they eat, from their religious celebration to their politics, Italians proudly maintain their local heritage. This is one of the reasons why the Piedmontese continue to prefer their beloved Barolo wine and their white truffles, the Umbrians their rich Sagrantino wine and black truffles, the Milanese their risotto and panettone, the Venetians their stockfish and polenta, the Bolognese their lasagne and pumpkin ravioli, the Florentines their bread soups and steaks cooked rare, the Abruzzese their excellent fish broth and seafood, the Neapolitans their mozzarella, basil, pizza, and pasta. As a result of its rich cultural diversity, the country's population also varies greatly in its customs from region to region, city to city, town to town. As you visit different cities and regions throughout Italy, you will see how the local personality and character of the Italians change as rapidly as the landscape does. Having lived for millennia with their great diversity and rich, highly heterogeneous culture, the Italians have taught us many things, foremost among them the age-old expression, "When in Rome, do as the Romans do."

NATIONAL HOLIDAYS

New Year's Day (1st January), Epiphany (6th January), Easter Monday (day after Easter Sunday), Liberation Day (25th April), Labour Day (1st May), Italian Republic Day (2nd June), Assumption (15th August), All Saints' Day (1st November), Immaculate Conception (8th December), Christmas Day and Boxing Day (25th-26th December).
In addition to these holidays, each city also has a holiday to celebrate its patron saint's feast day, usually with lively, local celebrations. Shops and services in large cities close on national holidays and for the week of the 15th of August.

EVERYDAY NEEDS

State tobacco shops and pharmacies
Tobacco is available in Italy only at state licensed tobacco shops. These vendors ("tabaccheria"), often incorporated in a bar, also sell stamps.
Since 11 January 2005 smoking is forbidden in all so-called public places - unless a separately ventilated space is constructed - meaning over 90% of the country's restaurants and bars.
Medicines can be purchased only in pharmacies ("farmacia") in Italy. Pharmacists are very knowledgeable about common ailments and can generally prescribe a treatment for you on the spot. Opening time is 8:30-12:30 and 15:30-19:30 but in any case there is always a pharmacy open 24 hours and during holidays.

Shopping
Every locality in Italy offers tourists characteristic shops, markets with good bargains, and even boutiques featuring leading Italian fashion designers. Opening hours vary from region to region and from season to season. In general, shops are open from 9 to 13 and from 15/16 to 19/20, but in large cities they usually have no lunchtime break.

Tax Free
Non-EU citizens can obtain a reimbursement for IVA (goods and services tax) paid on purchases over €155, for goods which are exported within 90 days, in shops which display the relevant sign. IVA is always automatically included in the price of any purchase, and ranges from 20% to 4% depending on the item. The shop issues a reimbursement voucher to present when you leave the country (at a frontier or airport). For purchases in shops affiliated to 'Tax Free Shopping', IVA may be reimbursed directly at international airports.

Banks and post offices
Italian banks are open Monday to Friday, from 8:30 to 13:30 and then from 15 to 16. However, the afternoon business hours may vary.
Post offices are open from Monday to Saturday, from 8:30 to 13:30 (12:30 on Saturday). In the larger towns there are also some offices open in the afternoon.

Currency
Effective 1 January 2002, the currency used in many European Union countries is the euro. Coins are in denominations of 1, 2, 5, 10, 20 and 50 cents and 1 and 2 euros; banknotes are in denominations of 5, 10, 20, 50, 100, 200 and 500 euros, each with a different color.

Credit cards
All the main credit cards are generally accepted, but some smaller enterprises (arts and crafts shops, small hotels, bed & breakfasts, or farm stays) do not provide this service. Foreign tourists can obtain cash using credit cards at automatic teller machines.

Time
All Italy is in the same time zone, which is six hours ahead of Eastern Standard Time in the USA. Daylight saving time is used from March to October, when watches and clocks are set an hour ahead of standard time.

Passports and vaccinations
Citizens of EU countries can enter Italy without frontier checks. Citizens of Australia, Canada, New Zealand, and the United States can enter Italy with a valid passport and need not have a visa for a stay of less than 90 days.
No vaccinations are necessary.

Payment and tipping
When you sit down at a restaurant you are generally charged a "coperto" or cover charge ranging from 1.5 to 3 euros, for service and the bread. Tipping is not customary in Italy. Beware of unscrupulous restaurateurs who add a space on their clients' credit card receipt for a tip, while it has already been included in the cover charge.

Foreign Embassies in Italy

Australia
Via A. Bosio, 5 - 00161 Rome
Tel. +39 06 852721
Fax +39 06 85272300
www.italy.embassy.gov.au.
info-rome@dfat.gov.au

Canada
Via G.B. de Rossi, 27 - 00161 Rome
Tel. +39 06 445981
Fax +39 06 445983760
www.canada.it
rome@dfait-maeci.gc.ca

Great Britain
Via XX Settembre, 80/a - 00187
Rome
Tel. +39 06 42200001
Fax +39 06 42202334
www.britian.it
consularenquiries@rome.
mail.fco.gov.uk

Ireland
Piazza di Campitelli, 3 - 00186
Rome
Tel. +39 06 6979121
Fax +39 06 6792354
irish.embassy@esteri.it

New Zealand
Via Zara, 28 - 00198 Rome
Tel. +39 06 4417171
Fax +39 06 4402984
nzemb.rom@flashnet.it

South Africa
Via Tanaro, 14 - 00198 Rome
Tel. +39 06 852541
Fax +39 06 85254300
www.sudafrica.it
sae@flashnet.it

United States of America
Via Vittorio Veneto, 121 - 00187
Rome
Tel. +39 06 46741
Fax +39 06 4882672
www.usis.it

Foreign Consulates in Italy

Australia
2 Via Borgogna
20122 Milan
Tel. +39 02 77704217
Fax +39 02 77704242

Canada
Via Vittor Pisani, 19
20124 Milan
Tel. +39 02 67581
Fax +39 02 67583900
milan@international.gc.ca

Great Britain
via S. Paolo 7
20121 Milan
Tel. +39 02 723001
Fax +39 02 86465081
ConsularMilan@fco.gov.uk

Lungarno Corsini 2
50123 Florence
Tel. +39 055 284133
Consular.Florence@fco.gov.uk

Via dei Mille 40
80121 Naples
Tel. +39 081 4238911

Fax +39 081 422434
Info.Naples@fco.gov.uk

Ireland
Piazza San Pietro in Gessate 2 -
20122 Milan
Tel. +39 02 55187569/02 55187641
Fax +39 02 55187570

New Zealand
Via Guido d'Arezzo 6,
20145 Milan
Tel. +39 02 48012544
Fax +39 02 48012577

South Africa
Vicolo San Giovanni Sul Muro 4
20121 Milan
Tel. +39 02 8858581
Fax +39 02 72011063
saconsulate@iol.it

United States of America
Via Principe Amedeo, 2/10
20121 Milan
Tel. +39 02 290351
Fax +39 02 29001165

Lungarno Vespucci, 38
50123 Florence
Tel. +39 055 266951
Fax +39 055 284088

Piazza della Repubblica
80122 Naples
Tel. +39 081 5838111
Fax +39 081 7611869

Italian Embassies and Consulates Around the World

Australia
12, Grey Street - Deakin, A.C.T.
2600 - Canberra
Tel. 02 62733333, 62733398,
62733198
Fax 02 62734223
www.ambitalia.org.au
embassy@ambitalia.org.au
Consulates at: Brisbane, Glynde,
Melbourne, Perth , Sydney

Canada
275, Slater Street, 21st floor -
Ottawa (Ontario) K1P 5H9
Tel. (613) 232 2401/2/3
Fax (613) 233 1484 234 8424
www.italyincanada.com
ambital@italyincanada.com
Consulates at: Edmonton,
Montreal, Toronto, Vancouver,

Great Britain
14, Three Kings Yard, London
W1K 4EH
Tel. 020 73122200
Fax 020 73122230
www.embitaly.org.uk
ambasciata.londra@esteri.it
Consulates at: London, Bedford,
Edinburgh, Manchester

Ireland
63/65, Northumberland Road -
Dublin 4
Tel. 01 6601744
Fax 01 6682759
www.italianembassy.ie
info@italianembassy.ie

New Zealand
34-38 Grant Road, Thorndon,

(PO Box 463, Wellington)
Tel. 04 473 5339
Fax 04 472 7255
www.italy-embassy.org.nz
ambwell@xtra.co.nz

South Africa
796 George Avenue, 0083 Arcadia
Tel. 012 4305541/2/3
Fax 012 4305547
www.ambital.org.za
ambital@iafrica.com
Consulates at: Johannesburg,
Capetown, Durban

United States of America
3000 Whitehaven Street, NW
Washington DC 20008
Tel. (202) 612-4400
Fax (202) 518-2154
www.italyemb.org
stampa@itwash.org
Consulates at: Boston, MA -
Chicago, IL - Detroit, MI - Houston,
TX - Los Angeles, CA - Miami, FL -
Newark, NJ - New York, NY -
Philadelphia, PA - San Francisco, CA

ENIT (Italian State Tourist Board)

Australia
Level 4, 46 Market Street
NSW 2000 Sidney
PO Box Q802 - QVB NSW 1230
Tel. 00612 92 621666
Fax 00612 92 621677
italia@italiantourism.com.au

Canada
175 Bloor Street E. Suite 907 –
South Tower
M4W3R8 Toronto (Ontario)
Tel. (416) 925 4882
Fax (416) 925 4799
www.italiantourism.com
enit.canada@on.aibn.com

Great Britain
1, Princes Street
W1B 2AY London
Tel. 020 7408 1254
Tel. 800 00482542 FREE from
United Kingdom and Ireland
italy@italiantouristboard.co.uk

United States of America
500, North Michigan Avenue
Suite 2240
60611 Chicago 1, Illinois
Tel. (312) 644 0996 / 644 0990
Fax (312) 644 3019
www.italiantourism.com
enitch@italiantourism.com

12400, Wilshire Blvd. – Suite 550
CA 90025 Los Angeles
Tel. (310) 820 1898 - 820 9807
Fax (310) 820 6357
www.italiantourism.com
enitla@italiantourism.com

630, Fifth Avenue – Suite 1565
NY – 10111 New York
Tel. (212) 245 4822 – 245 5618
Fax (212) 586 9249
www.italiantourism.com
enitny@italiantourism.com

An ancient land with an ancient language, Sardinia is a uniquely fascinating place, forged by many centuries of culture and history, in its strategic position at the center of the Mediterranean. Its awe-inspiring treasures of the past, such as the Nuraghic bronzes in Cagliari and the Megalithic tombs of the giants, can be admired in the island's many museums, or in its archeological areas, some dating back as far as the 7th century BC.

And standing silently ever-present across the island, the enigmatic nuraghs: these round fortresses built in pre-historic times still survive as powerful symbols of the tenacity of Sardinia and its people. All this combines with the breathtakingly beautiful and varied natural environment to create a truly special place.

Highlights

- The mystery of the nuraghs and the village of Su Nuraxi at Barùmini
- Tomb of the giants, Lu Coddhu 'Ecchju
- Superb ancient objects on display at the Museo Nazionale Sanna in Sassari

Bold, stars and italics are used in the text to emphasize the importance of places and works of art:

bold type ** → **not to be missed**
bold type * → **very important**
bold type → **important**
italic type → **interesting**

The city of Cagliari is Sardinia's main port and one of the island's "gateways"; it lies, among salt-pans and lagoons teaming with fish, in the middle of the large southern bay that stretches between Capo Spartivento and Capo Carbonara. The history of the city is contained in the meaning of the ancient place-name Càralis (or Kàralis), "bare and lonely stony ground", later changed into the plural Carales, probably to describe an inhabited area made up of various quarters. Phoenicians from Tyre and Carthaginians settled here before the Roman occupation of 238 BC. No remains survive of Carthaginian structures, but there are Roman ruins: tombs, villas, and an amphitheater. The city came under the Vandals from 455 to 533, and was then Byzantine for a long period; the central part of the basilica of S. Saturno (St Saturn) dates from that time. On top of the hill stood the Castello (Castle) which the medieval quarter is named after. Three gates are defended by three towers: S. Pancrazio (St Pancras), l'Elefante (Elefant) and Leoni (Lions). They, together with the cathedral, were built when Sardinia was ruled by the Pisans, who left their mark on the Castello quarter. The area lies north to south and is crossed by three main roads: Via Lamarmora, Via Canelles and Via dei Genovesi. Pope Boniface VIII subjected the whole of Sardinia to the King of Aragon, and the Aragonese took over the Castle in 1326. This was the start of four centuries of Spanish rule, which again influenced the

city's appearance and buildings. Next to the medieval quarters of Castello and Marina, the Villanova and Stampace quarters developed to the west and east. The Catalan Gothic church of Bonaria and the cloister of San Domenico (St Dominic) are the most important Aragonese monuments; the Renaissance church of S. Agostino (St Augustine) and the Baroque church of S. Michele (St Michael) were built later under the Spanish. In 1720, when Cagliari came under the rule of Piedmont, there were no significant changes. Under the city's first urban development plan in 1858, the walls were demolished and the three main roads were built: Via Roma, Largo Carlo Felice and Viale Regina Margherita. After the second world war, urban growth and industrial development meant that Cagliari spread further out into flat areas, spoiling some of its most attractive natural surroundings.

Our itinerary follows the topography of the city: firstly the Castello, from the Bastione di Saint Remy to the Cittadella dei Musei, and then the lower part of the town, for all the remaining monuments.

View of the Bastione di Saint Remy

Bastione di Saint Remy ❶

The Bastion was built between 1899 and 1902, altering the old Spanish bastions (Sperone and Zecca) at the southern edge of the Castle. It consists of two terraces: the largest, named after Umberto I, and the other, smaller and higher, dedicated to St Catherine. The Bastion links the Castle to the Villanova quarter; originally it was a promenade

and belvedere, enhanced by the impressive neo-Classical facade in granite and limestone, with triumphal arch and long flight of steps leading towards Piazza Costituzione. It was seriously damaged by bombing in the second world war, and has been faithfully reconstructed. Today, no longer used as a promenade, it is the location for the Sunday second-hand market.

The port of Cagliari. Its strategic position in the center of the Mediterranean means that since ancient times it has been a crossroads for trade

Le torri di S. Pancrazio ② e dell'Elefante ③

The two twin towers of St Pancras and the Elephant, in limestone ashlar, were built respectively in 1305 and 1307, and are landmarks that really stand out on Cagliari's landscape. The torre di S. Pancrazio (tower of St Pancras) on the northern side of the Castle, at its highest point, gave control of all the territory around the city; it was used as a prison from the 17th century to the end of the 19th century. The torre dell'Elefante (Elephant tower) marked entry to the lower part of the quarter; an elephant sculpted on the tower has become a symbol of the city.

CAGLIARI
IN OTHER COLORS...

BEACHES: page 74
ITINERARIES: page 98
FOOD: page 112, 119, 121, 124, 130
SHOPPING: page 138, 140
EVENTS: page 144, 148
WELLNESS: page 155, 156
PRACTICAL INFO: page 165

Cattedrale di S. Maria ④

The Cathedral of St Mary was built in Pisan style (along the Romanesque lines which developed in Pisa between the 11th and 12th centuries); it was extended at the end of the 13th century, and then modified to Baroque style in the 17th to 18th centuries. In 1933 a new facade was built, where sculptural work from the original church was recycled. The beautiful transept portals (there is a Roman sarcophagus front above the right portal) and the bell-tower also survive from the original building. **Inside**, on the counter-facade, there are two **pulpits***, originally part of a single ambo (raised platform in the presbytery, for giving readings from the Bible); they were created by Gugliemo da Pisa in 1159-62, for Pisa cathedral, and donated to Cagliari in 1312. The second chapel on the right has a statue of the Madonna Nera (Black Madonna), in gilded wood (14th century). In the right transept, there is a Gothic chapel built under the Aragonese. In the left transept, a small chapel dating from the original Pisan cathedral, and at the back, the magnificent mausoleum of Martin II of Aragon (1676).

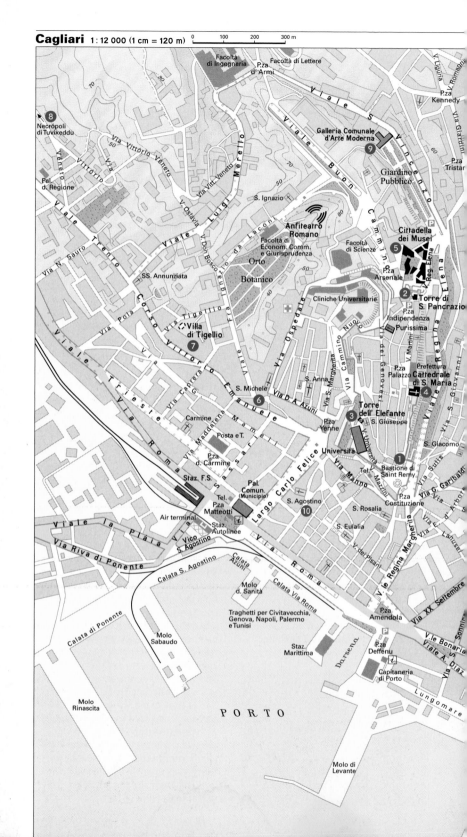

Cagliari 1 : 12 000 (1 cm = 120 m)

0   100   200   300 m

PORTO

18

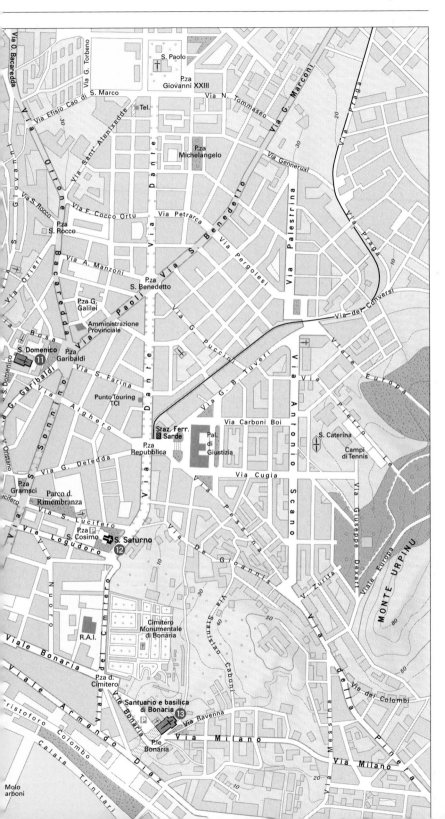

Cittadella dei Musei ⑤

This modern complex of museums has a great view and occupies a vast area which was used as a military arsenal until 1825; what remains of Pisan, Aragonese, Spanish and Savoy fortifications can be seen here. The museums are: the Museo Archeologico Nazionale (National Archeological Museum), the Pinacoteca Nazionale (National Art Gallery), the Museo d'Arte Siamese (Museum of Siamese Art) and the Raccolta delle Cere Anatomiche (Collection of Anatomic Waxes).

Museo Archeologico Nazionale

In 1993 the National Archeological Museum was moved from its historic site in Piazza Indipendenza, where it had been since 1905. The museum clearly shows the history of Sardinia, from before the development of the Nuraghic Civilisation, with finds from the Su Carroppu cave (5th millennium BC), ranging up to early Christian times, with finds from Corpus and S. Lussorio di Fordongianus. Objects are exhibited which date from pre-historic times, from the Copper and Iron Ages, from Phoenician-Carthaginian and Carthaginian-Roman times, and from Greco-Roman and Roman-Christian times. There is a very important collection of small Nuraghic **bronzes*** (9th-8th century BC), in the form of votive incense-boats, warriors, workers and priests, which provide valuable information about the social and religious life of the proto-Sardinians. There is also Phoenician material, such as a sacrificial altar and steles, from the Tharros Tophet (Phoenician-Carthaginian sanctuary).

Pinacoteca Nazionale

The National Art Gallery, on three floors, follows the history of Sardinian painting and the spread of the Catalan-Valencian school in the 15th and 16th centuries. The top floor contains 15th- and 16th-century retablos from Sardinian churches. Retablos (from the Latin retro tabula, meaning "behind the altar") are typical of 15th-century Sardinian art. They are large wooden structures, placed behind the altar, which were made by assembling various component parts in wood (panels, frames).

The oldest were made by Catalan artists who came to Sardinia during the Aragonese occupation; 16th-century retablos are by Sardinian artists, such as Michele Cavaro, with the Triptych of the Consolation and Pietro Cavaro, with his St Augustine in Meditation. The middle floor has 17th- and 18th-century paintings. On the lower floor, a varied collection ranges from 15th-century Flemish paintings to works by contemporary Sardinian artists.

Museo d'Arte Siamese "Stefano Cardu"

The Museum of Siamese Art is a municipal museum, with a collection of around 1300 pieces, including porcelain, arms, coins, and gold, silver and ivory objects, from Asia.

Raccolta delle Cere Anatomiche di Clemente Susini

The Clemente Susini Collection of Anatomic Waxes, in 23 display cabinets, consists of 80 models in colored wax, reproducing various parts of the human body. The models were made in Florence, between 1803 and 1805, by the well-known artist Clemente Susini (1754-1814), based on dissections by the Sardinian anatomist Francesco Antonio Boi (1767-1855). In recent years, because of their exceptional quality, some waxes have been exhibited in important museums in London, Milan, Paris and Tokyo.

Museo di Mineralogia "L. De Prunner" - Museo Sardo di Geologia e Paleontologia "D. Lovisato"

The Mineralogy Museum and the Sardinian Geology and Paleontology Museum are located in the Department of Soil Sciences; they were founded in 1802, when Carlo Felice, the Savoy king, exhibited his collections, which he then gave to the university in 1806. The mineralogy museum displays mineral and rock samples, such as silver from Sarrabus and Carlo Alberto Lamarmora's Sardinian rock collection. The geology and paleontology museum was improved and reorganised at the end of the 19th century, by Domenico Lovisato, who it is named after; it has a rich fossil collection.

S. Michele 6

This is one of Sardinia's finest examples of Spanish Baroque architecture; it was built by the Jesuits in the 17th century. A portico with three arches leads into the vestibule where the pulpit of Charles V, carved in bas-relief, is located. It is believed that it was here that the Emperor took part in religious ceremonies in 1535 before the expedition against Tunisia, which left from the port of Cagliari. The interior, with beautiful marble and wood ornamentation, has an octagonal ground-plan with radial chapels.

The ruins of the Villa di Tigellio, built when Cagliari was in Roman hands

Anfiteatro romano e Villa di Tigellio 7

The 2nd-century amphitheater is one of the most remarkable Roman buildings in Sardinia. It is almost entirely dug out of the rock; a considerable amount survives of the elliptical rows of seats, of the cavea, of the barriers and of the podium where the town worthies watched the games from. It is believed, although there is no concrete evidence, that the Villa di Tigellio (Tigellius's Villa) is named after Caesar's and Cleopatra's Sardinian musician friend, who lived in the 1st century BC. It consists of three 1st-century AD urban Roman houses.

Necropoli di Tuvixeddu 8

The Tuvixeddu necropolis is Phoenician-Carthaginian, and later was used by the Romans. It has over a hundred hypogeum-type tombs, where entry is gained through vertical shafts; burial goods have been found here dating from the 6th century BC to the 1st century AD. One of the best examples of Carthaginian tomb painting can be seen in the tomba dell'Ureo (Tomb of the Uraeus).

Galleria Comunale d'Arte Moderna 9

The Municipal Modern Art Gallery occupies a late 18th-century building, originally the royal powder magazine. It was converted to become the art gallery in the late 1920s, by a designer from Cagliari, Uboldo Badas. The elegant neo-Classical facade was built in 1828. The gallery houses the Ingrao Collection and the Sardinian Artists Municipal Collection. The Ingrao Collection consists of around 500 works including paintings, sculptures and drawings by early 20th-century Italian artists: these include Umberto Boccioni, Giorgio Morandi, and Fortunato Depero. The Sardinian Collection contains paintings and sculptures ranging from 1900 to 1970 by Sardinia's best-known artists. The gallery also contains the Biblioteca Ingrao, a library which provides a valuable complement to the collections of artworks. The library has around 4000 books on the history of art.

S. Agostino 10

The church of St Augustine was designed by the Swiss architect, Giorgio Palearo, in 1577, and is one of Sardinia's few Renaissance buildings. Excavation work has revealed Roman and late-Roman remains which suggest that the whole area may have contained an elaborate thermal baths complex.

S. Domenico 11

The first church of St Dominic, according to tradition, was built in 1254; today almost nothing remains of the late-Gothic church, started in the early 15th century. The damage inflicted during the second world war meant that the church had to be rebuilt, in 1954. The crypt contains parts of the late-Gothic building; next

S. Saturno in Cagliari, one of Sardinia's oldest churches; the ground-plan dates from the 5th-6th century

to the church, the beautiful cloister is partly late-Gothic (15th century) and partly Renaissance (16th century).

S. Saturno ⑫

The church of St Saturn is also known as the church of Ss Cosmas and Damian; it is one of the oldest and most important of early Christian buildings in Sardinia. It was built in the 5th-6th century, on the site where Saturn of Cagliari was martyred. In 1089 it was converted into a basilica: it consists of an eastern part, with nave and two side aisles, built in Romanesque style in the 11th-12th century by workers from Provence, and of a front section dating from the same time, which was converted into an atrium after the ceiling collapsed. Excavation has revealed a 2nd- to 5th-century pre-Christian and Christian necropolis.

Santuario e basilica di Bonaria ⑬

This large 18th-century basilica is dedicated to the Madonna, Protectress of Sailors, and is a place of pilgrimage. It has a modern facade, and stands beside the old 14th-century sanctuary (subsequently altered), the only building that survives to testify the presence of the Aragonese, during the siege of the Pisan Castle. The venerated wood statue of the Madonna dates from the 15th century, but according to legend the statue was washed up on shore in 1370.

Next to the sanctuary is the Museo di Nostra Signora di Bonaria (Museum of Our Lady of Good Wind); it contains the Treasury, archeological remains and a collection of historical model boats and of ex-votos offered over the centuries by sailors who came to pray here.

DAY TRIPS

NORA [32 km]

This was an important Phoenician settlement, then a Carthaginian town and later a prosperous Roman city; archeological **excavations*** have provided much valuable information about the past, and ongoing work still does. A sizeable Phoenician town certainly existed here between the late 8th century BC and the early 6th century BC. Little remains of the Carthaginian settlement, but the precious burial goods found in tombs suggest that it was a flourishing commercial center. Nora's status as a municipium (or independent city) under the Romans is demonstrated by an inscription, while numerous milestones show how important the city was, especially between the 2nd and 3rd centuries AD: this is the time that most surviving remains of buildings date from. Vandal raids and pirate attacks very probably caused the city's rapid decline. In the archeological area, you can see the remains of typical Roman city buildings, and some particularly beautiful and original mosaics, made using virtually only white, black and ochre colors.

QUARTU SANT'ELENA [8 km]

Quartu is the third largest city in Sardinia in terms of number of inhabitants. Now it has grown to include Quartucciu, which in turn now extends to Selargius, which reaches as far as Monserrato. Each of these towns has its origins in the old rural world; evidence of this can be seen in the houses with their large doorways and their mud-straw bricks, in the little medieval churches, and in the local festivals and customs. Wherever modern concrete buildings have not taken over completely, some precious historic remains survive, like lost pieces of an old mosaic. The **Museo etnografico Il ciclo della vita** (Cycle of Life Ethnographic Museum) is at 271 Via Eligio Porcu, in a house typical of the region. Exhibits are mainly equipment and objects related to rural and artisan life in Sardinia, from the 17th century to the 20th century.

TEULADA [62 km]

The town is situated in a valley surrounded by hills, and has an interesting and unusual layout. The church of the Madonna del Carmelo (Madonna of Carmel), with its neo-Classical forms and simple facade, dates from the late 18th century and has beautiful marble decoration inside. The church of S. Francesco (St Francis) is late-Gothic, with wood beams and a simple facade with an octagonal window on the portal and a bell tower. Teulada produces interesting arts and crafts: excellent needlework, tapestry, rugs, cork and leather articles and local terracotta pipes with brass-coated copper lids.

VILLASIMIUS [49 km]

Capo Carbonara is a promontory extending into the sea on the south-eastern corner of the island; Isola dei Cavoli lies off the end of the promontory, and the gulf of Carbonara to the west. The town of Villasimius, once a fishing village, lies in a protected position in the gulf; its location, latitude and climate have made it a popular seaside resort. As well as providing services for holiday makers, the town also has some interesting attractions, such as the Museo Civico (Municipal Museum), which exhibits objects found on the sea floor and Roman remains from the area.

Nora: excavations area

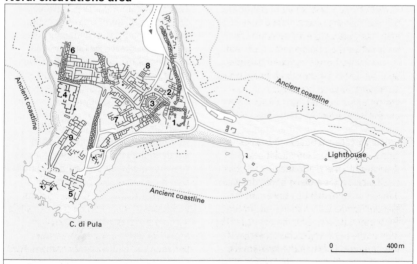

1	Forum	5	Esculapius complex
2	Temple	7	Central thermal baths
3	Theater	8	Temple of Thanit
4	Sea thermal baths	9	House with tetrastyle atrium

The new province of Carbonia-Iglesias was established recently, when Sardinia was reorganised into eight provinces. However the new system is not yet fully in operation: for example, road signs still follow the previous four-province system. The new province includes the old Sulcis and Iglesiente areas, which were previously part of the province of Cagliari. Carbonia-Iglesias is an area which hosted a variety of cultures and civilisations, drawn here by the existence of significant mineral resources. Today it is still Italy's main mining area. It has been inhabited for millennia: the Phoenicians and Carthaginians found it particularly suitable for their settlements in Sant'Antìoco, Nora, and Monte Sirai. The sea and the coastline, with long beaches of fine powdery sand, are fundamental to the area: the dunes of Piscinas, the magnificent bay of Chia, and the Colonne di Carloforte. There is also extensive woodland, with the state forests of Gùtturu Mannu-Pantaleo and Is Conneris; and some grottoes, such as Su Benatzu di Santadi, which was chosen by Nuraghic peoples as a place of worship.

The famous Colonne rising out of the sea at the island of San Pietro

CARBONIA

This "new town" was built from scratch in 1937-38 after a boost to growth was provided by mining policy. The town's appearance has changed considerably in recent years as a result of public and private housing programs. Carbonia has also been affected by the serious crisis suffered by the mining sector, and has gradually become a commercial and service center for the surrounding area. Carbonia's original buildings are concentrated around Piazza Roma, the central point from which the town spreads. The most important public buildings here are built in rough trachyte ashlar. The parrocchiale di S. Ponziano (parish church of St Ponzianus) stands on the east side of the square, with a smaller version of Aquileia's bell-tower. On the ground floor, a votive chapel dedicated to St Barbara, patron saint of miners. On the side to the right of the church you will find the Torre Civica (Municipal Tower), built during the Fascist regime, and the Theater. The City Council is on the side to the left. Opposite the church is the park, bordered by long avenues where grand

houses and the headquarters of the coal-mining corporations were built. At number 4 Via Napoli, set in spacious grounds, is the building which was the mines director's residence at the end of the thirties. It is now the **Museo archeologico Villa Sulcis** (Villa Sulcis Archeological Museum), which illustrates the history of the Sulcis region very well, from pre-historical to early Christian and medieval times (although the museum is currently being reorganised). There is a multimedia presentation describing the Phoenician and Carthaginian settlement of Monte Sirai. Not far away, in Via Campania, the *Museo Civico di Paleontologia e Speleologia "E. A. Martel"* (Municipal Museum of Paleontology and Speleology) has a paleontological collection ordered chronologically, from the pre-Cambrian to the Holocene, with particular attention given to Sardinian finds. It also has a section on speleology.

IGLESIAS

Although Iglesias was inhabited in Carthaginian and Roman times, it was only from the time of the Pisan conquest that it gained real importance, and became, as "Villa di Chiesa", the most important Sardinian city after Cagliari. It was at its greatest when it belonged to the powerful Counts of Donoratico: under the Della Gherardesca family, in fact, the city flourished, and was organised following the model of the Tuscan comuni or city states, with its own laws (the famous Breve of Villa di Chiesa) and the right to coin money. Laws also regulated mining, among other things. But the Aragonese conquest, which started in Iglesias itself in 1324, marked the beginning of the city's decline. In the 19th century, mining was again promoted by companies from mainland Italy; but the mining crisis in recent years has again affected Iglesias. The city is now creating a new economy, and this includes promoting tourism and interest in old mining towns and equipment. The town's three stages of development are clearly visible: the medieval layout, inside the Aragonese fortifications; the 19th-century layout resulting from the boom years in mining; and the post-war part of the town which fills all the previously unoccupied spaces. Most of the oldest buildings were replaced in the 19th century. This renovation of the city included various buildings in art nouveau style, including Palazzetto Spada in Via Matteotti.

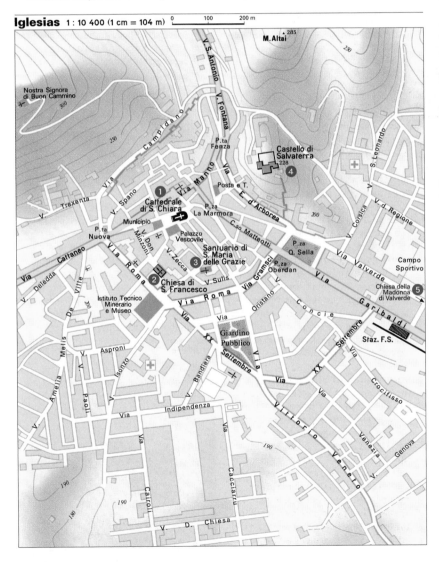

Iglesias 1 : 10 400 (1 cm = 104 m)

Iglesias: the 13th-century church of the Madonna di Valverde

Cattedrale di S. Chiara ❶

The Cathedral of St Clare* is in Piazza del Municipio, where the late 18th-century Palazzo dell'Episcopio (Bishop's Palace) also stands. The cathedral was built between 1285 and 1288, and extended and converted to Catalan Gothic style between 1576 and 1588; the cross-vaulted side chapels date from between 1600 and 1700, as does the retablo of St Antioch, with the paintings and statues that it contains. The cathedral's treasures, many in silver, include the Croce astile (a crucifix supported on a rod) with Pietà, a 16th-century work by a silversmith from Cagliari.

Chiesa di S. Francesco ❷

The church of St Francis dates from the 15th century and was altered in the 16th century. It has a simple facade, with a Gothic portal embellished with simple columns and two small rose windows. Inside, the capitals are decorated with a great variety of forms and themes. The capitals of the arch leading to the presbytery are decorated with various scenes from the life of St Francis.

Santuario di S. Maria delle Grazie ❸

The Sanctuary of St Mary of Graces dates from the early 14th century and was altered in the 18th century. The lower part of the facade - the portal with lunette, and trussed cornice with little arches - dates from the original church. The interior, a single nave with small side chapels, has a spacious square presbytery, with octagonal cupola, which an inscription dates to 1708. In the sacristy, there are a number of paintings and wood statues.

Castello di Salvaterra ❹

Salvaterra Castle was built in the 13th century and used for many centuries; once it lost its military importance, though, it fell almost completely into ruin, in the second half of the 19th century, with the destruction of the city walls. The castle was next to the porta di S. Antonio (St Anthony's Gate), one of the four gates in the city walls, which almost nothing remains of now.

Chiesa della Madonna di Valverde ❺

The church of the Madonna of Valverde is located outside the city walls and was built between 1285 and 1290; it is a less sophisticated copy of the Cathedral. The decoration on the trusses and flanks is new, with geometric motifs and animals in a Gothic setting. On the right side, the anthropomorphic trusses and leaves are similar to decoration in the church of S. Maria di Tratalìas (St Mary of Tratalìas). Inside, the presbytery, which was radically transformed at the end of the 16th century, has a fine cross vault with a carved pendent gem, and Madonna and Child in Renaissance style.

DAY TRIPS

FLUMINIMAGGIORE

The town was founded in 1704; the Museo Paleontologico (Paleontological Museum) is in the center, and has interesting fossils largely found in the Fluminese area. South of the town, along a scenic road in high, wild country, there are a number of mostly abandoned mines. A road to the left leads to the **tempio di Àntas**** (temple of Anthas),

The Roman temple of Anthas, near Fluminimaggiore

Isole sulcitane   1 : 255 000 (1 cm = 2,55 km)

0   2,5   5 km

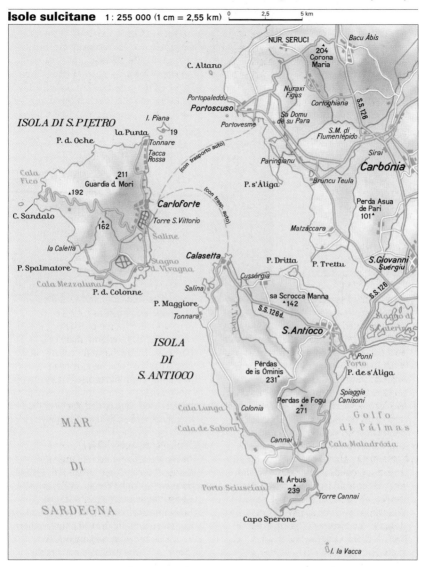

probably built under Augustus and reconstructed at the beginning of the 3rd century AD on the site of a Carthaginian temple, dating from 500 BC. It stands in the beautiful Àntas valley, which in ancient times was thickly wooded and had rich iron deposits. The building has undergone extensive restoration work, and today appears in Hellenizing style, with a tripartite, rectangular base, four columns at the front and a flight of stairs. Just after Fluminimaggiore, a track to the left leads to the **Su Mannàu grotto**, almost 6 km long, with various chambers and many concretions.

ISOLE SULCITANE

Sulcis is the area in south-west Sardinia between the golfo di Connessa and Capo Teulada; it includes the islands of San Pietro (St Peter) and of Sant'Antìoco (St Antioch). Originally Sulcis was the name of a Carthaginian town, then a Roman town, which was situated where Sant'Antìoco is now. It is harsh, bare terrain, with sheep pastureland alternating with cork forests; the marshy coastline has recently been drained and now is used for farming. Mineral resources, to varying degrees over the centuries, have affected the area's landscape, economy and social structure.

The **isola di Sant'Antìoco** (Sant'Antioch Island) is off the south-west coast, and linked to the mainland by a 3 km isthmus; it's the largest island off Sardinia, and the fourth largest in Italy after Sicily, Sardinia and Elba. Again the terrain is rugged; the highest point is Pèrdas de Fogu, a hill which is 271 m high. The island's inhabitants make their living from agriculture, and, like the inhabitants of San Pietro, were originally Ligurians from Tunisia, with some additional groups from Piedmont. Sant'Antìoco is the main town on the island, and spreads over the slopes of a hill to the east,

The beautiful colors of Carloforte, in a lane

which runs down to the sea. There was a Nuraghic settlement here, later Phoenician, called Sùlcis (8th century BC). The name Sant'Antìoco derives from the name of the African martyr who found refuge here; he was buried in the catacombs under the parish church, built in 1102 on a pre-existing early Christian Greek-cross church. The crypt houses a sarcophagus which is believed to hold the remains of the saint; the catacombs have very random and complex passageways. The Museo Archeologico (Archeological Museum) shows very clearly the main stages in the history of the town and the island, from the beginnings of the first Neolithic settlements (3rd millennium BC) up to late-Roman times. Most finds come from the Carthaginian-Roman necropolis. They consist largely of pottery, amphorae, oil-lamps, gold jewelry, and glass paste perfume holders. A great deal of space is devoted to material from the Tophet: cinerary urns and votive steles. The Tophet, 400 m from the Roman acropolis, was a sanctuary for Phoenician and Carthaginian divinities.

It consisted of a series of concentric courtyards enclosed by stone walls, at the center of which rose the sacrificial altar; the complex was surrounded by an area where terracotta urns with the ashes of the deceased were buried. Many of the cinerary urns are original and enable the site to be dated to Phoenician-Carthaginian times (7th-1st century BC). The Museo Etnografico (Ethnographic Museum), located in a typical 18th-century storehouse, exhibits tools and equipment used to carry out various trades: the cheese-making section, the agricultural equipment section, the viticulture section and wine-making section.

One exhibit is particularly interesting and unique: the Pinna Nobilis, the Mediterranean's largest mollusc. In Sant'Antìoco, it was used up until the 1930s to make byssus, a precious, very soft and transparent fabric. According to legend, the hilly **isola di San Pietro** (St Peter's Island) is named after the apostle Peter, who stopped here on his way to Cagliari. It was repopulated in 1738 by Carlo Emanuele III with a colony of Tabarkan Ligurians (prisoners ransomed by Tabarka in Tunisia), whose

Carthaginian stele at the Museo di Sant'Antìoco

speech and traditions the inhabitants still retain today. There are manganese mines and a salt mine on the island. The coast is largely rocky on the western side; on the eastern side, it's sandy and flat. The only town on the island is **Carloforte**, which lies on the slope of a hill on the east coast; its 18th-century layout was designed by the Piedmontese military engineer, Augusto de La Vallée. If you go to the small piazza in front of the lovely, simple parrocchiale di S. Carlo Borromeo (parish church of St Carlo Borromeo), you can see the oratorio della Madonna dello Schiavo (oratory of the Madonna of the Slave), whose interior has rococo-inspired forms. It's named after the simulacrum of the Madonna in gray linden wood on the main altar, which was probably once a ship's figurehead. The interesting chiesa di S. Pietro (St Peter's church) was rebuilt in the late 18th century, on the ruins of a 13th-century church.

PORTOSCUSO

This fishing town and seaside resort opposite the island of San Pietro was established in the 17th century, set among rocky shores and sandy coves. **Monte Sirai** (191 m) is a few kilometers away; on top of this hill there is an **archeological area** with the remains of a **Fortress***. This high place was occupied by Phoenicians, around 725 BC, in order to control access to the fertile plains of the Sulcis, as well as to the extremely rich mines of the area around Iglesias, and the roads leading to the Campidano plain. The position of the acropolis and necropolis dates from this first period, which lasted until the late 6th century BC. This was the time when Monte Sirai, like many other Phoenician settlements, was taken over by the Carthaginians. The tophet, with its adjacent temple area, dates from the early 4th century BC. When the Romans conquered Sardinia, the town's layout was significantly modified. Towards the end of the 2nd

century BC, it was abandoned for reasons still not understood. A good place to start our visit of the archeological area is at the outwork, or advance structure, a complex of buildings situated in front of the acropolis. Continuing on from here, you come to the main square, with numerous buildings built around it. The most important is the massive keep, built over the remains of an older Nuraghic tower. This stronghold was the linchpin of the settlement's defence, and also included a place of worship. The site's appearance today is as the town was when it was last inhabited. The necropolis and sacred area are outside the acropolis. Graves which held urns with ashes of the dead can be seen in the Phoenician necropolis; opposite, to the left, are the stepped corridors leading to underground tombs, dating from Carthaginian times, with loculi, where the dead were placed, along the walls, and niches where grave goods were sometimes placed. The great Carthaginian female goddess, Thanit, is carved back-to-front on a pillar in the rock. The sacred area consists of the tophet and an adjacent sacellum. A monumental stairway, at whose base urns and steles were placed, led to a temple built according to the Phoenician and Carthaginian model: vestibule, anticella, cella, and service area.

Monte Sirai: Phoenician-Carthaginian fortress

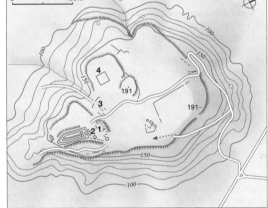

1 "Outwork"
2 Acropolis
3 Necropolis
4 Tophet

MEDIO-CAMPIDANO

Medio-Campidano is the name of a new province, established with the reorganisation of Sardinia into eight provinces, in July 2001. Although the new system was to be introduced in May 2005, this has not yet completely happened. For example, road signs still follow the previous four-province system. The Medio-Campidano province covers an area of 2000 square kilometers, and includes the central part of the Campidano area. It's situated between the Sulcis-Iglesiente province (to the south), the Oristanese (to the north) and the Cagliaritano province (to the east and south-east). To the west the province is bordered by the sea; this coastline, the Costa Verde, is one of Sardinia's most magnificent and unspoilt coastal areas. The crystal clear waters and marine vegetation play off each other to create superb emerald green reflections and colors. The natural environment here is unique and still largely undamaged. Sardinia's only medieval fortress is at Sanluri.

Barùmini

This agricultural town lies in the green, rolling countryside at the foot of the Giara di Gèsturi; it has a compact, almost polygonal layout. The chiesa di S. Francesco (church of St. Francis), in the highest part of the town, was built next to the Capuchin monastery in the 17th century (perhaps on top of an older church) by the aristocratic Zapata family. The parrocchiale dell'Immacolata (parish church of the Immaculate Virgin) is in the main road through the town, and was built after 1541 in late-Gothic style. The choir, renovated in the 17th century, has a large altarpiece with paintings around a statue of our Lady of the Assumption. In the sacristy, there is a remarkable 15th-century Catalan predella in carved, polychrome wood with half figures of the Apostles, and in the center a Spanish-school simulacrum of the Madonna. Barùmini's oldest building is the chiesa di S. Giovanni Battista (church of St John the Baptist), with two aisles and apse; it's near the parish church. Su Nuraxi, one of the most important proto-Sardinian Megalithic nuraghs and a UNESCO world heritage site, lies one kilometre to the west of the town.

Nuraghe Su Nuraxi

Just before entering Barùmini, you will see the four-lobed mass of the **Su Nuraxi**** nuragh complex, to the west of the town; this megalithic "palace" bears witness to many centuries of history, from the Middle Bronze Age (16th-13th

ORANGE FLAG
THE QUALITY LABEL FOR TOURISM AND ENVIRONMENT IN ITALY'S INLAND AREAS

The ORANGE FLAG is a label of quality for the development of tourism in Italy's inland areas. Municipalities with less than 15,000 inhabitants may be awarded it if selected criteria are achieved and maintained: cultural heritage, respect for the environment, hospitality, information and services, and quality local production. The ORANGE FLAG program is run by the Touring Club of Italy. The World Tourism Organisation has chosen ORANGE FLAG PROGRAM as a success in the sphere of environmental tourism. For more information: www.touringclub.it/bandierearancioni

ÀGGIUS (OLBIA-TEMPIO)
La Valle della Luna (the Valley of the Moon) is a barren expanse where enormous rocks rise out of the ground, and is an unusual feature of the small town with its granite houses. Interesting Museo Etnografico (Ethnographic Museum), illustrating the history of this ancient place.

GAVOI (NÙORO)
Lago di Gùsana is a lake, set in a wooded area with stark rocky peaks, not far from the large town whose attractions are its granite houses, arranged as if to form an amphitheater, and the 16th-century church of S. Gavino (St Gavin). Many archeological sites in the area.

LÀCONI (ORISTANO)
Renowned for the beauty of the surrounding area, and its fascinating history. The town, inhabited since Neolithic times (2700 BC), has the Parco Aymerich with the castle ruins, and the Museo Archeologico (Archoelogical Museum) with many menhirs.

SARDARA (MEDIO-CAMPIDANO)
The town is perched on a rocky limestone spur; it's known for its hot springs and the temple of S. Anastasia, an 8th-9th century BC Nuraghic temple built over a well. Votive objects found in the church of S. Anastasia and nearby Nuraghic sites are in the Museo Archeologico Villa Abbas.

The 14th-century castle of Eleonora d'Arborèa in Sanluri

centuries BC), which the original ground plan of the central tower dates from, up to the second Iron Age (6th-3rd centuries BC). Su Nuraxi has been a UNESCO World Heritage site since 1997. The impressive remains stand alone on a hill, overlooking the vast, unspoiled Marmilla area; they include the central multi-lobed nuragh, with three chambers, one above the other (16th-13th centuries BC), the later bastion with its four towers, the 20 m-deep well, and a more recent rampart. It was destroyed in the 7th century BC, then rebuilt and inhabited until Roman times.

Gèsturi

This densely-built village is situated on a gentle slope at the head of a small valley. As you enter the town, where the road branches off to the right and climbs up to the Giara, you will see on the left the chiesa di S. Maria Egiziaca (church of St Mary Egyptian), dating from around the end of the 16th century, with late-Gothic and Renaissance features on the facade. Next door is the chiesa del cimitero (Cemetery church), with a 16th-century tempera wood polyptych. In the town center, the parrocchiale di S. Teresa (parish church of St Teresa) retains parts of the late 16th-century, late-Gothic structure: the stone facade with inflexed arch and lateral curves, the bell-tower and the fine apse with stellar vault. Inside, the nave has five chapels on each side, typical of Sardinian churches of this time; in the third chapel on the right, there is a 16th-century wood polyptych.

The **Giara di Gèsturi** is a basaltic plateau, trapezoid in shape, with steep cliffs and escarpments; "giara" is the local name for this type of glacial formation. The plateau varies in height between 500 and 580 meters (with Monte Zeparedda rising to 609 m), and dominates the landscape; it is covered with Mediterranean maquis, cork forests and grassy pastureland, which provides grazing for the several hundred small wild horses which live here and are native to the Giara. Its height, steepness and inaccessibility made it a natural stronghold in ancient times; around its edges there were numerous nuraghs, which today are in ruins but are still interesting from a topographic point of view. The Bruncu'e Madili nuragh near the turnoff, which was surrounded by a large village, has been found by archeologists to have the oldest Sardinian Nuraghic structures ever identified (1800 BC).

Sanluri

The castle's square silhouette, with its four crenelated turrets, is the first landmark you notice in the town of Sanluri. It's the only medieval castle in Sardinia not only not to be in ruins, but to be actually inhabited and carefully restored. It was built in the 13th century, although it is known as the castle of Eleonora d'Arborèa. Rooms have been converted for use as a museum, exhibiting mementos, weapons and flags from the time of the Risorgimento, mostly from the Palace of Capodimonte in Naples, where they were kept until 1927. Part of the museum concentrates on the history of Italy during the two world wars. On the first floor there is an interesting collection of wax models. The parish church of Nostra Signora delle Grazie (Our Lady of Graces) is worth a visit in the town. It has a Madonna of Souls by Giovanni Marghinotti, as well as a remarkable 15th-century wood Crucifix in a carved, gilded retablo.

Tuìli

It's only 3 km from Barùmini to Tuìli, at the foot of the Giara. Tuìli is interesting because of its white chiesa di S. Antonio Abate (church of St Anthony Abbot)

The nuraghs have long been an unfathomable mystery. These monumental structures, built in stone in the form of towers, are now a universally-known symbol of Sardinian history and culture; they have for centuries been a real mystery to archeologists and scholars of ancient history. They were widely used as places of worship in Carthaginian and Roman times, and thus it was believed in the past that they may have been large tomb complexes. In the twentieth century, a clearer and more complete understanding of the Nuraghic civilisation emerged, especially with knowledge gained from archeological research and excavation campaigns carried out in the fifties. Research by Antonio Taramelli and later by Giovanni Lilliu revealed what the nuraghs really were: dwellings which also had a defensive function, and were the greatest expression of a culture which originated and developed thousands of years ago, in the wake of the great Megalithic civilisations of the Mediterranean.

Round fortresses

The first nuraghs were very probably built in pre-historic times, from the second millennium BC. Today, there are over seven thousand nuraghs all over Sardinia, and a large number of them have survived to our times in excellent condition. If we think of all the activities and works which have been undertaken on the island over the centuries, such as the construction of roads and aqueducts, and the development of towns, it is clear that much evidence of the Nuraghic civilisation must have been destroyed, and thus much precious knowledge lost forever. Most Nuraghic structures are situated in hill areas, but some are found in flat areas, along the coast, on plateaux and in rough, inhospitable terrain, such as for example high in the Gennargentu area, at over 1000 m. A nuragh consists of a tower which is shaped like a truncated cone; the ground-plan is thus circular. They were built with sedimentary or volcanic rocks and stones, sometimes of considerable size; these are placed in concentric rows that progressively get smaller and smaller as they get higher. Gravity keeps them in place, without any cement or mortar. The entrance is surmounted by an architrave: from here a corridor leads to a room in the shape of a cupola. Sometimes these rooms are on two or more levels, connected by spiral staircases constructed inside the walls. Other structures such as chambers or galleries are sometimes connected to the main tower. In most cases, simple forms prevail. In others, structures were architecturally very complex, such as those with a number of towers. Individual nuraghs were often part of a defence system which was highly structured and organised, within fortified town walls. Multiple tower nuraghs within fortified walls predominate at "Is Paras" north of the town of Isili, at "Arrubiu" at Orroli, and at "Su Nuraxi" at Barùmini, where the Marmilla and Sarcidano regions

Remains of a main building and a secondary building

Su Nuraxi nuragh and Nuraghic village at Barùmini

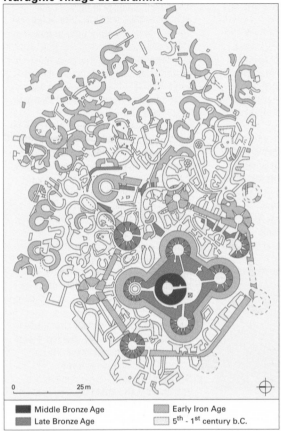

0 ———— 25 m

- ■ Middle Bronze Age
- ■ Late Bronze Age
- ■ Early Iron Age
- □ 5th - 1st century b.C.

The towers in turn are surrounded by a defensive wall with seven towers which appears to date from between the 10th and 8th centuries BC. An Iron Age village (9th-6th century BC) was found around these structures, with circular stone buildings, probably roofed with branches and leaves, which almost certainly served as dwellings for the soldiers' families. Extremely interesting objects, tools and ornaments have been found here. As Su Nuraxi gradually developed and grew, probably for military reasons, the oldest structures were incorporated and fortified. The Carthaginians made frequent raids into the interior, which meant that there was a strong need for defence.

In the center of the Mediterranean

Although there is evidence clearly indicating that the village of Barùmini was still inhabited in the early centuries of the Christian era (at least until the 3rd century AD), the nuraghs appear to have gradually diminished in importance, particularly after the Roman conquest of the island in the 2nd century BC. The difficulty encountered in attempting to understand the nuraghs is partly due to the fact that the Nuragh civilisation was totally different from the "classical" Greek civilisation which flourished on the coast of southern Italy and Sicily. However, recent studies have revealed that, although the Nuraghic civilisation was, curiously, extremely self-contained, it had important links with the Mycenean culture. And when this culture came to the end of its period of expansion, Nuraghic Sardinia, in the heart of the western Mediterranean, became an important point of reference for the Etruscan and Phoenician civilisations.

meet: rich, fertile areas. And this may explain why the nuraghs here are so impressive, and among the largest found on the island. It has also been noted that sometimes villages of round huts with stone foundations developed around the nuraghs.

The settlement of Barùmini

Many aspects of the history, life and society of the peoples who inhabited the nuraghs have become clearer since the Nuraghic complex "Su Nuraxi" on the western edge of Barùmini was excavated in the early 1950s. The heart of the settlement is a stronghold formed by a central keep which probably dates from the end of the second millennium BC, and was originally 18 m high. This is surrounded by four towers situated at the points of the compass and built between the 13th and 10th centuries BC.

surrounded by the usual enclosure, which "lollas" are built beside; these are shops used by traders and artisans during local folk festivals and celebrations. The church was built in 1582 and is one of the area's most interesting examples of rural church architecture, with its Latin-cross ground-plan, between two lateral porticos. The interior has a fine 17th-century altar in carved and gilded wood; the organ in the choir dates from 1753.

The center of town is laced with a complex network of roads; along them you can see the large arched portals of the traditional houses with their inner courtyards, built in stone or plastered unbaked bricks. The neo-Classical Palazzo Pitalis is in the center. In the high part of the town, opposite Villa Asquer, is the parish church of S. Pietro

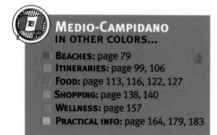

Apostolo (St. Peter the Apostle); one chapel (third on the left), with stellar vault, survives of the original late-Gothic construction. The first chapel on the right has a retablo by the Master of Castelsardo dating from 1500, which has been restored to its former splendid state. The town is the starting point for guided trips to the Giara di Gèsturi Park, and is benefiting from recent tourist and cultural initiatives, such as the rehabilitation of old buildings for the Museum of Ethnic Music and the Museum of Historic Cars.

Villacidro

This large agricultural town, situated at the base of towering pink granite rocks, divides into two parts. The higher part is the oldest; it extends around the piazza where the 16th-century parrocchiale di S. Barbara (parish church of St Barbara) stands, with its portal surmounted by a curved gable. The bell-tower is square in ground-plan and has single ogival or pointed windows. The interior, with its

barrel-vaulted nave, has 18th-century rococo style furnishings: the baptismal font, the main altar in polychrome marble and the white marble pulpit. There is an interesting pipe-organ, also 18th-century.

Opposite the parish church is the oratorio della Madonna del Rosario (oratory of the Madonna of the Rosary), built against what remains of Monte Granatico; at the corner of Via Parrocchia, the oratorio delle Anime (oratory of Souls) has a simple facade, with cornice in relief and a bell-tower. In the lower part of the town, in Piazza dei Mille, there is a magnificent iron public washing area built in 1893; it consists of two square canopies linked by a central section, with finely decorated pillars and arches.

Various day trips can be made from the town up into the hills, where Mediterranean maquis gives way to ilex or holm oaks, chestnuts, and walnuts; mushrooms, wild orchids and cyclamen grow very well in these woods.

One of the easiest walks goes to the **Sa Spèndula*** waterfall, and has lovely views of the high country.

Villanovaforru

This town in the Marmilla area is a creative center of ideas, initiatives and projects all revolving around the old Monte Frumentario building which has been turned into a Museo Archeologico (Archeological Museum). Here you can see objects such as askoi (vases shaped like animals, sacks or skins), ziri (large oil jars), pear-shaped vases with geometric decoration, oil lamps, ember-holders, and lead and copper smelting slag from the Genna Maria nuragh complex (15th-7th centuries BC); all these exhibits were found after much painstaking excavation work at the top of a hill not far away.

West of the town, you take an unsealed road that goes above and beyond the hill of Collinas (408 m), to the villaggio nuragico di Genna Maria (Nuraghic village of Genna Maria), a fortified complex which developed in the First Iron Age and was abandoned in the 8th century BC for reasons unknown. This sacred place was dedicated to the worship of Demeter and Core for over eight hundred years.

NÙORO

Nùoro straddles a rugged granitic ridge which extends out from Monte Ortobene. As the crow flies, the sea is about thirty kms away; the closest port, Olbia, over a hundred kms away. The city is the heart of inland Sardinia's special culture and traditions.

In 1975, a tomb dated some time between the 7th and 8th centuries BC was found during renovation work on an old building in Via Ballero: this is the oldest evidence of human occupation of the site where Nùoro stands today.

The first written documents date from the 14th century: in the *Rationes Decimarum* imposed by Pope John XXII, Nùoro figures as one of the most highly-taxed towns in the diocese of Ottana, and hence one of the most important. The place name Nùgor had already been recorded in various 11th-, 12th- and 13th-century records. In the 16th century, the town grew considerably; in the 17th century, it had 1600 inhabitants and many churches had been built in addition to those already in existence, S. Croce (Holy Cross) church and the late 16th-century chiesa del Salvatore (church of the Saviour).

Piazza Sebastiano Satta, featuring granite blocks by the sculptor Costantino Nivola

In 1777, with 2782 inhabitants, it was one of the area's largest towns; most inhabitants were shepherds and peasants. Its layout was simple, and it counted 15 churches. The early 19th century was a peaceful time. This came to an end with the royal directives forbidding common use of land (*"enclosures" decree*, 1820). In the late-19th and early-20th centuries, the town was a center for much original cultural and socio-political activity, which drew inspiration largely from the conflict between traditional Sardinian society and the new society of the nation state. Examples of some of those who were active: the poet Sebastiano Satta (1867-1914), the writer Grazia Deledda (1871-1936, Nobel Prize winner for literature in 1926), and the essayist and politician Attilio Deffenu (1890-1918). When Nùoro was made a provincial capital in 1927, it grew enormously: the population increased from 8,534 in 1921 to 16,949 in 1951. In the period after the second world war, Nùoro continued to expand, at the same time as it was gradually changing from an agricultural town into a more administrative and service-oriented center.

Duomo ❶

The Duomo, built between 1836 and 1854, has paintings by local 19th-century painters, and a Jesus among the Doctors, perhaps painted by Luca Giordano. An attractive nearby square, Piazza Sebastiano Satta, was renovated by Costantino Nivola in 1967, and named after the poet who was born in a house which still stands there.

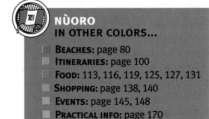

NÙORO
IN OTHER COLORS...

■ **BEACHES:** page 80
■ **ITINERARIES:** page 100
■ **FOOD:** 113, 116, 119, 125, 127, 131
■ **SHOPPING:** page 138, 140
■ **EVENTS:** page 145, 148
■ **PRACTICAL INFO:** page 170

THE GRAZIA DELEDDA LITERATURE PARK

There is a Literature Park dedicated to Grazie Deledda, who lived from 1871 to 1936, and won the Nobel Prize for Literature in 1926. Most of the park's sites are in the Nùoro area, and the "gateways" giving access are in Nùoro, Galtelli and Monteleone Rocca Doria. The park's theme trails relate to Deledda's life, and her works, to her novel "Canne al vento" (Reeds in the Wind), and to the Sardinian soul.

letters, information on films and plays based on her works, Italian and foreign first editions, personal objects, and a copy of her Nobel Prize for literature (1926). The kitchen and portico have been used to recreate environments typical of the agricultural society of her time, furnished with household and work implements and equipment.

Museo della Vita e delle Tradizioni Popolari Sarde ❹

The **Museum of Sardinian Life and Folk Traditions**** was founded in 1963 but has only been open permanently since 1976. It occupies a building that was specially constructed for the purpose, in Sardinian rural style. The museum shows aspects of domestic and social life. Exhibits include: objects, implements and furniture used in daily life; textile handcrafts (blankets, mats, a funerary rug); and gold and silver jewelry. There is an important collection of traditional costumes, some of which are extremely rare. The museum also has sections on carnival, with displays of costumes and masks, on traditional bread- and cake-making, and on musical instruments.

Museo dell'Arte della Provincia di Nùoro - M.A.N. ❷

The permanent collection in the **Museum of Art of Nùoro province*** (MAN) gives a good idea of 20th-century Sardinian art, with works by Sardinian artists such as Ballero Biasi, Ciusa Romagna, Delitala, Floris, Nivola, Pintori and Fancello. The museum organises at least 4 anthological contemporary art exhibitions every year.

Museo Deleddiano - Casa Natale di Grazia Deledda ❸

The **Deleddiano Museum*** is in Grazia Deledda's childhood home, a typical 19th-century Nuorese house belonging to a comfortably-off family. Papers and documents relating to the writer and her work are on display in her bedroom:

Museo Archeologico Nazionale ❺

The National Archeological Museum, which opened in July 2002, has a

Nùoro has been inhabited since the 8th century, and is the birthplace of some famous people in Italy's political and cultural life, including Grazia Deledda, who won the Nobel prize for literature

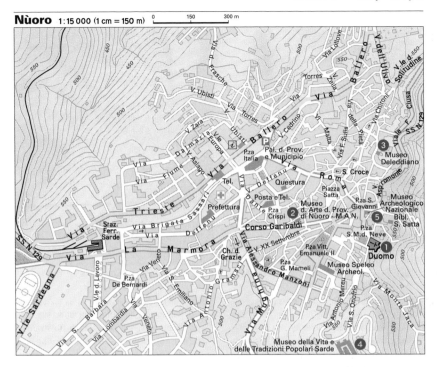

Nùoro 1 : 15 000 (1 cm = 150 m)

paleontological section with Plio-Pleistocene mammal fossils from the Monte Tattavista vertebrate deposit. There is an interesting hyena skull, and the skull of a type of monkey (Macaca majori) that was widespread in Sardinia at the time. Other rooms show archeological material from the early Neolithic Age up until historical times (stone implements, pottery, bone jewelry, shells, amber), found in areas further inland. The Nuraghic section is the most important; it has reconstructions of various funerary and ceremonial monuments, with mainly bronze materials that were found inside the monuments.

DAY TRIPS

ARITZO [74 km]
The town is surrounded by thick chestnut woods, and is Sardinia's best-known hill resort town. The attractive parrocchiale di S. Michele Arcangelo (parish church of St Michael Archangel) is on the main road, Corso Umberto I, on the right. It dates from the 14th century and has been extensively modified. Inside, there's a 17th-century wood statue of St Christopher, an early 18th-century Pietà, and some modern

paintings by the local artist Antonio Mura. Other buildings worthy of note: the stately home of the Arangino family, built in the early 18th century in neo-Gothic style; and, along a steep flight of stairs near the parish church, a solid austere edifice in dark schistose stone, built in the 17th century and used as a prison until after the second world war. Aritzo's municipal Ethnographic Collection is exhibited in some rooms at the primary school. There are two sections: the first on local costumes and clothing, and the second on typical local arts and crafts. The carved chestnut chests are especially renowned.

ATZARA [76 km]
The town lies in gentle hilly vineyard-covered countryside. It was founded in medieval times on the site of the ancient Roman Villa di Leonisa, and the town's layout reflects its ancient origins. The 16th-century parrocchiale di S. Antìoco (parish church of St Antioch), in a small square near the main road, has an austere crenelated facade with a trachyte rose window. A solid bell tower stands next to it. The church contains two superb Baroque-style wood altars, a 16th-century wood statue of the

Madonna and Child, and some precious 16th-century silver.

The Pinacoteca Comunàle d'Arte Contemporanea (Municipal Contemporary Art Gallery) is in Via Dante, in a historic mansion which has recently been renovated. The gallery has over 50 artworks by most of the most important 20th-century Sardinian artists; there are also some paintings by Spanish artists who worked here in the early 1900s.

Atzara is renowned for the rugs and tapestries made here, some of the finest in Sardinia.

Sòrgono lies just a few kilometers away, surrounded by woods and vineyards. In the town's old center, there are some fine examples of local rural architecture and some elegant 19th-century buildings. The bell-tower of the parrocchiale di S. Maria Assunta (parish church of St Mary Assumption) dates from 1580.

Rocks and coves in the Nùoro area

CALA GONONE [40 km]

Cala Gonone* was once a small fishing village, lying around a harbour where in the past wood, coal and cheese were shipped from; in the 19th century it was already a much-frequented summer holiday town for Nùoro's bourgeois families. Recent tourist development has turned it into an important seaside resort town. Its small port is used by many boats going to and from the superb beaches and coves in the vicinity, which can only be reached by sea.

Cala Luna* lies 7 km south of Cala Gonne and can be reached only by sea. This is an exceptional spot, with its white sandy beach about 800 m long, a small lake surrounded by a thick wood of colorful oleanders, and the mouths of eight large grottoes at the base of a steep rock cliff. The **grotta del Bue Marino****(Monk Seal Grotto), located 5 km south of Cala Gonne, is accessible by ferry. It is one of Sardinia's largest and most breathtaking grottoes.

The name derives from the fact that it was one of the last refuges of the Mediterranean monk seal (in local dialect "su boe marinu"). It extends for around 5 km; a 900 m-long section is illuminated and can be visited. The myriad and magical shapes of the grotto's concretions reflected in the waters create a spectacular effect.

DORGALI [32 km]

Dorgali is situated in a commanding position, halfway up calcareous Monte Bàrdia (882 m); you can't actually see the sea from the town, although it's very close. In recent years, Dorgali has grown enormously as a result of tourism. In the old center, there are some surviving old buildings in dark-colored stone and a number of 19th-century palazzi; there are many mostly 17th-century churches. The impressive 18th-century parrocchiale di S. Caterina (parish church of St Catherine) is a distinctive feature of the town. Inside, it has two impressive wood altarpieces. One, in the right transept, dates from 1770; the other, in the left transept, was made in 1957, faithfully following the model of the great 18th-century Sardinian retablos.

Dorgali has strong craft traditions, particularly in goldsmithery, in carpet weaving, in leather working and in ceramics. The Museo Civico Archeologico (Municipal Archeological Museum) in Via La Marmora contains a good proportion of the pre-Nuraghic, Nuraghic, Phoenician-Carthaginian, Roman and early-medieval finds from the area's numerous sites; they are well-presented with clear explanations and good photos. The Museo "Salvatore Fancello" is a museum located on the ground floor of the Municipality, in Viale Umberto. It's named after a local artist (1916-1941) who, despite his short life, produced over 400 ceramic works, as well as drawings, water-colors and engravings.

About 10 km from Dorgali, the **grotta di Ispinigoli (Ispinigoli grotto)** stretches for around 10 km, and is one of Italy's largest. The most amazing part of it is a large natural hall which was used in Nuraghic and Carthaginian times, almost certainly as a place of worship; at the center is an enormous stalagmite measuring over 38 m. A deep abyss opens at its base, known as the "Abyss of the Virgins" where propitiatory rites may have been performed in Carthaginian times, with human sacrifice; this is suggested by the fact that human bones and women's jewelry, now in Dorgali's Muncipal Archeological Museum, were found at the bottom of the abyss.

It is worth visiting the **villaggio nuragico Serra Órrios*** (Nuraghic village of Serra Órrios), which is near Dorgali on a basaltic plateau, set among centuries-old olive trees and lentisk or mastic trees. One of the better-preserved villages, it has a number of groups of round huts, arranged around courtyards with communal cisterns and wells. At the western edge, there are some particularly interesting remains of two rectangular buildings, perhaps small temples, which resemble Mycenean mègaron in their structure.

stairs, arches, pergolas, tiny balconies, and graceful chimneys in unexpected shapes. This spontaneous, dynamic style of building has inspired the design of many new tourist resorts. Another distinctive feature of Oliena's urban layout is the large number of churches, mostly small in size and simple in design, with small bell-towers. The two most noteworthy: the old 13th-century parrocchiale di S. Maria (parish church of St Mary) at the entrance to the town, which has been modified many times; and the parrocchiale di S. Ignazio di Loyola (parish church of St Ignatius of Loyola), built by the Jesuits in the early 18th century. It has some interesting 17th-century wood statues, and in the sacristy, a fine 16th-century retablo, known as St Christopher's retablo.

About 6 km from Oliena, on the road for Dorgali, a 2 km sealed road off to the right leads to the **sorgente carsica di Su Gologone*** (Su Gologone karstic spring). The spring gushes powerfully (300 liters per second) from an underground river through a natural cleft in the rock, and flows into a clear, deep pool below. A thick wood of colorful oleanders, and just above the spring, the small white country church of Nostra Signora della Pietà (Our Lady of Mercy) combine to make the place even more special.

OLIENA [12 km]

There are written references to Oliena in medieval times; from the 17th century it grew considerably as a result of the Jesuit settlement here. The Jesuits founded schools, and introduced silk worm cultivation, as well as more advanced methods of olive and grapevine cultivation. Still today, olives and vines are a considerable source of income. The well-known strong local wines were much admired and written about by Gabriele D'Annunzio.

The powerful bulk of Monte Corrasi (1463 m) looms over the winding alleys of the old town, with its small whitewashed houses and their little courtyards, outdoor

ORGÒSOLO [20 km]

Orgòsolo is a very old agricultural and farming center, one of the Nùoro area's most traditional, which has changed a great deal in recent years. The old town has steep, winding alleys with very simple country houses, sometimes with

Murals in Orgòsolo

ORGÒSOLO MURALS

The Spanish word Mural was first used in Mexico in the twenties, when messages related to the revolution were painted on walls. In 1969 Francesco Del Casino, an art teacher in Orgòsolo, produced a series of posters, picking up on the style of Mexican murals, to express the town's problems. In 1975 Del Casino and his pupils transferred these as murals to the walls of Orgòsolo.

(All Souls church), with cupola and fine lateral portico. Other noteworthy churches are: the santuario della Madonna del Rimedio (sanctuary of the Madonna of Remedy) a 19th-century reconstruction of a smaller 17th-century building, and the chiesa di S. Antonio Abate (church of St Anthony Abbot), dating from the 14th- to 15th-century, which has a superb 14th-century wood statue of St Anthony and frescoes dating from the same period, unfortunately in very poor condition.

little loggias or pergolas. The gray walls are made colorful by the many murals (around 150), most painted in the 1970s. They are generally on political or social themes, and express very effectively the strong contrast between the old pastoral world and the modern world. The town has a number of churches; two interesting ones are the rural oratorio di S. Croce (oratory of the Holy Cross), dating from the late 16th century, and the 17th-century chiesa dell'Assunta (church of Our Lady of the Assumption).

OROSEI [40 km]

The town is situated in a fertile plain between the sea and the eastern slopes of Monte Tuttavista, on the site of the Roman town of Fanum Carisii. The many churches and noble homes, mostly dating from the 15th to the 18th centuries, in the well-maintained and well-preserved old part of the town, demonstrate how wealthy and important Orosei was in the past. The Museo "Giovanni Guiso", in one of these houses, is a museum with an interesting collection of theater costumes worn by famous actors and actresses. The town's center is Piazza del Popolo, with its various churches. The parrocchiale di S. Giacomo Maggiore (parish church of St James the Elder) dominates the square from above; its pale plaster and unusual roof with small cupolas lend it an Arab-style appearance. The 17th-century chiesa di S. Croce (church of the Holy Cross) is beside St James's apse. On the opposite side of the square: the 17th-century chiesa del Rosario (church of the Rosary); and the 18th-century chiesa delle Anime

SINISCOLA [48 km]

The town lies in a fertile plain on the north-eastern slopes of Monte Albo, a calcareous mountain. Its economy has traditionally been based on farming. Recent building development has considerably altered the old town layout. Interesting monuments include the 18th-century parrocchiale di S. Giovanni Battista (parish church of St John the Baptist), which is entirely frescoed on the inside. It has an unusual plaque, dated 1627, which bears carved footprints and a height measurement, said to be those of Jesus Christ.

SANTUARIO DI S. FRANCESCO DI LULA [32 km]

The Sanctuary of St Francis of Lula is very white, and surrounded by green woods. With the white heights of Monte Albo above, it is one of Sardinia's most beautiful and important rural churches. According to tradition, it was founded in the 17th century by Nuorese bandits. St Francis of Assisi, known as St Francis of Lula by Sardinians, is worshipped as the protector of bandits and "balentes" (the brave): he was often called on for protection during gunfights. Today's church, built in 1795, is a reconstruction of a smaller 17th-century church, and has a 17th-century Neapolitan-school wood statue of St Francis. The church is surrounded by a large number of "cumbessìas"; these shelters were traditionally used by novena participants, and they make an attractive sight.

OGLIASTRA

The province of Ogliastra was recently founded as part of the reorganisation of Sardinia into eight provinces; the new system was supposed to start in May 2005, but has still not been completely implemented. The road signs for example, still follow the previous four-province system. Ogliastra is on the east coast of Sardinia. The name may derive from the many "ogliastri", or wild olives, that were once cultivated here and which holy oil was made from. Some believe that the name derives from "Agugliastra" (or Sa Pedra Longa"), a small rocky island. The province extends from the Tyrrhenian Sea to the slopes of the Monti del Gennargentu. The landscape includes beaches of very fine white sand, crystal-clear water, steep rocky coastline, centuries-old woods and arid flat plains. The area is still unspoilt and wild, much to the inhabitants' pride, and is a destination that is highly sought-after by tourists. The economy is still largely based on farming and agriculture, as well as the production of wine and cheese.

Àrbatax

Àrbatax lies at the base of Capo Bellavista, a picturesque cape; in the center, there is a solid 17th-century coastal tower. It has become an important port and lively tourist town, and has grown so much in recent years that it virtually reaches as far as Tortolì. The town is known especially for its attractive cliffs in red porphyry which rise up from the sea near the port. There is a superb view from the belvedere at the Capo Bellavista lighthouse (150 m). Àrbatax is a port of call for ferries sailing between Cagliari and Genoa, and Cagliari and Civitavecchia. There is also a railway line from Àrbatax to Cagliari: a narrow-gauge railway which follows an incredibly beautiful and varied route. Part of the trip, starting from Àrbatax, can be made on a very popular tourist train drawn by a steam engine, known as the "Treninio verde" (Little Green Train) (see children's itineraries).

Baunei

The town is dominated by a dramatically steep calcareous rock wall; it looks more like a mountain village than a seaside village, despite its position near the sea. It's alway been a farming town, and according to tradition was founded by a goatherd. Today Balnei is making efforts to develop a tourist industry, drawing on its splendid and unspoilt coastline, and is setting up a marine nature reserve. The vast area inland is also extremely beautiful, especially the Golgo, a wild and empty calcareous plateau lying above the town.

In the charming, steeply-sloping old town, the parrocchiale di S. Nicola (parish church of St Nicholas) stands out in the main street. Originally built in the 17th-century, it has been modified many times; it has an attractive cupola, and an original decorated portal, detached from the body of the church, which acts as a false facade.

A 4 km-long sealed road off State Road 125 leads to **Sa Pedra Longa**, the distintive 128 m-high pointed pinnacle, which soars skyward out of the sea like a spire. Behind stand the three peaks of Argennas (711 m), Girabili (757 m), and Ginnircu (757 m), also plunging steeply down into the waters of the Tyrrhenian Sea.

Jerzu

There is a pleasant place to stop, with a great view, just before Jerzu: the

The impressive sight of the red porphyry rocks known as the Rocce Rosse of Àrbatax

Bau'e Munsa spring, in a lovely green and natural setting.

Jerzu is a country town which has grown largely as a result of flourishing grape-growing and wine-making activity. From the main street through the town, Via Umberto, there are some lovely views over the deep valley of the Rio Pardu, to the north-east. There are groups of domus de janas in the neighbouring localities of Perda Puntuta and Sa Ibba s'Ilixi.

A short detour of less than 2 kilometers leads to **Ulàssai**, a peaceful town high in the hills. A road continues on above the town, and then climbs steeply through a narrow valley planted with crops and thick pine forests, among towering rock masses. These are the precipitous walls of the limestone plateaux which are a distintive feature of this area, and are known as "tacchi" or "tònneri". A sealed road, just over 1 km from the town, leads through an impressive gorge to the **grotta Su Màrmuri*** (Su Màrmuri grotto). Its superb concretions make it definitely worth a visit, although this is only possible with a guide.

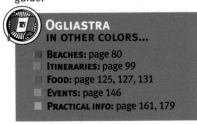

OGLIASTRA
IN OTHER COLORS...

▪ **BEACHES:** page 80
▪ **ITINERARIES:** page 99
▪ **FOOD:** page 125, 127, 131
▪ **EVENTS:** page 146
▪ **PRACTICAL INFO:** page 161, 179

Santa Maria Navarrese

This tourist town is famous for its splendid and exceptional location. It began originally as a group of country houses around the rural church it's named after. According to legend, the church was built in the early 11th century by a daughter of the King of Navarre, to express her gratitude for narrowly escaping shipwreck. It has a central nave and two side aisles, with a semi-circular apse. A centuries-old olive tree grows beside the church. There's a torre spagnola (Spanish tower) on the shore, which has both sandy stretches as well as many rocks and little islands. The tiny red porphyry island lying offshore is the isola dell'Ogliastra (in Roman times known as "Agugliastra") which the region is named after.

Seùi

Seùi is the main town in the Barbàgia di Seùlo area; the Gennargentu is in the distance. Today Seùi's economy is largely based on farming and agriculture. But from the late 19th century to the 1950s, the town prospered from the mining of a rich deposit of anthracite. The mine's old wash-plant, 3 km from the town, is an interesting example of industrial architecture. The local Museo della Civiltà contadina, pastorale, artigianale, della Miniera e dell'Emigrante (Museum of Peasant, Farming and Craft Culture, of Mining and of Emigration) has a section which concentrates on the town's mining history. The museum is located in an attractive art nouveau building in Via Roma in the center.

The old town has some elegant 19th-century palazzi, and fine examples of local rural stone buildings, with arches, wooden balconies and slate roofs. There is an interesting old building in Via Sassari: the carcere baronale (baronial jail). It was built in the early 18th century and used until 1975 as a prison. It has been restored, keeping the original interior structure, and furnished according to 19th-century taste. The 18th-century parrocchiale di S. Maria Maddalena (parish church of St Mary Magdalen) has been significantly altered over the years; inside there is a fine wood altar, and a 17th-century baptismal font.

A short unsealed road off the provincial road to Seùlo leads to the **grotta di Is Janas** (Is Janas grotto); it's located in a superb natural setting, surrounded by a thick forest of ilex, or holm oaks. The grotto extends for over 200 m, and has some fascinating chambers and an underground lake. The largest and most spectacular chamber has numerous stalactites hanging down, and walls that look as if they are decorated with fine lacework. The grotto is called "sa 'omu 'e is janas" (the house of the fairies) because it has three stalagmites which, according to legend, are petrified fairies. It's open to the public; guides lead visitors along an illuminated trail.

OLBIA-TEMPIO

Olbia-Tempio is one of Sardinia's eight provinces, although in reality the transition from the old four-province system to the new system is not complete. The province covers 3,300 square kilometres, in the north-east of Sardinia. Tourism is important: the Costa Smeralda is a world-renowned tourist destination. The cork and granite industries are fundamental to the province too, and its geographical position makes it an important point of connection with peninsular Italy. Some successful food and wine industries are based here too: Vermentino di Gallura and Moscato are two renowned wines produced here; mussels are produced in the Gulf of Olbia; and there is a tuna-canning factory. Cattle, pig and sheep farming is carried out, and there is a scheme to establish a local produce trademark. The province also has some nature and wildlife reserves (Riserve di Capo Figari e Figarolo; Oasi di Cosuccia e Saloni; Riserva naturalistica di Monte Nieddu). Three marine and mountain nature parks have been created (Parco Marino di Tavolata, Molara e Capo Coda Cavallo; Parco Internazionale dell'Arcipelago della Maddalena; Parco di Monte Limbara).

OLBIA

Olbia is situated on a stretch of coastal plain which slopes towards the inner part of the gulf.of Olbia; the imposing mass of the **isola di Tavolara*** (Tavolara Island) towers over the town. It was an important port in antiquity; with the growth of the tourist industry in Sardinia over the last thirty years, it has recovered its traditional function as the port linking Sardinia with the Italian mainland peninsula. Olbia's important seaport and airport make it the busiest Italian city in terms of numbers of passengers passing through. Its new transport functions and facilities have produced extremely rapid growth, and this has compromised the town's historic appearance and layout.

A view of the lively and picturesque town of La Maddalena

The bay of Olbia was densely populated in pre-Nuraghic and Nuraghic times, as revealed by dozens of nuraghs, giants' tombs, megalithic fortifications and sacred wells found here. The city originated on a square-shaped terrace slightly higher than the sea: it was almost certainly founded by the Carthaginians (5th-4th centuries BC).

OLBIA-TEMPIO
IN OTHER COLORS...

From Roman times, Olbia's growth went hand in hand with the growth of the port. For many centuries, it was an important and prosperous town; the area inland from Olbia was farmed intensely and dotted with numerous agricultural towns. Acte, the emperor Nero's powerful concubine, owned land, villas and a brick factory here. After the fall of the Roman Empire, Olbia suffered the same destruction and ruin that all coastal Sardinian towns suffered with the barbarian invasions. In the few early-medieval documents surviving, it is referred to as Fausiana. New information about Olbia's history is emerging as a result of an exceptional archeological find made when a tunnel was built in the port area: the remains of around ten Roman boats were found.

In the 11th century, under Pisan rule, the town was rebuilt on the ancient Carthaginian site. It prospered as Terranova (the name it was known by until 1939): sea trade and traffic increased again, and agricultural activity on the plain flourished. Terranova was a bishop's see; a number of churches were built here, including the fine Romanesque church of S. Simplicio (St Simplicius) built between the 11th and 12th centuries, in an unusual position in relation to the town center. There then followed a very long period of stagnation in economic, demographic and construction terms, which famine, disease and malaria contributed to. This continued until the 19th century, when the road linking Olbia to State Road 131 (the Carlo Felice road) was built; the railway was opened and streams flowing to the sea were channelled. Again, the city grew as its port gained importance again. A number of dairy factories were established, and the mussel-farming industry developed in the 1920s. As the city's economy improved, immigrants arrived from the central and southern areas of peninsular Italy. In the last thirty years of the 20th century, strong demographic growth has lifted Olbia to its position as Sardinia's fourth largest city, and lent it a very distinctive ethnic and cultural mix.

Our itinerary provides a clear picture of Olbia's origins and of its development over the centuries. The town also has a marina, a yacht club (near the old port), and many beautiful beaches both to the south and the north; hence it is a good starting point for trips to renowned tourist destinations on the north-east coast (Golfo Aranci, 18 km) and south-east to Caletta in the Siniscola area (54.4 km).

Chiesa di S. Paolo ❶

The church of St Paul is just past the art nouveau Municipality. It was built immediately after the second world war, in granite ashlar with a majolica-tiled cupola. The urban fabric around Corso Umberto is also noteworthy; many buildings have their original granite

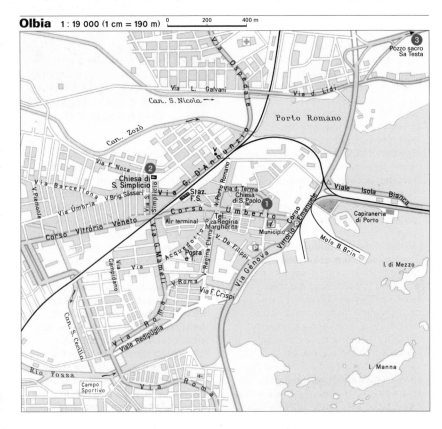

Olbia 1 : 19 000 (1 cm = 190 m)

architraves. The "Simpliciana" Biblioteca comunale (Municipal Library) has a collection of Nuraghic finds; it's in a restored late 19th-century Umbertine-style palazzo at the intersection between Corso Umberto and Via della Terme. In Piazza Regina Margherita, a Carthaginian cistern has been discovered and excavated.

Chiesa di S. Simplicio

The church of St Simplicius is one of Sardinia's most interesting examples of Romanesque architecture. It was built in stages between the 11th and 12th centuries on a Christian burial area, entirely in granite ashlar; it's simpler than other large Romanesque churches in Sardinia. The interior has pillars and columns supporting the trussed roof and the side aisle vaults. There is an interesting collection of funerary inscriptions, from necropolises in the area, and of Roman milestones.

Olbia, the church of S. Simplicio with its Romanesque facade

Pozzo sacro Sa Testa ❸

This sacred well is situated a few meters from the scenic road to Golfo Aranci. It is considered to be one of the most interesting monuments of the type in Sardinia, and is dated to the middle Nuraghic period (7th-6th century BC). The vestibule on the lower floor is reached from the large circular enclosure. A 17-step stairway leads from the vestibule to the tholos chamber (in the shape of a truncated cone) where water gushes from the ground.

TEMPIO PAUSANIA

Tempio Pausania was founded by the Romans; the settlement was formed when two stations along the road between Olbia and Tibula – Gemellae and Templum – were joined. It was a tiny village in terms of population and area. But it became more important from the 16th century, and between the 18th and 19th centuries, the population grew steadily as immigrants arrived from Corsica. The town expanded, and many important churches and civil buildings were built by the town's most important families.

The cork-making industry first began here in the mid-19th century: abandoned factories and offices, "monuments" to industrial architecture, can still be seen in various areas of the city. Today Tempo Pausania is a diocesan see, and a center for legal and financial services. It is also a center for the processing of local resources such as cork and granite. In the sixties, the Experimental Cork Station was founded here, and gained a Europe-wide reputation.

Via Roma is the busiest part of the town, linking Piazza Gallura and Piazza d'Italia. It passes the small square of S. Pietro (St Peter) with its austere granite buildings, and the town's most interesting churches: the Cattedrale (Cathedral) and the oratorio del Rosario (oratory of the Rosary). The Cathedral of St Peter was rebuilt in the 19th century: only the portal and apsed bell-tower survive of the previous 15th-century structure. Inside, in the third and fourth left chapels, there are two finely carved and gilded 18th-century wood altars. The elegant facade of the 18th-century oratorio del Rosario (oratory of the Rosary), looking onto the cathedral, combines a variety of different styles. The Museo Bernardo De Muro, recently annexed to the Biblioteca comunale (Municipal Library), is a museum commemorating the life and work of the local tenor Bernardo De Muro (1881-1955), a famous interpreter of works by Mascagni and Verdi. The collection includes stage costumes, personal objects, photos and portraits, and posters advertising performances.

DAY TRIPS

ARCIPELAGO DELLA MADDALENA

The La Maddalena Archipelago is situated at the far north-eastern tip of Sardinia, and is named after the main island in the group. The islands are granitic, and cover a total surface of 49.3 km². They were inhabited in pre-historic times, and acquired importance under the Romans as bases for ships sailing the Tyrrhenian Sea. After centuries of abandonment, they were once again used in the 12th century by the Pisans and Genoese; then the first inhabited town was established on La Maddalena in the 16th century, when shepherds migrated from Corsica. When Sardinia came under the Piedmontese, the resistance of the rebellious Corsican community was overcome by a military detachment sent to occupy the archipelago in 1767. La Maddalena became more important, with the presence of the Sardinian navy there. The town's main structures were built at this time, starting from the original settlement at Cala Gavetta. In 1887, the Italian government chose the island as a strategic naval base, and as such it was important until the end of the second world war. The naval base and dock had a great influence on the town, and the population increased. Since the 1970s, there's been a US base for atomic submarines in the strait between the islands of La Maddalena and Santo Stefano.

The breathtakingly beautiful islands and sea, as well as the various bird species found here, make this stretch of the coast one of the Mediterranean's most outstanding and exceptional in terms of landscape and natural life. The need to protect and enhance the area's natural, environmental, and historic resources led to the establishment in 1996 of the **Parco nazionale dell'Arcipelago della Maddalena*** (La Maddalena Archipelago National Park). It covers an area of over 20,000 hectares - both land and sea – and 180 km of coastline, and includes all the islands (and islets) which are part of the La Maddalena administrative area. One especially interesting island is Caprera, which was registered by the European Union as one of Europe's most important nature conservation sites, and has been a nature reserve since 1980. In the last thirty years, tourism in the area has received a strong boost from hospitality facilities on some islands; these include the Centro Velico Caprera (Caprera Sailing Center) and the TCI (Touring Club of Italy) tourist resort. Four of the seven largest islands (Santo Stefano, Spargi, Maddalena, Caprera) are near the Gallura coast; the other

La Maddalena, the port. With a coastline of 45 km, it is the largest island in the archipelago of the same name

Arcipelago della Maddalena   1 : 140 000 (1 cm = 1,4 km)   0   1,5   3 km

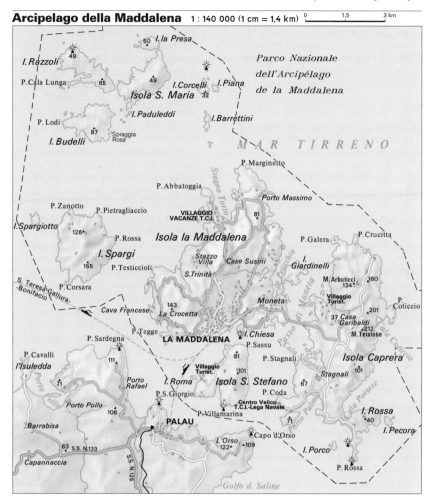

three (Budelli, Razzoli, Santa Maria) are nearer the Bocche di Bonifacio, the strait between Sardinia and Corsica.
La Maddalena. Covering an area of 19.61 km², and with a 45 km coastline, this is the archipelago's largest island. It's triangular in shape, rising to a rugged plateau in the center; its highest point (Guardia Vecchia) reaches 156 m. Lively Piazza Garibaldi, close to the seafront, is full of crowded bars and cafés, and the island's main official buildings, such as the Municipality. The charming old town is nearby, with the parrocchiale di S. Maria Maddalena (parish church of St Mary Magdalen): it has two silver candleholders and a silver Crucifix donated by Horatio Nelson who anchored off La Maddalena with the British fleet before the Battle of Trafalgar.

Via Vittorio Emanuele leads to the little fishing port and marina of Cala Gavetta. Piazza Umberto I, where the Navy buildings are, is just past the port. The Museo Archeologico Navale "Nino Lamboglia" is an archeological naval museum which exhibits finds from a Roman boat shipwrecked in 120 BC near the island of Spargi. A reconstruction of the hull contains a remarkable number of amphorae arranged according to the method of loading used by the Romans. Objects displayed include nails, tiles, pieces of hull, shipboard implements and equipment used by the crew, illustrating how sailors lived and methods of navigation.
Today the town is the base for the Sardinian Autonomous Navy Command and the Navy Non-commissioned Officers School.

Caprera. The island is believed by geographers to be Ptolemy's ancient Phintonis, and is situated east of La Maddalena. It is the second largest island in the archipelago, with a surface area of 15.75 km² and a coastline 34 km long. The east coast of the island, where Monte Teialone rises to 212 m, is very rugged; the west coast is flatter, with pastureland and pine forests. The island was partially acquired in 1855 by Giuseppe Garibaldi who built a house and some outbuildings here. In 1978 a museum was established here, the Museo Nazionale del Compendio garibaldino (National Garibaldi Compendium Museum). It occupies the west side of a courtyard, over which the pine tree towers that Garibaldi planted on the occasion of his daughter Clelia's birth. The museum consists of a number of intercommunicating rooms, relating to the domestic life and interests of Garibaldi, with doors giving direct access outside. The rooms have been preserved with the functions they originally had, and contain objects, furnishings, paintings and numerous mementos. The bed in the room where Garibaldi died is surrounded by a balustrade donated by the Livorno Società Reduci (Livorno Veterans Association). The oven and windmill built by Garibaldi himself can be seen behind the house.

Santo Stefano. The island of Santo Stefano is situated between the town of La Maddalena, and Palau on mainland Sardinia. The forte di S. Giorgio (fort of St George), also known as Napoleon's fort, can be seen from the ferry. It was part of the system of fortifications built at the end of the 18th century. Napoleon Bonaparte, who at the time was a young lieutenant-colonel in the Corsican National Guard, directed the bombardment of La Maddalena from here during the 1793 French attack. There are two large cannon balls in the La Maddalena municipality.

Spargi. The island is round, with rugged terrain. Its highest point is Monte Guardia Preposti (155 m). There's a small settlement of shepherds and a lovely, much-visited beach, Cala Corsara.

Budelli. This island lies north of Spargi and is uninhabited. It's well-known for its pink beach; the color comes from minute particles of coral. It's also famous because the Italian director Michelangelo Antonioni shot some scenes for "Red Desert" here. In 1992, there were controversial plans to build a tourist resort on the island. Its uniqueness is now protected by a protection order as part of the Geo-marine Park of La Maddalena. The islands of **Razzoli** and **Santa Maria** lie to the north-west and north-east, facing the Bocche di Bonifacio, and separated by a passage (Passo degli Asinelli). The former is completely uninhabited; its coastline is steep, and is only accessible on the western side. The latter is almost all flat; it's inhabited and partly cultivated.

ARZACHENA

The town lies on a rocky ridge, and grew up over the Roman settlement of Turibulum Minor. Up until the late 19th century, it was merely a group of houses gathered around the country chiesa di S. Maria (church of St Mary), built in 1776, which has now been restored according to the original structure. Arzachena has grown rapidly, from the second half of the 20th century, in its new role as "capital" of the Costa Smeralda; the number of houses increased rapidly, along with strong growth in the business, construction and tertiary sectors. The area around Arzachena has many archeological sites, some of great interest. One example is the **tomba di giganti di Lu Coddhu 'Ecchju** (Lu Coddhu 'Ecchju giants'

Arzachena, Giants' tombs

tomb), also known as the "Capinera giants' tomb". The enormous front of the tomb is largely occupied by a granite stele, over 4 m high. The tomb could have held dozens of deceased. Nearby there is an interesting nuragh, La Prisgiona, and the **necropoli di Li Muri** (Li Muri necropolis). Excavation work began in 1940; it consists of five large dolmenic cists (tombs built on stone slabs surrounded by small circles of closely-placed stones). Here

west end, past Punta della Volpe. Porto Rotondo is also the name of the luxury seaside resort and tourist town situated here, with its tasteful buildings centered around the small square. It is worth visiting the chiesa di S. Lorenzo (church of St Lawrence) designed by Andrea Cascella, with 20 wood statues by the sculptor Mario Ceroli. The excellent marina makes this the best-known of the coastal resorts to have sprung up over the last twenty years north of Olbia.

Porto Cervo has developed as the Costa Smeralda has developed, and is the biggest town in the area

archeologists have found evidence of an early culture known as the Li Muri culture, or the circle tomb culture, which was contemporaneous with the very first Nuraghic civilisation. The **tomba di giganti di Li Lolghi*** (Li Lolghi giants' tomb) is close by. These two giants' tombs are among Sardinia's largest, finest and best preserved.

GOLFO ARANCI

The shores of this small gulf in the Gallura region, near Capo Figari, are riddled with grottoes. The name Aranci derives from a mistranscription of "di li ranci", which means "of crabs". It was a fishing village; now it has become the final port of call for ferries from Civitavecchia. It is also a seaside resort, and popular for underwater diving. The large bay of **Golfo di Marinella***, north-west of Golfo Aranci, has Mediterranean maquis vegetation, rocky little promontories, and steep hills. The little bay of **Porto Rotondo** is at the north-

PORTO CERVO

Porto Cervo is an internationally known resort, set in an isolated bay. It consists of luxury accomodation, restaurants and bars, and a modern marina. The town revolves around the famous "piazzetta" (little piazza), and culminates in the chiesa Stella Maris (Star of the Sea church), with a bronze portal by the artist Luciano Minguzzi. The marina has excellent facilities and berths for 500 boats, on seven berthing jetties.

SANTA TERESA DI GALLURA

The town was once a fishing village but today is a seaside tourist resort. It lies on a rocky terrace, on the west side of a deep bay called Porto Longonsardo, on the northern tip of Sardinia. The bay lies opposite the windy Bocche di Bonifacio separating Sardinia from Corsica . The town was founded in 1808 under the Savoys (Vittorio Emanuele I's wife was called Teresa), to control smuggling and as a strategic defence against Napoleon.

Oristano is situated just inland from the gulf of Oristano, halfway along the west coast of Sardinia; it lies at the western end of a large, flat flood plain, bounded to the north by the river Tirso, to the west by coastal dunes, and to the south by a lagoon or lake (lo stagno di Santa Giusta). As early as the 7th century, the Byzantine writer George of Cyprus referred to Oristano's lake *(Aristianes limine)*. In the 12th century, the city's name was wrongly assumed to derive from the words "Aureum Stagnum" (meaning "golden pond" in Latin); the city's coat-of-arms shows a piece of land emerging from a golden lagoon. In fact, the names derives from *Aristianum*: in Roman times, large tracts of land here were owned by a man named Aristius. There were three towns in the area inland from the gulf, in ancient times: Tharros on Capo San Marco to the north, Neapolis south-east of Capo Frasca, and Òthoca near today's town of Santa Giusta.

The first traces of the new town date from around the 6th century, and the beginning of the Byzantine age: a necropolis developed around the church of S. Maria Assunta (St Mary Assumption), which became the town's cathedral in the 11th century. A number of reasons (ports silting up, piracy, decreasing population) led to the abandonment of Tharros and Neapolis. Òthoca, renamed Sancta Justa, became less important than Aristiane which was protected from the sea and lagoons. From the end of the 13th century, the center of the medieval city was surrounded by a turreted city wall. There were two points of entry: Porta Manna (Great Gate) to the north, and Porta Mari (Sea or Lagoon Gate) to the south-west, which was destroyed in 1907, and was near the torre di S. Filippo (tower of St Philip) which once stood in Piazza Manno. In the 12th century Oristano sided with the Aragonese, thus avoiding alliance with the city of Pisa; in 1323 it supported the establishment of the *Regnum Sardiniae et Corsicae (Kingdom of Sardinia and Corsica)*. In the mid 14th century, the great ruler Marianus IV and, subsequently, his children Ugone III and Eleonora d'Arborèa were forced to fight against the Catalan-Aragonese armies. The war ended with the defeat of the d'Arborèa dynasty at Sanluri (1409). The three centuries of Aragonese and Spanish rule brought about a steep decline in the city's fortunes. In the 18th century (and even more in the 19th) the city underwent a remarkable transformation in terms of building and urban layout. The cathedral was rebuilt in Baroque style, the chiesa del Carmine (church of the Carmine) and chiesa di S. Efisio (church of St Ephisius) in late 18th-century style, and S. Francesco (St Francis) and S. Vincenzo (St Vincent) in neo-Classical style.

Oritano's new areas (Città Giardino, San Nicola, Torangius) changed the town's appearance, with their enormous buildings in làdiris (or mud bricks), surrounded by high walls.

Duomo ❶

The Duomo is dedicated to St Mary Assumption. Although it has an 18th-century appearance, it was built in the 13th century; the bell-tower dates from the 15th century. The first chapel on the right has a polychrome wood Annunciation by Nino Pisano (14th century) and parts of two 12th-century Romanesque ambos (an ambo is a raised platform in the presbytery, for reading holy texts), which were recycled and used again by a 14th-century Catalan artist. The presbytery has 19th-century paintings by Giovanni Marghinotti, and an 18th-century oval (Assumption) by Vittorio Amodeo Rapous. The 14th-century cappella del Rimedio (Chapel of Remedy) is on the right. The large chapels at the end of the two arms of the transept date from 1830; four standards captured from the French during the 1637 siege hang from the walls. A passage behind the 18th-century main altar leads to the adjacent Aula capitolare (Capitulary Hall) which has thirteen 13th- to 14th-century illustrated anthem books.

The nearby chiesa del Carmine (church of the Carmine) is also 18th-century.

The Duomo bell-tower

Oristano: Cathedral of S. Maria Assunta (St. Mary Assumption)

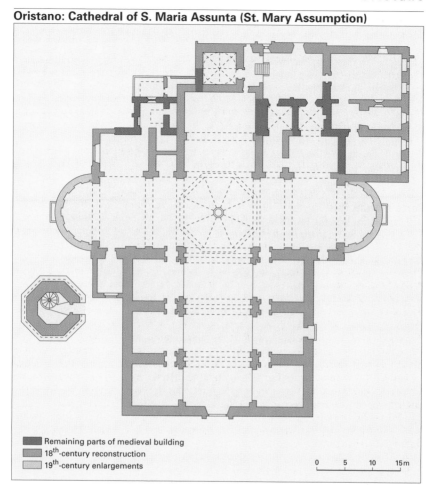

■ Remaining parts of medieval building
■ 18th-century reconstruction
■ 19th-century enlargements

0   5   10   15m

S. Francesco ❷

The church of St Francis was originally built in the 13th century, and later rebuilt in neo-Classical style. The left altar has a 15th-century wood **Crucifix*** of the Catalan school. The central painting in the sacristy altarpiece is by Pietro Cavaro (1533); the others are in the Antiquarium Arborense. There's a superb mid-13th-century Gothic **cloister***, modified according to Catalan style in the 16th century. The nearby Piazza Eleonora is named after Eleonora d'Arborèa, mistress of the city from 1383 to 1404 and famous for the Logu charter, an important medieval legislative codex.

Antiquarium Arborense ❸

The Antiquarium was founded in 1938, when the State acquired the collection belonging to Efisio Pischedda, an archeologist and lawyer. The collection has been housed since 1992 in the historic Palazzo Parpaglia, which was specially renovated for the purpose. There are three main sections. The first contains prehistoric finds from the Sinis area: Nuraghic bronzes; Etruscan, Greek and Roman pottery; and Phoenician-Carthaginian finds exhibited in a reconstructed Phoenician tomb from Tharros. A large model at

ORISTANO
IN OTHER COLORS...

the center of the room recreates the ancient town of Tharros. The second section has three retablos from churches in Oristano: one by a 15th-century Catalan painter (St Martin), one by Pietro Cavaro in 1533 (Stigmata of St Francis), and one by Antìoco Mainas in 1565 (Madonna of the Councillors). The third section has two late 13th-century inscriptions by Marianus II d'Arborèa which refer to the construction of the city tower and walls.

Porta Manna ❹

Porta Manna was the town's main gate. It's also known as the torre di Mariano II (tower of Marianus II), after Marianus II d'Arborèa who had it built in 1291, although the upper part dates from later. The gate is also known as the torre di S. Cristoforo (St Christopher's tower), since inside there a retablo of St Christopher, the patron saint of travellers, which was placed inside possibly in the 15th century. The niche for the small retablo,

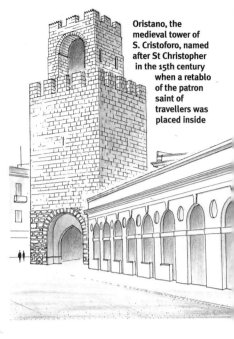

Oristano, the medieval tower of S. Cristoforo, named after St Christopher in the 15th century when a retablo of the patron saint of travellers was placed inside

recently carefully restored, is on the right as you enter through the Gothic gate.

Oristano 1:12 300 (1 cm = 123 m)

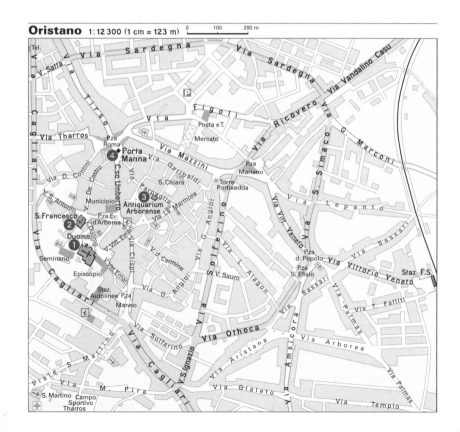

Bosa: Serravalle Castle

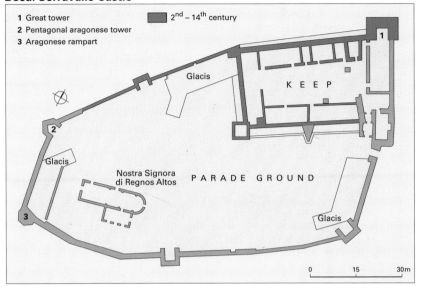

1 Great tower
2 Pentagonal aragonese tower
3 Aragonese rampart

2nd – 14th century

Glacis

K E E P

Glacis

Nostra Signora
di Regnos Altos

P A R A D E   G R O U N D

Glacis

0   15   30m

DAY TRIPS

BOSA [62 km]

The town was founded in ancient times, according to some scholars as far back as the 9th century BC. It was a strongly fortified town, from around the year 1000, and enjoyed considerable prosperity as a result of its strategic position, which meant that it was seen as the "key to the whole island".
Its decline began in 1528, partly because of the silting up of the mouth of the Temo river. The Savoys supported the town's revival, and promoted coral harvesting. But the town's real economic rebirth came in the 19th century with an increase in craft activities (especially leather working and precious metals). The medieval town grew around the unusual conical conformation of the Serravalle hill, and clustered around the castle for protection. The originally late-medieval quarter of Sa Costa, with its various layers of building history, conveys a strong feel of the past. Its distinctive lanes and alleys follow the contours of the hill, the stairways asymmetrically intercept the horizontal paths, and its centuries-old layout and structures are fascinating.
The massive complex of the **Castello di Serravalle or dei Malaspina ❶**

(Serravalle or Malaspina Castle) was built in various stages, from the second decade of the 12th century, when some of the castle's towers were constructed following a design similar to that of Cagliari's Castle of S. Michele (St Michael). The large tower is built in pale pink trachytic tufa; the base is in pink trachyte ashlarwork. Two subsequent enlargements extended the complex's perimeter to 300 m, with seven polygonal and square towers, covering an area of over a hectare. Other important modifications, such as for example the three glacises for gun placements, were made in 1468.
The restored chiesa di Nostra Signora di Regnos Altos (the church of Our Lady of Regnos Altos) was built in the 14th century in the parade ground within the castle walls. In 1972 a remarkable fresco cycle was found in its interior, dating from 1350 to 1370. The cycle is painted on the three main walls of the original building, on two levels separated by a trussed cornice.
A Carmelite monastery (today the Municipality) and the adjacent **chiesa del Carmine ❷** (church of the Carmine), consecrated in 1810, were built in 1779 on the ruins of the chiesa di nostra Signora del Soccorso (church of Our Lady of Succour). The church has a single nave with four chapels on either

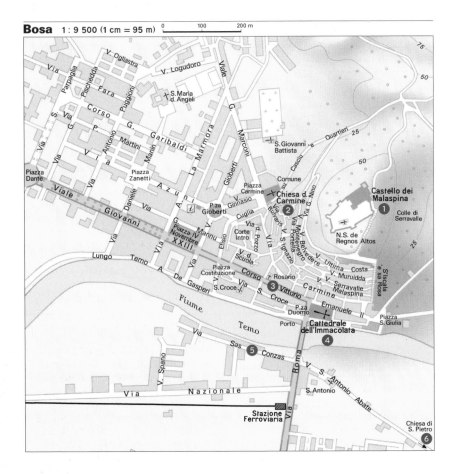

Bosa 1 : 9 500 (1 cm = 95 m)

side, and is built very simply. There is only one concession to Sardinian taste, seen in the sophisticated use of color in the pink trachyte framework structures. The church has a bell-tower and three cupolas placed asymmetrically, on the presbytery and on two side chapels. Inside, there is an exquisite Baroque-style wooden door. One of the town's main streets, **Corso Vittorio Emanuele** ❸, is an elegant urban thoroughfare which crosses the 18th-century Sa Pitta quarter. The corso is flanked by 18th- to 19th-century houses with attractive balconies and wrought iron railings. Don't miss Palazzo Don Carlos in Piazza Costituzione; other buildings to look out for are the Scarpa house and the recently-restored Uras house. The side streets, paved in cobblestones and basalt, are often reached through arches on the Corso. The **Cattedrale dell'Immacolata** ❹ (Cathedral of the Immaculate Virgin),

on Corso Vittorio Emanuele was rebuilt in the 19th century by Salvatore Are; its original 12th-century structure had already previously been modified in the 15th century. The facade is divided into two orders by a solid cornice; it has a distinctively light and elegant roof over the main door. The interior is long and very spacious. Rising above the choir, the octagonal cupola was decorated in 1877 with a scene from Dante's Paradise by the painter Emilio Scherer, who also painted the frescoes in the apse and the presbytery. The colorful artisan area, **Sas Conzas** ❺, is on the left side of the river. The large buildings here were used for tanning hides from the 18th century, and today are fine examples of industrial architecture. The complex was still in use immediately after the second world war, and was classified as a protected site in 1989. The group of buildings cover around 4000 square meters overall, for

Bosa, the cathedral of S. Pietro. Constructed between 1062 and 1073, it is one of Sardinia's most beautiful Romanesque-Gothic buildings

CABRAS [8 km]

Cabras is a medieval town, referred to as «masone de Capras» in a 12th-century document; it lies on the shores of the vast Cabras Lagoon. A few brick remains survive of the castle belonging to the d'Arborèa family which once stood by the lagoon waters, behind the 16th-to 17th-century parrocchiale di S. Maria (St Mary's parish church). The Cabras Museo Civico (Municipal Museum) was opened in 1997. It's a solid square building in pink trachyte, standing by the lagoon, in Via Tharros. It's organised in two sections. The first recreates the various phases of human settlement in the Sinis area, from pre-history to early-medieval times. The second section exhibits pre-Nuraghic and Phoenician-Carthaginian archeological finds. They come from excavations at Cuccuru Is Arrius and at Tharros, which was founded by the Phoenicians around 800 BC; the area had been occupied in the second half of the second millennium BC by Nuraghic settlements, and later came under Roman rule in 238 BC. The museum also has temporary exhibitions. The Cabras lagoon is referred to in 13th-century maps as Maris, derived from Mar' 'e Pontis, or sea and bridge in Latin; it is like a sea because of the enormous area it covers (around 2000 hectares), and there was a large Roman bridge which linked the important towns of Tharros and Òthoca.

a volume of around 27,000 cubic meters. Currently they are in very poor condition. They make a fine sight though, with their gables ranged in ranks by the river. The **chiesa di S. Pietro** ⑥ (church of St Peter) is also on the Temo river. This was the old cathedral of Bosa, started between 1062 and 1073; an inscription inside bears the name of the bishop, Costantino de Castra, who had the church built. The facade is attributed to Anselmo da Como, and is topped by a small columned aedicule on the cusp. The facade also boasts three four-lobed rose-windows, which have been altered, and three pointed arches with the symbols of the four evangelists. The architrave in limestone bears the archaic figures of St Peter and St Paul, of the Madonna and Child, and of the emperor St Constantine. Very interesting pre-Christian inscriptions from the nearby Roman necropolis, and medieval inscriptions are embedded in the apse wall.

Cabras, a large village of medieval origin on the banks of the lake of the same name

FORDONGIANUS [26 km]

This small, predominantly agricultural town has some very appealing houses in reddish trachyte, and is known for its hot springs. It has some important pre-historic remains, and interesting monuments dating from historic times. The town probably came into being towards the end of the 1st century BC, because of the hot springs. Its ancient name was Aquae Ypsitanae, and later Forum Traiani, which its current name derives from. From the 5th century, it was a bishop's see. In Byzantine times, it acquired new fortifications and was a place of residence for Sardinia's military commanders, probably known as Chrysopolis (golden city). There are various Roman ruins, such as the remains of an aqueduct, of an amphitheatre, and of civic buildings: the most important is the thermal complex situated near the left bank of the Tirso. The oldest part is the large pool with portico, which made use of the natural hot waters (54°C/130°F) and which dates from the 1st century AD.

The picturesque remains of the Roman baths at Fordongianus

GHILARZA [37 km]

The Romanesque chiesa di S. Palmerio (church of St Palmerius) is situated in Piazza Palmerio in delightful medieval surroundings. It was built between 1200 and 1225; it has alternating ashlar bands in dark and white trachyte, and a fine tripartite arcaded facade. To the side, there is a solid 15th-century tower, an excellent example of Catalan military architecture; it was used from the 17th century as a prison, then abandoned, and later used as a prison again from 1893. The Centro documentazione e ricerca Casa Gramsci (Gramsci House Documents and Research Center) is at Corso Umberto 57. This house, where Antonio Gramsci (1891-1937) lived from 1898 to 1908, is now a museum and cultural center, with a library. The library on the ground floor contains Gramsci's works (foreign-language editions too), and books on the history of the workers' movement and the Communist Party. On a wall, there is a copy of the letter he wrote to his mother on the 10th of May 1928 from San Vittore prison, in Milan. In the Casa del Forno (Oven House) there are artworks donated to the museum by contemporary artists. On the first floor, there is a presentation of Gramsci's life from his childhood years to imprisonment and death, together with the testimony of people who shared political activity and imprisonment with him.

NURAGHE LOSA [40 km]

The Losa Nuragh complex near Abbasanta is one of Sardinia's most important pre-historic sites. It reveals two stages of construction, both probably dating from the second half of the 2nd millennium BC. The oldest part consists of a two-level tower. It has central chambers one above the other (the lower one with three niches), with false ceilings, and connected by a spiral staircase starting from the corridor. Subsequently this structure was incorporated in a triangular bastion with three towers, two accessible from corridors starting just past the main entrance, and the third from a secondary entrance on the north side. Another two towers, with slit openings, and joined by massive curtain walls, protect the back part of the complex; opposite the main entrance there is a tower with two entrances opposite each other, whose purpose is still not entirely clear. A wider circle of walling would have protected the village lying around the complex.

PENISOLA DEL SINIS [20 km]

The **penisola del Sinis** (Sinis Peninsula) stretches north to south between the Cabras lagoon and the sea, with a slimmer promontory and Capo San Marco forming the northern part of the

Golfo di Oristano (Oristano Gulf). It is 20 km long and 5 km wide, and sparsely populated, with high steep coastline interspersed with long beaches.

San Salvatore is located at around 8 km, along a short road off to the right; it's a religious village which grew in the 17th- to 18th-century around the church of the same name. A staircase inside the church leads to a pagan **hypogeic sanctuary***, partially excavated in the rock and mostly constructed (around 300 AD). Here the cult of the waters was practised by the members of a religious group. Divinities from the Roman pantheon (Hercules, Venus, Mars, Eros, a Muse) are depicted on the walls, along with charriot races, gladiator scenes and ships, symbolising the struggle the gods fought against evil. The church's name of San Salvatore (St Saviour) also appears to relate it to the cult of salvation.

SANTU LUSSURGIU [10 km]

The chiesa di S. Lussurgiu (church of St Luxurius) was built by Vittorini monks around 1100, above an early Christian hypogeum. St Luxurius was buried here, according to tradition, after his martyrdom in 304 under Diocletian's persecution campaign. The site is in the extra-urban burial area of Forum Traiani (Fordongianus). The church retains the north flank and apse of the original Romanesque building, with Provençal influence. The south flank, which collapsed with the original barrel-vaulted ceiling, was rebuilt between 1250 and 1270, while the facade was rebuilt even later (15th century). Access to the hypogeum, where the bodies of the martyrs St Luxurius and St Archelaus are supposed to lie, is gained from inside the church. The hypogeum consists of a long corridor with a barrel-vaulted ceiling; remains of frescoes and mosaic flooring can be seen, dating from the 4th and 5th centuries. Excavations carried out during restoration work have brought to light the foundations of a 7th-century Byzantine church.

SANTA GIUSTA [3 km]

Santa Giusta was the Phoenician town of Òthoca, which means "old town" in Semitic. Its current name is recorded as being used from the 12th century, in connection with the worship of a local martyr. Òthoca was founded by the Phoenicians around 730 BC to draw benefit from the agricultural and farming resources of the Campidano area, as well as the plentiful supply of fish which the lagoon provided. Excavation work, which began in the second half of the 19th century, has revealed remains of the ancient city walls on the hill where the cathedral is, traces of the inhabited area (today's area of Is Olionis), and most of all, the necropolis. It was used until the 1st century BC. A Phoenician chamber tomb, built in sandstone blocks, and part of the necropolis, can be visited at the chiesa di S. Severa (church of St Severa). The Romans built the bridge over the Rio Palmas, with five arches (only two survive), and a stretch survives of the paved Roman road which linked Òthoca and Kàrales (Cagliari).

The Romanesque **cattedrale di S. Giusta** (Cathedral of St Justine) stands on the area's highest point, once the site of the ancient acropolis. It was built in 1135-45 by skilled craftsmen who used the golden Sinis sandstone together with more austere white marble and ferruginous basalt. The facade has three arches which frame the portal, with its zoomorphous pillar capitals and triple window. The gable top is decorated with rhomboid motifs. Arches along the top of the flanks are accompanied alternately with trusses and pilasters. The austere interior has a central nave and two side aisles separated by marble and granite columns, whose capitals and bases were mostly removed very probably from Roman buildings in Òthoca. The presbytery is built over a crypt.

The cathedral of S. Giusta, built at the top of the acropolis in the first half of the 12th century

The Losa di Abbasanta Nuragh

The word "losa" means "tomb" in Sardinian. The Losa Nuragh is one of Sardinia's most important nuraghs. It is an example of a complex form of these monuments built by the Nuraghic civilization, which lasted almost a thousand years from 1500 BC to 500 BC); they are the most obvious expression of that Sardinian diversity which has always made the culture and history of the island distinctive. A nuragh is a conical-shaped tower, built of rows of large stones placed one above the other, without using any cement. The towers were normally four to five meters high, although sometimes they could also be over ten. Single tower structures normally measured a few meters across at the base. Generally the structures were more complex, and also included bastions, courtyards, ramparts, and smaller towers. The term nuragh may derive from "nur", a term used in Proto-Sardinian (the language

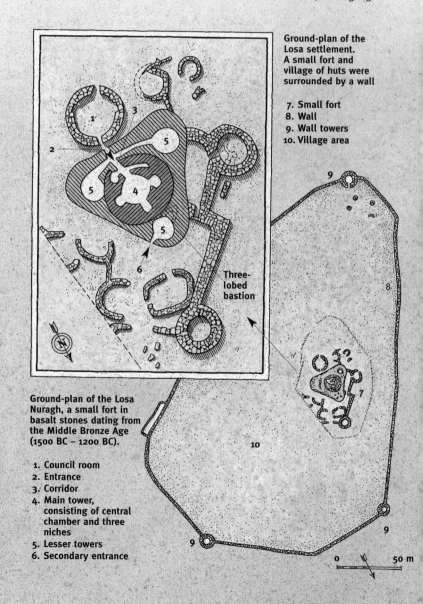

Ground-plan of the Losa settlement. A small fort and village of huts were surrounded by a wall

7. Small fort
8. Wall
9. Wall towers
10. Village area

Three-lobed bastion

Ground-plan of the Losa Nuragh, a small fort in basalt stones dating from the Middle Bronze Age (1500 BC – 1200 BC).

1. Council room
2. Entrance
3. Corridor
4. Main tower, consisting of central chamber and three niches
5. Lesser towers
6. Secondary entrance

0   50 m

spoken before the Roman conquest); it probably meant "hollow mound of stones, cavity", describing the structure of the monuments. They may have been castles for tribal leaders, buildings symbolising the aristocratic power of the clan, safe strongholds for the elderly and people of the village, or the temple-tombs of tribal heroes. But whatever they were, the nuraghs survive as evidence of a unique and original culture. The Losa Nuragh consists of a central tower on two levels, and a three-lobed bastion with a concave-convex outline. A wall with two towers surrounds both the small fort and the village of circular or oval huts, which dates from the Nuraghic age. There is a small antiquarium in the area, with exhibits that bear witness to life on the site, from the Nuraghic age up until the time when it was last inhabited, in Roman and early medieval times.

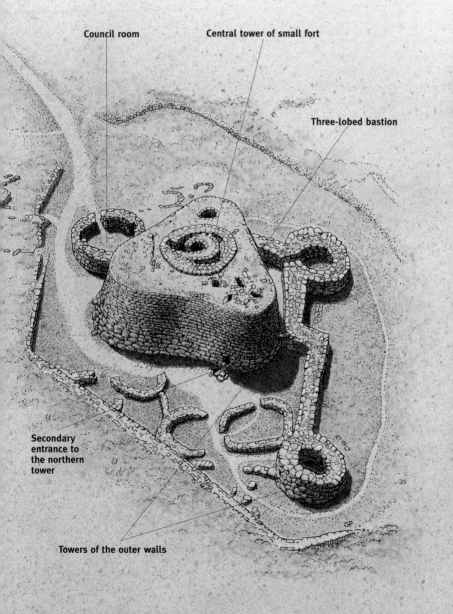

Council room

Central tower of small fort

Three-lobed bastion

Secondary entrance to the northern tower

Towers of the outer walls

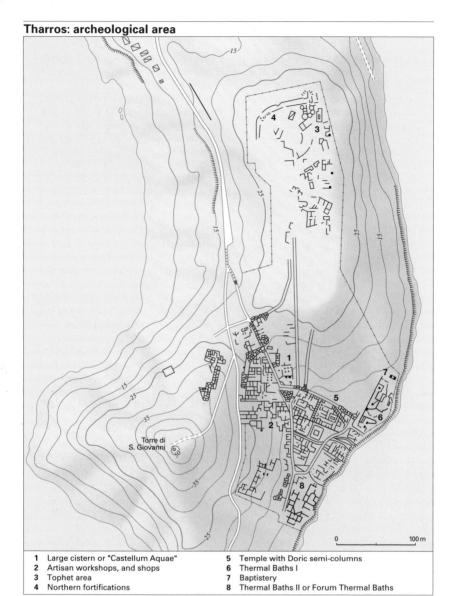

1	Large cistern or "Castellum Aquae"	5	Temple with Doric semi-columns
2	Artisan workshops, and shops	6	Thermal Baths I
3	Tophet area	7	Baptistery
4	Northern fortifications	8	Thermal Baths II or Forum Thermal Baths

THARROS [15 km]

Tharros was a town with the sea on two sides, like Corinth. The Phoenicians had a preference for small tapering peninsulas, where they founded their colonies. These promontories enabled them to always have their ships protected from the waves, whichever way the wind was blowing. Tharros was built around 730-700 BC, essentially as a port. In the 7th and 6th centuries BC, the reach of Tharros traders was enormous; they ranged from Cyprus to Egypt, from Ionia to Etruria, and from Spain to the Celtic world.

The Carthaginian conquest of Sardinia in 510 BC did not affect Tharros's control of the sea. But the Roman occupation in 238 BC marked a change in the fortunes of the ancient city: the new commercial trade routes, centered on Rome, meant that the city declined from around 77 BC. The first Christian communities are recorded from the 4th century; from the 6th century, the town had a bishop. The dangers of sea travel in Byzantine times meant Tharros was reduced to a castrum or military camp; the civilian population had to establish a new town at Sines, near the chiesa di S. Giovanni di Sinis (church of St John of Sinis). Saracen raids brought about a further decrease in the population, until Tharros-Sines was abandoned in 1070, in favour of Oristano, not far away.

Our visit of the **archeological area** starts from the small display center at the entrance to the site; here you can see the town layout, ground-plans of the main buildings, and photographs of Phoenician-Carthaginian objects found during excavation work carried out here, from 1956. The town is substantially as it was in late Roman times (3rd- to 4th-century AD), although there is some evidence of the Carthaginian town and of the early medieval town.

From the display center, follow the road on the right paved with basalt, as far as a small piazza (compitum), which had a shrine consacrated to the Lares compitales, or gods who protected crossroads. On the north side, there is a large four-sided building, which was the cistern, or castellum aquae, the water reservoir which the 2nd- to 3rd-century AD aqueduct flowed into, and which supplied the public fountain.

From the square the main road leads north; drains ran down the middle (today covered over) and on either side there would have been artisan workshops, shops and various eating and drinking places.

Further on there is an arena, and outside the arena, walls supporting embanked earth, where wooden steps would have been arranged. This, the

Ancient ruins, the sky and the sea at Tharros

Tharros amphitheater (2nd- to 3rd-century AD), was located on the edge of town, possibly to protect the community from attack if the wild beasts used in the games escaped. The arena partially occupied the area occupied by the tophet, the sanctuary which was a feature of Phoenician-Carthaginian towns. The tophet held cinerary urns of children who were born dead or died young; they were consecrated to the god Baal and, from the 5th century BC, also to the Phoenician goddess Thanit.

The Tharros tophet was used between the 8th and 2nd centuries BC; it had been built over the ruins of a Nuraghic village formed of circular huts, dating from the 15th- to 14th-century BC. The northern fortifications of the town can be seen past the tophet. Excavation work has revealed the remains of Carthaginian walls with square towers built in regular sandstone blocks (late 6th-century BC), overlaid by a wall made of polygonal basalt blocks dating from republican Roman times (2nd century BC). A walled trench dates from the same time; it was filled in, in the 1st century BC, and then by the 1st century AD was being used as a cemetery. Returning along the road from the amphitheater to the compitum, there is a sweeping view southwards, over the steep promontory of San Marco at the end of the Sinis peninsula, and past the gulf of Oristano, over the long Frasca promontory with the blue Arcuentu and Linas mountains above. From the compitum, the road goes left towards the gulf. Along the paved road, the large thermal baths III complex (not completely excavated yet) is on the left; on the right, the remains of a Carthaginian temple can be seen, with Doric semi-columns, carved partly in sandstone, dating from the early 3rd century BC.

The road comes to an end opposite the 2nd-century AD thermal baths, used by Christians in the 5th century to build a basilica with a hexagonal baptistery. This can be seen north of the baths. To the right, from the baths, two columns have been re-raised and restored. There was probably a four-columned Corinthian temple here, dating from around 50 BC.

The road leads to a trapezoid-shaped piazza which still has Roman paving on the right side: the Foro di Tharros (Tharros Forum), the business center around which the main public buildings were located. The south-east side of the piazza was flanked by a portico leading to themal baths II, also known as the Forum baths, dating from 200 AD. From here, the road leads up to the left, and returns to the compitum, and then to the exit.

SASSARI

Sassari lies on a gently sloping calcareous plateau, at the edge of the plain that goes down to the sea. It's the second largest city in Sardinia in terms of population and of economic, political and cultural importance. In the middle ages, in the place where today's city stands, there was a small village called *Tathari*; it grew as people fled here from the Saracens, from the Pisans and from the Genoese. In 1378 Sassari was occupied and remained under the control of the d'Arborèa family until 1420. Then in the 15th century it became part of the new institutional and administrative system of Sardinia which, as an independent kingdom, was part of the Catalan-Aragonese federation. The flourishing of the Catalan Gothic style in civil and church architecture dates from this time, and today is still a distinctive feature of the old town. Under Spanish rule, the city suffered hard times, largely due to the Mediterranean wars and stagnating trade and commerce. Sassari, of all the towns and cities in Sardinia, was the closest to humanism and the cultural models of the Italian Renaissance. Echoes of 16th-century classicism can be identified in some buildings in the old town, such as Palazzo d'Usini in the old city square known as the *carra manna* (today Piazza Tola), or in the facade of the Jesuit church of Gesù e Maria (Jesus and Mary), today known as S. Caterina (St Catherine).

In 1652, in the midst of a fierce dispute with Cagliari, Sassari was struck by a terrible plague epidemic which decimated the city's population. The second half of the century, however, was not a period of decline: the population increased and the introduction of new types of agriculture laid the foundations for 18th-century prosperity. Signs of growth in the agricultural economy and in cultural life were evident, especially during the reign of Carlo Emanuele III (1730-73): new crops were promoted (mulberries, potatoes), the port of Torres was rehabilitated, commerce was encouraged and the University was reopened (1765).

In the first half of the 19th century, the city grew considerably, as a result of the 1836 plan for expansion to the south-west, towards the "royal road" from Sassari to Cagliari, completed in 1829. In the second half of the century, almost all the city walls were demolished and the Aragonese castle (built around 1330) was demolished. The end of the century was a time of much cultural activity, in literature, music, art and politics. The population continued to increase in the twenty years of the Fascist regime and much public and private building was carried out. Three new town development plans, drawn up between 1929 and 1942, provided for suburban expansion and the creation of the new working-class quarter of Monte Rosello, and the residential area of Viale Italia-Porcellana. After the second world war, Sassari was fairly lively culturally and politically, despite the limits and contradictions of it economic growth. Three men from Sassari, Antonio Segni, Enrico Berlinguer and Francesco Cossiga, were key players in Italy's post-war political life.

Sassari from above: in the foreground Piazza Castello, then Piazza d'Italia and Via Roma in a straight line

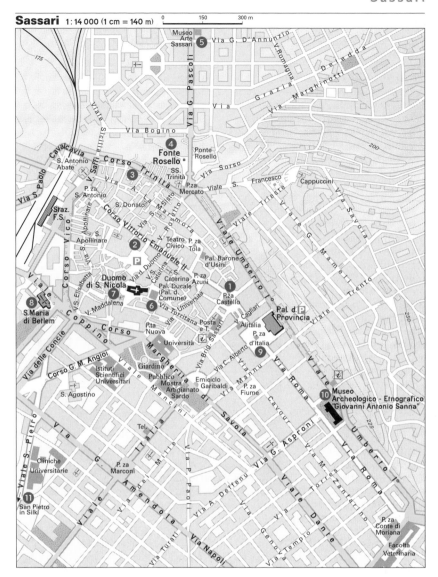

Sassari 1 : 14 000 (1 cm = 140 m)

Piazza Castello ❶

The piazza is named after the old Aragonese castle built around 1330, and once the seat of the Court of the Inquisition. It was demolished in 1877, and the La Marmora barracks (1878-1881) was built in its place. Coats-of-arms from the castle facade can be seen in the courtyard. Inside the barracks, the Museo storico della Brigata Sassari (Sassari Brigade Historical Museum) tells the story of the heroism of the Sardinian infantry in the first world war. The Politeama Giuseppe Verdi (Giuseppe Verdi Theater), built in 1884,

is in nearby Via Politeama. On the left side of the square, the chiesa della Madonna del Rosario (church of the Madonna of the Rosary) has an

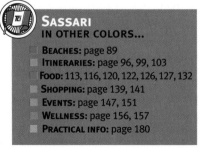

SASSARI
IN OTHER COLORS...

☐ **BEACHES:** page 89
☐ **ITINERARIES:** page 96, 99, 103
☐ **FOOD:** 113, 116, 120, 122, 126, 127, 132
☐ **SHOPPING:** page 139, 141
☐ **EVENTS:** page 147, 151
☐ **WELLNESS:** page 156, 157
☐ **PRACTICAL INFO:** page 180

early 18th-century facade, and inside a superb Baroque main **altar*** in gilded wood, made by local artisans (1686).

Corso Vittorio Emanuele II ❷

The Corso was the main street running through the medieval city from north to south. It was called Platha de Codinas (carved in tufa); Piazza del Comune and Palazzo di Città were halfway along, where the Teatro Civico (Civic Theater) stands today. The chiesa gotica di S. Caterina (Gothic church of St Catherine) and the palazzo del Podestà (Podestà Palazzo) were located in the upper part of the Corso. Some 15th-century Gothic houses have survived: one, at 20 Via Canopolo, and especially another, Casa Farris (Farris House), at 23 Via Canopolo. They have lovely Catalan Gothic double windows, and their old porticos can be seen embedded in the walls now. The 15th-century casa di Re Enzo (house of King Enzo) is in similar Catalan style, and has a splendid portico with sculptured capitals. The old municipality was replaced in 1826 by an elegant neo-Classical building which now houses the Teatro Civico (Civic Theater). Opposite the theater is the neo-Classical palazzo di S. Sebastiano (St Sebastian Palazzo) built in the 1820s. To the right, the Baroque facade of the chiesa di S. Andrea (church of St Andrew) was built in 1648 and inspired by Ligurian models. The street then ends as it widens into Piazza S. Antonio; on the left there are some remains of the medieval city walls with a crenelated tower. The chiesa di S. Antonio Abate (church of St Anthony Abbot) is in front of the piazza. It was completed in 1709, and has a simple, well-proportioned facade in Baroque style. The church's furnishings feature the main altar **retablo***, in inlaid gilded wood, by the Genovese artist Bartolomeo Augusto. The Holy Deacon, a painting attributed to Giovanni Muru (early 16th century) and Our Lady of Sorrows by Giovanni Marghinotti are in the sacristy.

Le mura medievali ❸

The remains of the medieval walls can be seen in Corso Trinità. The walls were started in the 13th century, and completed in the first decades of the 14th century. The walls' interior walkways and an unusual series of small houses built against the walls are visible from Vicolo Godimondo (Godimondo Lane). A tower, only slightly higher than the wall, appears to be a kind of outwork or advance structure. Just beyond, three 14th-century coats-of-arms can be seen embedded into the walls. In front, the chiesa della Trinità (church of the Trinity) has an interesting early 18th-century Baroque facade.

Sassari: the monumental fonte Rosello (1605-1606)

Fonte Rosello ❹

The Rosello Fountain already existed in 1295; it was modified to its current monumental form in 1605-1606. Built in Renaissance style, it consists of two parallelepipeds, one above the other, in white and green marble, crowned by two crossed arches, on top of which was placed an equestrian statue of S. Gavino (St Gavin). The original statue has been lost; the copy there now was made in 1975. At the corners of the base, the statues of the seasons are 1828 copies of the originals which were destroyed.

Museo Arte Sassari ❺

The Sassari Art Museum is located in the large Casa professa della Compagnia di Gesù (Professed House of the Society of Jesus), whose restoration was completed in 2001. It was originally built between 1597 and 1668. The museum exhibits paintings and sculptures belonging to state and local government collections, and donations from private collections. It provides a detailed picture of Sardinian figurative art from the middle ages to the 20th century. Works from the 14th to the 16th century are exhibited on the ground floor: the most interesting are paintings by Sardinian artists such as the Maestro of Ozieri (second half of the 16th century), and traditional retablos of Catalan origin. Works from the 17th to the 18th century are shown on the first floor, and include paintings by local artists. Artworks by 19th and 20th century Sardinian artists are on the third floor.

Palazzo Ducale (o del Comune) ⑥

The Ducal (or Municipal) Palazzo has been the Municipality since 1900; it's the city's most important example of 18th century civil architecture. It was probably Carlo Valino who oversaw its construction from 1775 to 1805, and who introduced some Piedmont-style features in the process. The austere facade has three levels, horizontally divided by bands and vertically by pilasters; the windows on the first floor are surmounted by rounded gables with cusp, and on the second floor by a rococo motif. The hallway has a double curved staircase, and leads to a well-proportioned courtyard.

Duomo di S. Nicola ⑦

The cathedral of St Nicholas is located in the heart of the medieval town, and was rebuilt over a 12th-century Romanesque church between 1480 and 1505. The facade was built between 1681 and 1715 by skilled workers from Milan. The interior, with its single central nave and cupola on drum, has kept its Gothic appearance. There is a Sienese-school, 14th-century tempera painting at the main altar. A 17th-century silver statue of St Gavin is on the left, in a showcase. The choir was built by Sardinian cabinet-makers in the early 1700s. The adjacent Museo del Tesoro del Duomo (Cathedral Treasury Museum) has a standard that was used during processions at the end of the 15th century.

S. Maria di Betlem ⑧

The lower part of the facade of St Mary's of Bethlehem is all that remains of the original church, which was built in 1106. The upper part of the facade, with its rose-windows, dates from 1465. The interior was modernised in the 18th- to 19th-century. However, the cappella dei Muratori (Stonemasons' Chapel), left of the entrance, has retained its Aragonese form. The chapel on the left of the high altar has an early 15th-century wood sculpture group (Madonna and Child). The cloister, now almost entirely walled up, has the 16th-century Fontana del Brigliadore (Spurting Fountain: "brillador" in Catalan means "spurt").

Piazza d'Italia ⑨

Sassari's growth in the 19th century centered around Piazza d'Italia, which was created in the 1870s. The buildings around the symbolic area of a hectare together create an attractive harmonious environment; in the middle stands the monument to Vittorio Emanuele II by Giuseppe Sartorio (1899). The most impressive building is the majestic and elegant Palazzo della Provincia, designed by Eugenio Sironi and Giovanni Borgnini, and built between 1873 and 1880 in late neo-Classical style. The facade is massive but well-proportioned, and consists

The Duomo, Sassari, dedicated to S. Nicolò, was built in its current form from the second half of the 15th century

of three orders of windows, and a frieze above. It's possible to visit the aula consiliare (council hall) on the first floor. It was decorated in 1881 with salient episodes from Sassari's past. The royal apartment is next door. Opposite Palazzo della Provincia, at number 19, is the neo-Gothic Palazzo Giordano. It was built in 1878 and has two rooms frescoed by Guglielmo Bilancini.

Museo Archeologico-Etnografico "Giovanni Antonio Sanna" ⑩

Sassari's Museo Archeologico-Etnografico (Archeological and Ethnographic Museum) is the result of a considerable series of acquisitions and donations, such as the collection of paintings left by Senator Giovanni Antonio Sanna, who the museum is named after. It was taken over by the State in 1931. Two artworks worthy of note are a Madonna and Child by Bartolomeo Vivarini, and a St Sebastian by the artist known as Mastro di Ozieri. The archeological section has numerous pre-historic finds from northern and central Sardinia, the altar from Monte d'Accoddi (2450-1850 BC), hypogeian tombs or domus de janas (4th-2nd millennium BC), and megalithic tombs (1000-900 BC). In addition there is a Nuraghic hall, with scale models illustrating the two types of nuragh: tholos and corridor nuraghs. There are many displays of pottery and bronze objects for votive use. The ground floor contains materials from historic times. For the Carthaginian period, there are funerary steles from Sulci, clay objects and numerous amulets. For the Roman period, a considerable collection of oil lamps, pottery, blown glass and gold objects. There are some important pieces of writing, including a bronze tablet from Esterzili (near Seùlo). A few steps lead down to the large lower hall, where late-Roman material is exhibited: marble sarcophaguses decorated with figures, and sculptures and mosaics from Turris Libisonis (the Roman colony situated where Porto Torres is now). In Rooms XI and XIII, there is an

Rare Nuraghic bronze, one of the treasures at the Museo G.A. Sanna

excellent collection of coins, ranging from rare and precious Carthaginian examples, to coins minted under Vittorio Emanuele I of Savoy (1814-1821).

S. Pietro in Silki ⑪

The St Peter's in Silki condaghe, Sassari's oldest manuscript, dates the church of the same name from the 12th century, although the oldest part surviving today is the lower part of the bell-tower (13th century). The nave masonry dates from around 1477, and the facade from 1675. The interior has a barrel-vaulted roof. The chapel of the Madonna delle Grazie (Madonna of Graces), the first on the left, is a well-proportioned example of Sardinian Catalan Gothic style (around 1470). The fourth chapel contains the venerated 14th-century simulacrum of the Virgin of Graces.

DAY TRIPS

ALGHERO [36 km]

Although Alghero is situated in an area which has been inhabited for thousands of years, the town itself only really came into existence after the Catalan-Aragonese conquest of Sardinia in 1323. Once Cagliari and Sassari had been occupied, a firm foothold was required in the north-west of the island. So, in 1354 the king, Peter the Ceremonious, sent a large Catalan-Aragonese force. A few months later, Alghero was entirely populated by peoples from the Iberian peninsula. Over the years, according to military requirements, the many little Genoese towers were demolished, the walls were strengthened and extended, and higher larger towers were built. Alghero was raised to the status of city in 1501 and always enjoyed the privileges the Catalans guaranteed to their overseas colonies. Its worst sufferings were caused by the discovery of America and the plague. In the 16th century the gates were opened to outsiders again; palazzi and churches were crowded on top of each other, in order not to keep within

Alghero 1 : 9 000 (1 cm = 90 m)

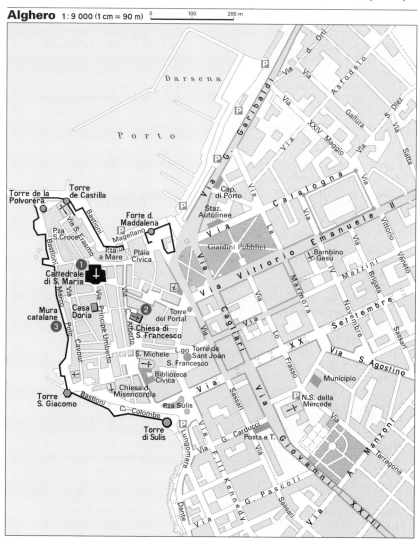

the city walls. In 1720, Sardinia came under the Savoys, but Alghero did not lose its taste for Catalan culture. So much so, that in 1850 a catechism was printed in Catalan for the use of the people of Alghero. In the 19th century the city mushroomed: so in the late 1800s, the walls were demolished on the landward side. It is paradoxical, but it was only when Alghero began to change that the inhabitants began to take an interest in the old town. It was damaged by allied bombing on 17th May 1943, and by the ravages of uncontrolled building and development. The most important signs of the past are found in the old Mediterranean

and Catalan city. By following the walls that once enclosed the town, you can really gain an idea of its history. Many of the towers now are used for exhibitions, and you can still see the remains of the walls in between. They were demolished or swallowed up by buildings on the landward side, but still survive on the seaward side. The **Cattedrale di S. Maria ❶** (Cathedral of St Mary) was built in the second half of the 16th century. The late-Gothic Catalan apse and bell-tower remain of the original building, as well as, inside, the nave and side aisles, the cupola and the chapels off the presbytery. The cathedral's tetrastyle pronaos dates from 1862. The Museo Diocesano d'Arte Sacra (Diocesan Museum of Sacred Art) is next door. It contains the cathedral's treasury and artworks from the churches of the diocese. The **chiesa di S. Francesc** or **S. Francesco ❷** (church of St Francis) is a must to visit. It was built at the end of the 15th century in Catalan Gothic style, as evident in the presbytery, some chapels and the polygonal bell-tower with spire, that was saved from collapse in 1593. The single original nave was modified to form a central nave and two side aisles. It has been recently restored, and has a fine 15th-century cloister. The late Baroque main altar (1773) in polychrome marble is noteworthy, as well as the 18th-century wood sculpture of Christ at the Column, originally in the chiesa di S. Croce (church of the Holy Cross), which now no longer exists. The **Mura catalane ❸** (Catalan Walls) still surround the old town center, on the seaward side. The walls have towers at regular intervals and are pleasant to walk along. The forte della Maddalena (Magdalen Fort) overlooks the port; it was modified in the 18th century. Behind is the porta a mare (sea gate), one of the points of entry to the old quarter. The towers are: torre della Polvorera is on the north-west corner of the bastions, and the octagonal torre di S. Giacomo in Gothic style, on the south-west corner; to the south-east, the torre di Sulis, or de l'Esperò reial, mentioned as early as 1364, but modified to its current appearance under the Spanish; the 16th century torre de Sant Joan and the 14th-century torre de Portal look towards the new part of Alghero.

View from the sea of Alghero, a fortified port from the 12th century

BURGOS [72 km]

Burgos's main feature is the picturesque ruins of the **Castello di Gocèano** (Gocèano Castle), also known as Burgos Castle, built in the 12th century. Maria Adelasia, wife of King Enzo, illegitimate son of Federick II, died here in 1255. Continuing 10 km northwards, you reach the **Foresta di Burgos** (Burgos Forest), where an organisation with its headquarters in Ozieri works to promote the breeding of prized Anglo-Arab-Sardinian horses.

CASTELSARDO [32 km]

Castelsardo looks over the Golfo dell'Asinara (Asinara Gulf) from a trachyte cliff, on the north coast of Sardinia. The old town above the harbour and the beach is surrounded by bastions, and criss-crossed by steep flights of steps. It once belonged to the Genoese Doria family, who turned it into a fortress. It was called Castella Jane or Castelgenovese, and then Castellaragonese until 1767. It is worth stopping at the **Roccia dell'Elefante** (Elephant Rock) not far out of Castelsardo, after Sèdini and a long downhill stretch. The large trachyte rock, at the side of the road, named after its strange shape, also has some domus de janas in its lower part. You will see, carved on two opposite walls in the chamber to the right, two pairs of taurine horns, the symbol of a male divinity who was reputed to bring life after death. The area was densely inhabited in Nuraghic times. The nuraghe Paddaggiu (Paddaggiu nuragh) – not the Su Tesoro nuragh, as indicated by the signs – is located beside the old road for Codaruìna, which turns off immediately afterwards on the right (at the sign for Terme di Casteldoria). Partly underground, the nuragh retains many of its original structures.

On the right two kilometers after Castelsardo, you come to the **church of S. Pietro delle Immagini** (St Peter of Images), or of Simbranos, which once belonged to the Benedictine monks of Montecassino. The facade has alternate bands of light and dark stone, and a dynamic series of partly Romanesque and partly Gothic arches arranged on three levels. It is always open. The interior shows clearly the two stages in which it was built: the first in the early 12th century, and the second a century later. Once there was a Deposition here, with 13th-century colored wood statues.

The Grotta di Nettuno (Neptune's Grotto), one of the marvels of the sea in Sardinia

PORTO CONTE [50 km]

Porto Conto is the Portus Nimpharum mentioned by Ptolemy in his Geographia. This unspoilt gulf with clear water reaches inland for 6 km (average width 2.5 km), and at the end almost looks like a lake; it's situated between Capo Caccia and Punta del Giglio, west of Alghero. The sea floor is a natural habitat for fish repopulation, because of the vast stretches of the Posidonia oceanica alga species found here.
To the south-west, after a charming wine-growing area, the road follows the sea shore to Monte Timidone (361 m), almost at the top of the calcareous promontory of **Capo Caccia***. The escala del cabirol (goat stairway) is daringly carved out of the rock of the west wall, which plunges vertically down towards the sea. Its 656 steps lead to the entrance of the **grotta di Nettuno** (Neptune's grotto). The grotto can also be reached via sea; many ferries come here from Alghero in the tourist season. The grotto is illuminated, and is one of the most picturesque to be found in the

Mediterranean. It consists of a series of pools, narrow passageways, wide chambers with columns, and fairytales scenes created by nature's arrangement of stalactites and stalagmites.
The little island of **Foradada** is almost opposite the grotto; it is crossed from one side to the other by a natural tunnel at water level. The entrance to the Grotta Verde (Green Grotto) is in the rock wall opposite Neptune's Grotto; it's reached from the high part of the promontory near the 17th-century Torre del Bulo (Bulo Tower). The grotto is 80 m below, in the heart of the rock, almost at sea level. Evidence of human occupation has been found inside, dating from the early Neolithic age. The Grotta dei Ricami (Needlework Grotto) can only be reached by sea; it's in the wall of Capo Caccia that faces Alghero. The snowy white crystalline formations inside are extraordinarily varied and beautiful.

PORTO TORRES [20 km]

Porto Torres lies on a plateau that slopes gently down towards the gulf of Asinara. With its busy port, it's one of the most important towns in the north of Sardinia. The town, named Turris Libisonis, first emerged probably around the second half of the 1st century BC, when a Roman colony (the only one in Sardinia at that time) was established there. The city was rectangular in shape, and oriented north to south, an orientation which still survives today. The last stretch of its main street, Corso Vittorio Emanuele II, was probably part of the most important of Roman Sardinia's roads. It was known as the "A Turre Kàrales" ("from Porto Torres to Cagliari") road; today's the Carlo Felice road is the modern equivalent, in terms of importance. The port guaranteed the town's economic prosperity. During the persecution that took place under the Roman emperor Diocletian in 304, the saints Gavin, Protus and January were martyred at here. This episode resulted in the 11th-century construction of the splendid basilica of St Gavin. In medieval times the town went into decline; it was reduced to two small parts, one near the basilica and the other near the port. The town can be visited in half a day, starting from the basilica of St Gavin. From Corso Vittorio Emanuele, the town's main street, go to the port where a 14th-century Aragonese tower stands. Then follow the road along the seafront (Lungomare Balai), until you come to a calcareous rock where the little church of St Gavin stands, on the presumed site of martyrdom of the three saints. The **basilica di S. Gavino** (basilica of St Gavin) is the oldest, largest and certainly the most important example of Pisan Romanesque architecture in Sardinia. It's built on the hill known as Monte Agellu, on the site of an older sepulchral basilica. It has two apses at opposite ends of the church, the only example of this in Sardinia and extremely rare in peninsular Italy. There is an entrance on both of the two longer sides. The outside wall is in limestone ashlar, with arches and narrow single windows. The north side, with the 17th-century structures of the so-called "atrio Comita" (Comitas atrium), has the only surviving Romanesque door, dating from the second half of the 11th century. It's decorated with human and animal figures, and shows Lombard influence. The superb double portal, dated 1492, is on the south side. Inside, the nave and two side aisles are divided by solid cruciform pillars and columns taken from elsewhere, with arches above. The 17th-century wood statues of the town's martyrs are displayed on a catafalque in the east apse. There's an early 17th-century equestrian statue of St Gavin in the north aisle, and a 7th-century Greek-Byzantine inscription commemorating the victory of Duke Constantine over the Longobards who attempted to invade Sardinia. The anticrypt houses some precious Roman sarcophaguses decorated with figures. From here it is possible to enter the remains of the 6th-century sepulchral basilica, and the crypt where the bones believed to be of the three martyrs killed under Diocletian are kept in three Roman sarchophaguses.

Archeological finds from the Turris Libisonis excavations and the interesting municipal Collection are kept in the Antiquarium Turritano. On the ground floor there is a fascinating marble altar by C. Cuspius Felix, dedicated to the Egyptian divinity Bubastis under the emperor Tiberius, which was found near the Palazzo di Re Barbaro. On the floor above, there is a noteworthy late imperial Roman polychrome mosaic, with funerary inscriptions accompanied by Christian symbols; it was part of the covering of two tombs found in the Balai area.

Porto Torres, the basilica of S. Gavino is Sardinia's best example of Romanesque architecture

The **Palazzo di Re Barbaro** (Palace of King Barbar) is not a palace, but the area where the Central Thermal Baths are located. The area was named after the mythical governor who, according to tradition, condemned the three martyrs of Porto Torres to death. Immediately past the entrance to the area, which is in the Antiquarium, you will see the remains of a residential area which was probably part of the original Roman colony. After a street paved in basalt (decumanus), you reach the massive thermal baths building, which was built in two separate stages: the 2nd century, and the late 3rd to early 4th century. The frigidarium (cold water room), with two rectangular pools and geometric mosaic decorations, and then the tepidarium (warm water room) also with mosaics, and part of the ceiling still in place. Then come the three calidaria (hot water rooms). Outside, paved roads flank the thermal baths; near the north-south road (cardo), there was a portico with many public shops and buildings. At present, the thermal baths building is closed to the public, but you can walk along the roads around it.

STINTINO [48 km]

After Porto Torres, the road leaves the sea and heads for Stintino, a small picturesque fishing village and now a well-known seaside resort, almost at the end of the little peninsula that points towards the island of Asinara. It has a fishing port, and a marina. The town was founded in 1885, for the inhabitants of Asinara; today it retains its attractive original town center, a regular grid of roads, and neat pastel houses. Flamingoes, dwarf herons, herons and cormorants stop in the stagno di Casaraccio (Casaraccio Lagoon) near the town, which covers around 10 hectares, and is surrounded by Mediterranean maquis and European fan palms.

The **isola dell'Asinara** (Asinara Island) was known by the Romans, who called it Herculis insula, Hercules's Island. It was a point of reference for sailors navigating between Spain and Rome, or out of the rough Bocche di Bonifacio (the strait between Corsica and Sardinia). From the late middle ages it was inhabited by families of Sardinian shepherds who tended their flocks there, and by Ligurian fishermen who fished for tuna off the coast. Sometimes they had to defend themselves against raiding pirates, and in the second half of the 16th century watchtowers and forts were built on the shores. In June 1885, the Italian government decided to establish an international quarantine station here, and a penal colony. The island was expropriated from its inhabitants, who were forced to leave. With the small amount of compensation they were given, the 45 "deported" families moved to the closest land they could find, which was Stintino. In 1976, the government put a protection order on

the island, and on 28th Novembre 1997 the **Parco Nazionale dell'Asinara** (Asinara National Park) was established. There are beaches of crystal clear water, and almost totally unspoilt natural beauty, herds of mouflon, and a small herd of white donkeys. Permission is required for access to the island.

VALLE DEI NURAGHE [60 km]

The Valley of the Nuraghs is distintive for the exceptional number of nuraghs found here, on average one every two kilometers. To the south-east, very near, is the complex of the **reggia nuragica di Santu Antine**** (Nuraghic Palace of Santu Antine). The central keep, despite progressive disintegration and destruction, is still over 17 meters high; there are three smaller towers nearby, linked by a series of long corridors and walkways with narrow slit openings; there is also a large courtyard with well. A passageway, stairs and chambers complete the structure: there is a round corridor on the ground floor in the wall of the main room, which has the typical tholos ceiling (in truncated cone shape) with circles of stones getting narrower and narrower, and the staircase leading to the upper rooms. The complex was built in various stages, and was still used in Roman times.

The **Museo della Valle dei Nuraghi del Logudoro-Meilogu** (Logudoro-Meilogu Valley of the Nuraghs Museum) is in the town of Torralba, a few kilometers away. The Santu Antine room in the archeological section has material found in nuraghs, stone bullets, foundry pincers, cookers and oil lamps. It also has an ethnographic section where theme exhibitions are held.

The three-lobed Burghidu nuragh near Ozieri; the 15m-high keep in the middle is still standing

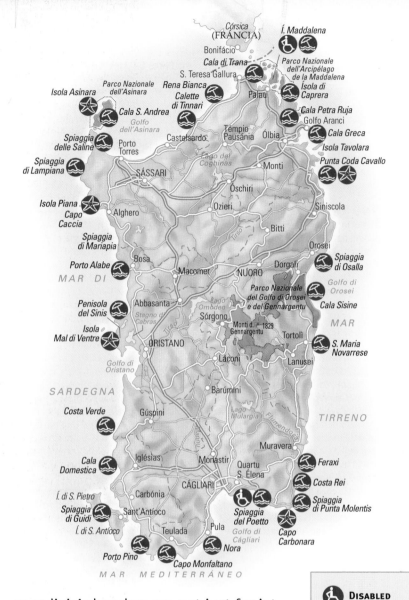

Córsica
(FRÁNCIA)

Í. Maddalena

Bonifácio

Cala di Trana

Parco Nazionale
dell'Arcipélago
de la Maddalena

S. Teresa Gallura

Rena Bianca

Palau

Ísola di
Caprera

Parco Nazionale
dell'Asinara

Calette
di Tinnari

Isola Asinara

Cala S. Andrea

Golfo
dell'Asinara

Cala Petra Ruja
Golfo Aranci

Témpio
Pausánia

Ólbia

Cala Greca

Castelsardo

Spiaggia
delle Saline

Porto
Torres

Isola Tavolara

Punta Coda Cavallo

Spiaggia
di Lampiana

SÁSSARI

Lago del
Coghinas

Monti

Óschiri

Ozieri

Siniscola

Isola Piana
Capo
Caccia

Alghero

Bitti

Spiaggia
di Mariapia

Orosei

Spiaggia
di Osalla

Porto Alabe

Bosa

Macomer

NUORO

Dorgali

Golfo di
Orosei

MAR DI

Abbasanta

Parco Nazionale
del Golfo di Orosei
e del Gennargentu

Cala Sisine

Penisola
del Sinis

Stagno di
Cabras

Lago
Omodeo

Sórgono

Monti d. ▲ 1829
Gennargentu

MAR

Isola
Mal di Ventre

ORISTANO

Láconi

Tortolì

S. Maria
Novarrese

Golfo di
Oristano

Lanusei

SARDEGNA

Barúmini

Costa Verde

Gúspini

Lago
Mulargia

TIRRENO

Cala
Domestica

Iglésias

Monástir

Muravera

Feraxi

Í. di S. Pietro

Carbónia

Quartu
S. Élena

CÁGLIARI

Costa Rei

Spiaggia
di Guidi

Sant'Antíoco

Spiaggia
del Poetto

Spiaggia
di Punta Molentis

Í. di S. Antíoco

Teulada

Pula

Golfo di
Cágliari

Capo
Carbonara

Nora

Capo
Carbonara

Porto Pino

Capo Monfaltano

MAR MEDITERRÁNEO

	DISABLED
	PROTECTED MARINE AREA
	BEACHES

Sardinia's beaches are not just for jet
setters and their yachts. Wild, untamed
and stretching for miles: the beaches
of Sardinia are vast and varied, from high
craggy cliffs to gentle sweeping dunes and
juniper-sheltered coves. The crystal clear sea
is unsurpassed in its sparkling translucence
and beguiling colors ranging from deep cobalt
blues to sheer emerald greens. With a little
effort, an adventurous spirit, and a few detours,

you can find large stretches of beach that are often deserted and spend the day in seclusion with the sea and sky as your companions. In addition to its pristine coastline, Sardinia also has protected marine habitats, inland lakes and underwater caves waiting to be explored.

Highlights

- 5 Protected Marine Areas set up by the Ministry of the Environment
- Capotesta: the forces of the wind have, over millions of years, produced unusual rock sculptures
- The Saline beach, a long stretch of the finest white sand and an emerald-green sea
- The Cala Luna beach exquisitely is the beautifully shaped in form of a candid crescent moon
- Lake Baratz, the only saltwater lake on the island, can be reached from the Porto Ferro beach, and has lovely deserted bays

In the middle of the Mediterranean sea Sardinia is still wild and mostly rocky with plains, coasts, mountains and hills. Along its 1731 kilometers of shoreline there are some of the most beautiful marine habitats. Its coasts are generally high and rocky, stretching for miles with headlands and deep inlets fringed by islands and islets, extremely long beaches with powdery sand, from dazzling white to pink to granite red. The crystal-clear sea has many different hues: turquoise, cobalt blue, azure, emerald green. Inland, near the low-lying plains there are pools, swamps and large expanses of dunes which are impassable for long stretches from the north west to the north east. Sardinia also has numerous islands: Asinara, La Maddalena and Caprera; Tavolara and Molara in the north east: San Pietro and Sant'Antìoco in the south west (actually the latter is joined to the island by an isthmus). Five protected marine environments have also been established to safeguard the sea, the coast and the flora and fauna described on the following pages.

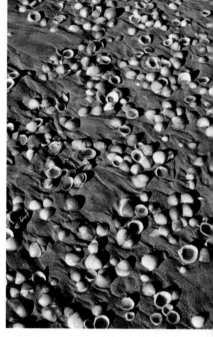

CAGLIARI

Poetto Beach

Cagliari's beach, which stretches to the beach of Quartu, is the most famous beach in Sardinia, in the middle of the vast Golfo degli Angeli. Locals and holidaymakers both use this long, spacious and dazzling white beach between the pool of Molentargius, famous for its flamingos, and the sea. Having been exploited for a long time it is now being cleaned up.

CASTIADAS
Silias o S'ilixi

Take the road from Castiadas to Capo Ferrato. As you head towards the sea you will find a dirt road which crests a hump and ends in a car park. Leave your car here and continue on foot. You will soon reach the beach, a cove which was once a small harbor for transporting wood by sea. The place-name is telling: S'Ilixi is the Latin for Ilex or holm-oak. The sand is powdery but dark and ferrous. The sea is made more beautiful and interesting by some sandbanks which emerge here and there which you can take an invigorating swim to. It is an unforgettable beach.

Feraxi

This delightful little beach is off the beaten track and therefore quite enchanting. Feraxi is easy to reach and there is more than one way to get there. The simplest thing to do is to take the road which snakes from Costa Rei to Capo Ferrato, and then head north on the chalk road for 4 or 5 km. After a series of bends you will come to a fork. Turn right and you will reach the small beach of Feraxi. It is worth taking a short hike which, in just a few short minutes, will bring you to the headland which overlooks the beach and from which you can enjoy a magnificent view of Costa Rei.

Costa Rei

You can get there from Muravera on the road to Castiadas, turning right at the fork if you are heading north and then continuing south. The beach is extremely long, about 8 km of limy shore. Beyond the beach there is the pool of Piscina Rei and the fascinating archaeological landscape of the megalithic complex with its string of menhirs (totems dating from the Neolithic age). There has been some unsubtle tourist development in the area but, towards the south, the beach is still intact and secluded, ending with Porto Pirastru.

2-3-2

Lovers of large, empty beaches will adore spending a few hours on the 2-3-2 beach, otherwise known as Quirra beach, near an army camp. To reach it you must go to Villaputzu and, after a series of hairpin bends, continue northwards until you reach the bar of Castello di Quirra. Here you must turn right onto a military road and follow it for a couple of kilometers until you are almost at the beach of coarse sand, large dunes and a deep blue sea. This is where the river Sa Flumini Durci runs into the sea.

TEULADA

Chia - Su Giudeu and Cala Cipolla

From Teulada the Costa Sud scenic route leads to the sea where you can see Torre di Chia, built in the 16th century as a defense against Saracen incursions, of which the whole area bears traces. Beneath the tower are the ruins of the Phoenician city of Bithia. West of the tower stretch the splendid beaches of Chia. Access is from coastal villages along dirt roads. The most beautiful beaches are at Chia opposite the cliff of Su Giudeu and the beach of Cala Cipolla. Chia is stunning due to its crescent-moon shape and its dazzling white sand. The gentle landscape is broken to the east by the rugged and granite ramparts of Capo Spartivento.

Nora

Travelling along the coastal road you will reach the headland of Pula, near the settlement of ancient Nora, extraordinary evidence of a city-state which was first Phoenician, then Punic and then Roman and of which there are still traces. Its geographical features are also curious as it is a causeway joined by a narrow isthmus to the mainland, which runs out into the sea providing wonderful opportunities for bathing and mooring boats, however strong the wind is. This is one of the most fascinating places on the island due to the presence of archaeological remains: Phoenician temples, spas, Punic settlements which rise from the sea as, over time, the coast receded, submerging part of the city and lapping the higher parts. And on rare days if the sea is especially clear you can see the underwater ruins.

Porto Pino

On the road from Carbonia to Giba, head towards Sant'Anna Arresi. Before you get to this little village, which also deserves a visit, there is a detour for Porto Pino. The beach is stunning due to its dunes: mountains of golden yellow sand (like those at Piscinas), a large pool sheltered by a pinewood, crystal-clear, azure water. Not far off is the road leading to the pool, cared for by fishermen, a fascinating wetland which makes the area more interesting and lively.

Chia with its crescent-shaped beach

POETTO BEACH
Golfo degli Angeli Cooperative

Visitor center tel. 070522055
www.sardiniapoint.it

Open from June 15th to September 15th, from 9 to 18.30.

Getting there Shuttles with wheelchair access connect the beach with the center of Cagliari.

Description

The long, white beach of Poetto (about 4 km) stretches along the seafront of Cagliari. The vastness of the sandy shore makes it highly attractive. It is heavily patronized by all kinds of sea and sun enthusiasts. There are numerous small restaurants and places providing refreshment on the beach.

Accessibility

There are 7 bathing establishments managed by the Golfo degli Angeli cooperative, equipped with a private car park, beach walkway into the sea, changing rooms, showers and a solarium, all accessible to and especially suitable for wheelchair-users. The lifeguards and beach staff are trained to assist people with various disabilities, including mental disabilities. JOB chairs, wheelchairs for entering the water, rigid air beds for bathing quadriplegics and H shaped lifejackets for bathing paraplegics are all available.

Poetto, a beach famous for its flamingos

LA MADDALENA (WATER SKIING)

Visitor center tel. 0789727768
www.flyforlife.it

Open From May to September.

Getting there Maddalena opposite the bridge to Caprera.

By boat: From Palau with Saremar, Enermar and Toremar ferries.

By air: Olbia airport is about an hour from Palau. There is train link operated by Sardinia Railways and a coach link provided by Turmotravel, Sun Lines and ARST.

Description

Fly for Life is the first federal school in Italy (a member of FISN and FISD) which teaches water skiing to the disabled. It has been managed for 13 years by Jeff Onorato, a disabled person himself, who earned the title of federal water skiing instructor, overcoming considerable obstacles. The courses, which are open to everyone, disabled or not, consist of 5 lessons, each lasting 30 minutes. All it takes is a week to attain a basic level of competence. Disciplines taught are: slalom, figure, barefoot and wakeboard, tube, water games and kneeboard.

Accessibility

Water skiing courses are open to both mentally and physically disabled people. The latter are taught using seats which enable them to ski in a seated position. The center has a catering facility with tables, beach umbrellas, refreshments and wheelchair access.

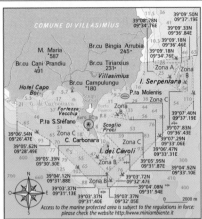

COMUNE DI VILLASIMIUS

Access to the marine protected area is subject to the regulations in force:
please check the website http://www.miniambiente.it

CAPO CARBONARA

YEAR OF FOUNDATION: 1998

PROVINCE: CAGLIARI

COMUNE: VILLASIMIUS

SURFACE AREA: 8598 HECTARES

TYPOLOGY: ROCKY HEADLAND STRADDLING
TWO GULFS AND ARCHIPELAGO OF ISLANDS
AND SAND BARS.

MANAGEMENT: COMUNE DI VILLASIMIUS,
VIALE COLOMBO 2, TEL. 070790234,
WWW.COMUNE.VILLASIMIUS.CA.IT

The protected marine area is on
the coast of Cagliari and stretches
from Capo Boi to Punta Porceddus.
In the middle, towering over the
surrounding sea, is the headland
of Capo Carbonara which separates
a large gulf into two distinct basins
which take the name Porto Giunco,
in the east, and Golfo di Carbonara
in the west. In front of the headland
there are the islands of Cavoli and
Serpentara, the west of which makes up
zone A of the reserve.

Beneath an ancient sea

Studies carried out on the seabeds of
Capo Carbonara, which still bears traces
of numerous shipwrecks (the oldest
dates back to 250 BC) have revealed the
existence of well-preserved underwater
meadows of posidonia sea grass
covering a total of approximately forty
hectares. In the northern part of Cavoli
(cabbage) Island, which probably owes
its name to the fact that the so-called
Sardinian cabbage (*Brassica insularis*),
grows there plentifully, there is an
interesting bio-construction of worm
shells (a peculiar mollusk with

a cylindrical and convoluted shell),
the northernmost example we know
of to date about on the Italian coasts.
The seabeds have steep walls which
reach depths of 40 m and which
sometimes generate underwater
landslides or ridges of rock below
the surface of the sea, forming sand
bars at various depths out towards the
open sea such as the Berni sand bar,
which is next to Cavoli Island.
The underwater granite rocks are
affected by currents, sometimes made
more violent by the coastal features
and seabeds which create bottlenecks
where the water is funneled,
increasing its speed.

This makes an ideal environment for
migratory fish such as amber-fish, tuna
or barracuda and for the settlement
of benthic filtering fish such as
sponges, sea fans, sea squirts etc.
On walls full of fissures grow large red,
yellow or white sea fans. The waters
teem with shellfish and on a dive you
can observe, as well as the inevitable
damselfish, shoals of steentjie, various
species of dassie, wrasse, combers,
moray eels and goldblotch groupers
such as those which live near the Santa
Caterina sand bar. Close to Serpentara
Island you may also come across
dolphins and sea turtles.

S. Margherita di Pula Beach
The beach can be reached from the convenient coastal road SS 195. Very large, with an intensely farmed hinterland and a large farming and tourist centre, as well as international standard hotel accommodation, the beach is not totally unspoiled but makes up for this with powdery sand and a crystal-clear sea. The setting, dominated by the cape of Pula and the ruins of the Punic city of Nora, is enchanting.

Teulada and Capo Malfitano Beaches
The heart of the Costa Sud, Capo Teulada is one of the most beautiful spots in Sardinia, inaccessible and only visible from the sea, as it is a military zone. Taking a short detour from the Costa Sud scenic route you can instead easily get to the beautiful beach of Teulada, known as Porto Tramatzu. If you continue along the scenic route eastwards towards Domus de Maria you will reach the headland of Capo Malfitano. The headland runs into the sea, creating a sort of marine basin which is extremely picturesque. Below it there are delightful little coves with pebble beaches, the typical amber color of the "Sulcitano" coast. There is also the small island of Taurredda which rises to a height of about 30 m.

VILLASIMIUS
Giunco Beach
To get to the beach of Giunco from Villasimius take the road which leads to Capo Carbonara. The first approach to the sea is on the left, starting from the little tourist harbor. A dirt road skirts the lagoon of Notteri and ends near the dunes, which tower over the shore. Another approach can be found if you continue towards the lay-by of Capo Carbonara: you must go down a dirt road on your left, which leads to the sea and which ends in eucalyptus groves and dunes. The beach of Giunco is separated from Cava Usai by a headland, where there is a tower bearing the same name.

Porto Sa Ruxi Beach
The beach of Porto Sa Ruxi, like the other beaches of Giunco and Punta Molentis, is part of the Protected Area of Capo Carbonara which will also include the Islands of Cavoli and Serpentara, in the environs of Villasimius. To get to the beach you must follow the coastal road for Villasimius from Cagliari. Once beyond the headland of Capo Boi and after a few bends you will see a chalk road on your right which leads to the beach of Porto Sa Ruxi. Actually this stretch of coast has three different little beaches, towered over by soft sand dunes and sheltered from behind by the maquis and juniper shrubs.

Punta Molentis Beach
From Villasimius head towards the sea. After travelling for 1.5 km turn left towards the coast for Costa Rei. After a further 2 km and on reaching a tight bend turn left towards the hotel "L'Oleandro" then turn right and go under the road bridge. On Punta Molentis beach you can lunch on barbecued fish, a service offered by fishermen.

CARBONIA-IGLESIAS

CARLOFORTE
Spalmatore Beach (Isola di San Pietro)
You can reach Isola di San Pietro from Portoscuso or from Calasetta (on the Island of Sant'Antìoco) with ferries which dock in the port of Carloforte.

Once you disembark, to reach the beach of Spalmatore (also called "La Caletta") on the south west side of the island, you must turn left and continue along the B-road 7 bis for about 7 km. Then turn left again and follow the signs for Cala Spalmatore, which is another 2.5 km. You can also get to the beach from Carloforte on the SP 7.

Guidi Beach (San Pietro Island)

Once you have disembarked from the ferry, to reach the beach of Guidi on the south coast of the island, you must turn left and follow the B-road 7 bis for almost 5 km. Leave your car on the road and then take the path which leads to the sea on your left.

S. ANTÌOCO

Cala Lunga Beach

To get to Cala Lunga beach, which is dominated by rocks and Mediterranean vegetation, you must first reach Sant'Antìoco Porto and then turn left immediately after a petrol station and follow the sign for the beach. After about 5 km you must turn left again near a bend and take the coastal road. After another 1.5 km you will reach Portixeddu. Leave the car on the road and continue on foot along a small path about 70 meters long, which takes you to the sea at Cala Lunga.

The extraordinary Piscinas beach

ARBUS

Cala Domestica

To reach Cala Domestica you must take the SS 126 as far as the village of Fluminimaggiore. From here you drive for another 2 km before turning left towards Baggerru. The beach is 1.4 km beyond the village

Scivu Dunes

From Fluminimaggiore, the road takes you to Is Arenas, an old mining center, and from there to the south coast, known as Costa Verde, where there are various beaches. The most beautiful is Scivu, where there is an ancient farm and sheepfold. The sea is blue and sometimes green. The beach has pale sand and consists of large dunes which are a foretaste of the even vaster ones of Piscinas-Ingurtosu. The dunes are desert-like, with sparse shrubby vegetation. The place is stunning due to its powerful backdrop of the Colle della Vedetta which can be reached by hiking.

Piscinas Beach

Famous thanks to its wonderful setting but not too crowded. Reaching the shore is not so simple if you are coming from the east, from inland that is. The journey to this stretch of dunes which can reach heights of 20 m is something of an adventure. It is easier to get there if you take the road from Costa Verde. After about 3 km you will reach Piscinas. You can get to the sea if you continue along the dirt road for another 4 km, crossing a dry stream bed which once contained mining effluent. The interior belongs to Parco Geominerario della Sardegna.

Torre dei Corsari and Costa Verde Beaches

Continuing along the SS 126, turn left towards S. Antonio di Santadi and eventually Porto Palma. From here you can reach the panoramic headland of Torre dei Corsari, dominated by the red beach of Is Arenas. After another 1.5 km of dirt road you will reach the sea. For Costa Verde keep to the SS 126 and after Guspini take the turning for Montevecchio. You will reach a fork with a sign post after about 15 km. Turn left for Costa Verde and after 7 km you will see a large stretch of sand dotted here and there with the green of juniper shrubs. The sea is emerald green.

NÙORO

DORGALI

Cala Cartoe

Continuing north, 1 km after Cala Gonone you will find the small beach of Cartoe where the sand is darker than it is on nearby beaches. Behind the beach there is a pool, while opposite it there is a sand bar. You can get there from Dorgali if you drive along the SS 125 towards Orosei for almost 5 km, as far as the fork to Ispinigoli. Once you reach the small surfaced road continue for another 1.5 km, leaving the fork on your right for the caves of Ispinigoli. Continue for another 2.5 km and you will reach the end of the surfaced road. Proceeding along a dirt road for another 500 m you will eventually come to tarmac again. After 400 m turn left and drive for another 3 km. The tarmac will run out but you must continue along 1 km of dirt road before leaving your car on the coast road and walking a short distance. Do not miss a visit to the Bue Marino cave, which you can get to by boat from Cala Gonone. You can also reach the famous Cala Luna beach from the sea.

OROSEI

Bèrchidda

Towards Capo Comino, on the coast road which takes you to Posada, you can admire the amazing beach of Bèrchidda, near a pool. Turn at the 65.3 km marker. Drive down a short stretch of dirt road and you will suddenly emerge onto an almost unspoiled stretch of shore which has a string of coves and sand banks. It stretches north to Capo Comino (which you can get to by walking for some distance along the shore) and south almost as far as Orosei. The whiteness of the sand and the light reflected by the crystal-clear sea are dazzling. There are pools along the shoreline, and rolling meadows and hills behind. On the long stretch of coast there are numerous coves and inlets you can visit.

Capo Comino

From Siniscola, head south on the SS 125. A detour to the left takes you to Capo Comino. The beach consists of many dunes with juniper thickets. The shore has limey white sand. The landscape is deserted and the sea is a transparent blue. June and September are the best months to visit this beach if you want to lose yourself in unspoiled nature.

Osalla Beach

From the village of Orosei a dirt road heading south leads to the large beach of Osalla, the northern part of the gulf of Orosei. The alluvial beach formed from the mouth of the river Cedrino is made up of fragments of various origins. The 5 km long beach, which is usually deserted even in the summer, is hauntingly empty. Behind it is the pool of Cedrino where you can observe waterfowl from dawn to dusk.

OGLIASTRA

BAUNEI

Cala Goloritzè

Not far from Baunei which is only 15 km from Tortolì, you can easily get to the coast, where you will find a delightful little cove named Cala Goloritzè, with calm, crystal-clear waters which you can enjoy in the solitude of caves and crags where birds of prey come to nest.
The path (long but not too difficult) has a lot of vegetation and holm-oaks.
To get there from Baunei take the road which leads to Golgo, an ancient ravine about 200 m deep, surrounded by grazing land. Leave the car here and follow the path which sets off from the only farm holiday center in the area. The route is sign-posted.

Cala Luna

This is the most famous beach in Sardinia and should preferably be reached by boat from Cala Gonone, skirting 5 km of towering cliffs which have deep caves at their base, a karst system which is one of the most important in the Mediterranean. Hiking enthusiasts can also get there on foot. The gentlest path snakes between the two seas through a lush maquis which can make the going rough in some places. Eventually, when the hill slopes down to the sea the beach appears like a crescent moon, snow-white in contrast to the blue of the sea. This is why it is called after the moon and why it is so famous. Cala Luna has a poignant beauty with its dazzling light and its treasured sandy shore between the

Cala Luna, where the white beach is set off by the blue sea

rocks and cliffs. Behind it a natural freshwater pool provides an alternative to the sea for bathing. Still further back on the edge of the pool there is an exotic copse of oleanders with Polynesian colors. Unfortunately, recent residential complexes, restaurants and tourist facilities have destroyed part of its beauty.

Cala Sisine

Best to arrive from the sea with a boat trip which leaves from Cala Gonone and visits amazing nature spots, including the famous Bue Marino cave. The shore of Sisine is made up of sheer cliffs reaching heights of up to 500 m and a series of large natural caves along the shore. The beach of limey sand is large and bright, the water is an extraordinary transparent azure color.

Torre di Bari

Barisardo is a village in Ogliastra a few miles from the coast which it retreated from in ancient times fearing Saracen incursions. To reach it take the fork sign-posted from the SS 125 (also known as the Orientale Sarda). From the village turn towards the sea and you will eventually get to the coast. The beach is extremely long, towered over by the Torre di Bari. Built to repel Barbary pirates at the end of the 16th century, it was armed with a garrison to defend the population from Moorish attacks and could send signals to other coastal towers on the eastern shores. The beach is pleasant and easily accessible. The red rocks which surround it make it unique. The deep, dark red color comes from mining intrusions and

is typical of the coast between Santa Maria Navarrese and Àrbatax.

Santa Maria Navarrese

From the SS 125 two sign-posted detours lead to Santa Maria Navarrese which, legend has it, was built in the Middle Ages by Isabella, daughter of the king of Navarra, shipwrecked on that coast. Once past the center of the village, where you can see an extraordinarily large thousand-year-old olive tree, the beach is just beyond the last houses, where the land shelves gently. You can get there on foot to find pale sand embedded between pink crags and transparent green water. In the distance, on the same line of coast, you can glimpse the red rocks of Àrbatax.

OLBIA-TEMPIO

ARZACHENA

Cala Petra Ruja

Sand, rock, green maquis and crystal-clear seabeds, so transparent it is often difficult to judge their depth. We are in Costa Smeralda, where reckless development, resorts and "Made in Sardinia" sea are the order of the day. There are a great deal of beaches along the coast, some of which aren't yet overrun with tourists. Driving along the SS 125 on the scenic route which takes you from Olbia to Porto Cervo, turn at the fork Liscia Ruja to find an enormous crowded beach, white sand and pink rocks of splendid granite, almost natural sculptures. From here, after a further 1 km on foot you will get to Petra Ruja,

TAVOLARA
PUNTA CODA CAVALLO

YEAR OF FOUNDATION: 1997

PROVINCES: NÙORO, OLBIA-TEMPIO

COMUNI: LOIRI PORTO SAN PAOLO, OLBIA, SAN TEODORO

SURFACE AREA: 15,091 HECTARES

TYPOLOGY: GRANITE ISLANDS AND STRETCHES OF COAST WITH MEDITERRANEAN VEGETATION.

MANAGEMENT: MANAGEMENT IS TEMPORARILY LEFT TO A CONSORTIUM OF THE COMUNI DI OLBIA, LOIRI SAN PAOLO, SAN TEODORO, VIA DANTE 1, OLBIA (SS), TEL. 0789203013.

Situated close to the north-east coasts, not far from the famous Costa Smeralda, the islands of Tavolara, Molara and Molarotto are the major elements of this marine area, with its wealth of Mediterranean colors, which starts from Capo Ceraso and, after a string of inlets, beaches, small coves and headlands, reaches as far as Capo Coda Cavallo.

Costa Smeralda, named after its transparent green sea

A very popular destination

Underwater there are breath-taking sights: places like la Secca del Papa at Tavolara, covered with red and yellow sea fans, la Secca di Punta Arresto or the sand bar north of Molarotto with its barracudas have now become scuba-diving legends. The importance of this area in terms of its environment and as a tourist attraction has been boosted by the fact that many dive sites allow you to see what beautiful and spectacular sights the

Mediterranean has to offer within a depth of 20 m. The north-west coast of Tavolara shelves less suddenly underwater while, in the south-east, the seabed rapidly slopes to 15-20 m and is often found to be perforated with caves and cracks or arches, which are proof of the limestone karstification of the island. Underwater the granite Molara and Molarotto are quite different from each other. The western coast of Molara has rounded features while in the east there are needles and gullies which are also seen at Molarotto, and in the sand bars and spurs which connect it to the bed. Deep fissures and through holes dot the underwater granite, offering welcome shelter for good sized groupers and moray eels alongside which swim corbinas and tadpole fish.

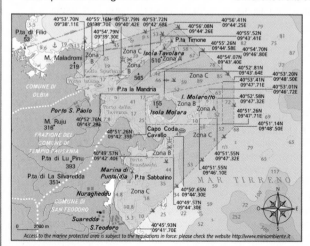

Access to the marine protected area is subject to the regulations in force: please check the website http://www.miniambiente.it

a delightful little pebble beach, not too busy, even in the month of August. This is a critical month for the whole island and especially for Liscia Ruja, where the entrance is controlled by road blocks: no more than 500 cars are allowed through per day.

Razza di Iuncu

Arzachena has 125 km of coast. Taking a detour from the Olbia-San Pantaleo road you will find the scenic route with smaller roads which take you to the beaches. Razza di Iuncu and Liscia Ruja are two of the most interesting. The most picturesque element is the coast with its assorted gullies and outcrops, a myriad of headlands, gulfs, little islands, fjords. Continuing along the coast road the headland of Capriccioli also deserves a mention. Its white beach is very crowded in August but empty in June and September.

Ulticeddu Beach

After Cannigione, take the SS 125 towards Palau. After driving for about 3.5 km you will reach Tancamanna. This spot has the most transparent and green sea in the whole of Costa Smeralda and a beach framed by two outcrops of red granite with splendid deep blue streaks. To get there just leave your car in one of the supervised car parks which are found along the beach. Not far from the sea is Padula di Salomi, a nature attraction. It is a large pool in an oasis, in the deepest part of the gulf of Arzachena. Inhabited by colonies of purple gallinules and flamingoes and visited by purple and gray herons, as well as ospreys, the area is not recommended in the summer due to the enormous clouds of insects and ticks.

GOLFO ARANCI

Cala Greca

Take the road from Golfo Aranci to Cala Moresca, passing the embarkation point for "Sardinia Ferries" and going over a level crossing. Turn right straightaway and continue for about 500 m along a surfaced road which then becomes a dirt track. Leave the car after a few meters when you see the signs for Cala Greca and continue on foot for about 1 km. Not far from Cala Greca, opposite Cala Moresca, is the small island of Figarolo, an area famous for its fauna,

which is inhabited by mouflon.
To reach it you can hire a boat from local fishermen or attempt to swim across. You only need to be reasonably fit as it isn't too far from the coast.

Cala Sabina

Here is a beach you can get to by train. Take one of the trains which leave from Olbia or from Golfo Aranci and alight at Cala Sabina, a few meters from the beach. The view is very easy on the eye: a white beach, blue water and a crown of juniper shrubs close to which you may put up a tent. To get there by car take the road from Olbia to Golfo Aranci and turn at the fork for Golfo Aranci. On the right you will see a gate with a sign for a carpenter's workshop (Falegname). After leaving your car near the crossroads walk along the path for about 1.5 km. Once you have reached the railway track you are there.

Punta Capo Ceraso Beaches

At Punta Capo Ceraso you will find a series of pretty little beaches: Cala sa Figu, Sos, Passizzedos, Porto Lucas and Porto Vitello. These are short stretches of shoreline surrounded by maquis and rocks, as well as pink granite. They are easy to get to. Leave the SS 125 which leads to Olbia and turn right for Porto Istana, well-known for the variety of colors in its bay: from white to sea green to midnight blue.
After another 500 m turn towards Punta Ceraso. From here continue for another 2 km and then turn onto the only road there is, which ends at the Hotel "Li Cuncheddi". Once you have passed the hotel continue along a dirt road (800m) which is only impassable in winter or after many days of rain.

LA MADDALENA

Maddalena Archipelago

To visit the beaches of Maddalena you can go by boat from Cannigione, from Palau or from Maddalena itself, with one of the tours which offer you a whole day at sea, lunch included. You will normally leave at about 9 in the morning and return at about 5 in the afternoon. Once you have disembarked in the port on the island just turn right and follow the scenic route to get to the beaches. It is 5 km to Maddalena and 6.5 km to Porto Massimo. The whole archipelago is protected by the Parco Nazionale

Geomarino and bathing and pleasure boating are regulated by the Park Authority.

PALAU
Budelli and Santa Maria
Of the other islands of the Maddalena archipelago, both Budelli and Santa Maria have a string of small, quiet white beaches. You can get to them by taking a boat from the small harbors of Cannigione, Baja Sardinia, Palau and Santa Teresa Gallura. On Santa Maria the most beautiful beaches are the small cove of the same name, and Cala di Fosso, both close to Punta Vecchio Marino. The local sailors will know, but make sure you ask to land there. Don't risk missing them. They have something special compared to the other beaches on the island. On Budelli Rosa Beach is enchanting. Its name derives from the color of the sand - a strange reddish mixture made of shells transported by the marine currents. In the past tourists almost entirely stripped the beach of sand to take it home as a souvenir. This is another reason it is forbidden to bathe on the beach and pleasure boating is regulated by the Park Authority.

Cala di Trana
This is a little beach which you can only get to from the sea, hiring a boat in Palau. By land, access is forbidden. The road which leads to the shore is private. If you intend to go to Palau, you must follow signs for Porto Raphael and Punta Sardegna. Once there, park your car on the road and continue on foot. The important thing is not to be discouraged by the difficulties you will meet on your descent. Despite a bumpy path and overgrown vegetation, with a little prudence you will manage to get to the beach from where you can swim to Cala di Trana, surrounded by granite rocks and a thick and impenetrable maquis. This is precisely the reason it is practically deserted.

Caprera Island
From Palau there are ferries to Maddalena every ten minutes. From there you can drive to Caprera, over a long bridge straddling Passo della Moneta. Inland there are thick forests sheltered by granite rocks and towered over by three mountains: Monte Teialone, Poggio Stefano and Poggio Zonza. Cala Brigantino and Cala Coticcio are two small beaches you simply must see. You can get to them after an hour's walk from the bridge, near where you can leave your car. The paths are sign-posted.

Culuccia Island
This small islet is near Santa Teresa Gallura, which it would be joined to by an ancient small bridge if this weren't now almost totally demolished.
To get there take the main road which connects Palau with Santa Teresa and then follow signs for Porto Liscia. Leave the car here and then walk across the small isthmus to reach the islet where, as well as a pleasant swim, you won't be able to resist the temptation of an easy hike into the interior.

Spargi Island
If you don't go on one of the hottest days in August, the small island of Isola di Spargi is an oasis of peace. It is an uninhabited and lovely spot which can be reached from Punta Sardegna by canoe. The important thing is to cross on a calm and sunny day as the area is subject to sudden currents and strong winds. Don't miss a stopover on one of the most beautiful beaches on the island, Cala Granara or Cala Conneri, where boats from Cannigione also dock.

SANTA TERESA DI GALLURA
Cala Li Cossi
Also known as Costa Paradiso Beach. To get there from Santa Teresa Gallura continue along the road to Castelsardo until you reach the fork for Costa Paradiso. This is a piece of authentic Sardinia which stretches from punta Cruzitta to Monte Tinnari, famous for its barren terrain made up of rocks eroded by the wind and the thick vegetation of junipers and tamarisks. After just a few kilometers you will reach the hotel "Li Rosi Marini" where, after leaving your car, you must take a path on the left and walk along the coast for about 0.5 km. Eventually you will find a white beach in the shape of an amphitheater on a still rugged stretch of coast, softened by golden sand. Behind the small cove there is a large expanse of maquis.

Calette di Tinnari
This string of little inlets can be reached from Santa Teresa by taking the road which

leads to Castelsardo. After driving for about 30 km and once you have passed the crossroads for Trinità-Isola Rossa, you must turn right and continue along a dirt road for another 2 km. At this point follow the sign for the hotel "Tinnari". Go straight on through the first gate. After another 3 km there is a second gate, where a sign invites you to leave your car and continue on foot. The path, which is about 1 km long, descends steeply to the sea.

Capo Testa

From Santa Teresa di Gallura, a sign-posted road on the left takes you in just a few minutes to Capo Testa. This isn't a beach but a headland joined by an isthmus, with a cliff and sea suitable for bathing. You reach it by crossing a hilly landscape of maquis. Down below, the

low scrub. To the west the beach is protected by Municca Island and on the opposite side by the barren crags of Porto Longone and Punta Falcone.

Rena Majore Beach

From Santa Teresa Gallura, drive along the main road to Porto Torres and turn at the fork for Castelsardo. Head towards the sea and, after tunneling through a long stretch of forest, you will find yourself on another surfaced road which, after 8 km, takes you near the beach of Rena Majore. To get to the sea you must turn about 200 m before the fork which leads to the village. After another 400 m of dirt road you will find yourself on the large white beach in a lovely dip surrounded by Mediterranean maquis.

BEACHES

Wind erosion has turned the rocks of Capo Testa into sculptures

headland suddenly appears, a staggering world of rock and wind with a thousand shapes. In Roman times ships loaded with slabs of granite for great building works in the capital sailed from here.

Rena Bianca

This is Santa Teresa's principal beach, located near the outskirts of the town, used by local people and holidaymakers. It is a sandy cove in the shape of a crescent, with granite colored sand, set between cliffs on both sides and dark thickets of maquis behind. It is easily reached on foot from the town on a little dirt road bordered by

Valle della Luna

To reach Valle della Luna from Capo Testa, near Santa Teresa, you will have to turn back before you reach the isthmus and head right. You will find a small road on your right which belongs to a tourist resort. Walk along the road until you see the lunar landscape of Valle della Luna. The valley is actually a geological fracture, the result of earthquakes some millions of years ago. It meets the sea with Cala Francese. On both sides the eroded rocks create an extraordinarily enchanting environment, unique on the island. The granite appears to be very pale, almost white, as though it were permanently bathed in moonlight. The impression is of an exotic and tough environment, not a pleasant, gentle landscape at all. This uniqueness has given the Valley the reputation of an "alternative" beach, visited by travelers in search of something different.

SAN TEODORO
Impostu Beach
About 8 km north of San Teodoro this is a large beach with white sand, surrounded by oleanders and mimosas. It is quiet except for in the middle of the summer season. To get there take the road from San Teodoro to Puntaldie or Capo Coda and turn at the fork for Lu Impostu (also called Porto Brandinchi). You will reach the beach after driving along 2 km of surfaced road.

Isuledda Beach
The beach of Isuledda is busy but still very lovely, stretching for about 500 m with powdery white sand and emerald green water. It is encircled by maquis and gorse, heather and myrtle. To get there take the SS 125 towards San Teodoro and turn at the fork for Ottiolu, then continue for about 2 km and turn right towards the port of Ottiolu. After another 300 m leave the surfaced road and turn left. About 1.5 km of dirt road will take you to the beach of Isuledda. Alternatively, if you decide to continue to the village of San Teodoro along the main road, you are sure to find the beach. The view, with its sweep and deep colors, is unmistakable. You can see the walls of the town from some way off, if you take the main road which skirts Stagno San Teodoro, from which there are various ways onto the beach.

Cala Girgolu Beach
Cala Girgolu is a small sandy cove where peace and quiet are guaranteed. To get there follow the SS 125 towards Olbia and, shortly before the restaurant "La Tombola", turn right onto a dirt road. Continue along 1.5 km of chalk road and then 500 m of tarmac. Then turn left and keep driving for 100 m until you reach the beach car park.

Capo Coda Cavallo Beach
Another white beach with a crystal-clear sea and no facilities, about 20 km from Olbia. You can get there from the other side of Punta di Tamarigio where the enchanting headland begins, whose point faces the small island of Proratora. By car just follow the SS 125 towards Olbia, the signs for Capo Coda Cavallo and then a stone which bears the legend "Villaggio est Capo Coda Cavallo". Another 1 km of dirt road takes you to the beach.

Punta Molara Beach
To get to this beach, surrounded by vegetation, follow the SS 125 towards Olbia and turn towards Punta Molara. Continue for 1.5 km, turn left and drive for another 2.5 km. Leave the car and walk down to the sea, which is very close. You will get to the beach by walking along the coast for another 150 m towards the left.

San Teodoro, a unique expanse of sand with amazing colours

ORISTANO

BOSA
Compoltitu
Towards Bosa, 5 km before you get to the little town, you will see a large car park. Leave the car and walk for a few hundred meters towards the sea. Go down to the shore, following the path, and all of a sudden you will see the sandy white beach in a partly enclosed roadstead where the water is crystal-clear, framed by a setting of rocks. The surprise is the stretch

SINIS PENINSULA - MAL DI VENTRE ISLAND

YEAR OF FOUNDATION: 1997

PROVINCE: ORISTANO

COMUNE: CABRAS

SURFACE AREA: 32,900 HECTARES

TYPOLOGY: PENINSULA WITH DUNES AND WETLANDS OF INTERNATIONAL IMPORTANCE.

MANAGEMENT: COMUNE DI CABRAS, P.ZZA ELEONORA 1, TEL. 0783290071.

WEB.TISCALI.IT/COMUNE-CABRAS

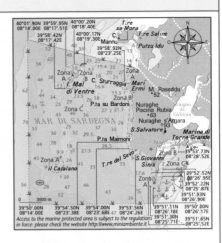

Now the marine area, which includes Sinis Peninsula, the small Mal di Ventre Island and the Scoglio del Catalano, contributes to preserve and protect a territory which ends in the dunes of Sinis and Is Arenas, and continues

Sponges and posidonias in the water beneath the Scoglio del Catalano

with the walls of sandstone eroded by wind and water, producing the symbol of this coastal landscape, S'Archittu, a large natural arch which has sea on either side and which is connected to the pools of Cabras (the largest natural sheet of water on the island), Mistras and Sale Porcus, one of the largest areas of marshes and lagoons in Italy.

The underwater landscape

The underwater environment is just as varied as the mainland with sand, sand bars and granite cliffs alternating with erosion channels, terraces and underwater landslides. The shallow seabeds of the marine area- between the peninsula and the islands they rarely exceed 40 m in depth – are largely sandy and covered in thick underwater meadows of posidonia sea grass interrupted by rock outcrops and sand bars like those which join the Scoglio del Catalano, split in two by a deep fissure, and Mal di Ventre which also has many fissures and small caves. If the meadow works as a lung and nursery for numerous fish species, many others instead make themselves at home on the rocky bed, like the nocturnal cardinal fish, the scorpion fish, the sea bass and gilthead which, with the gray mullet, regularly migrate to the nearby coastal pools. And to color the seabed there is no lack of corbinas, tadpole fish and invertebrates. Deep-sea fish and turtles are also quite frequent and off the Sinis Peninsula whale calves and sperm whales have been sighted.

of lily-white limey rocks worn and smoothed by the sea, which you can sit on to paddle your feet, or which you can use as a diving board to dive into the sea to swim to the isolated white reef which emerges from the roadstead.

Porto Alabe

Take the coast road which heads from Bosa south towards Turas to Marina di Tresnuraghes (Sardinian for "three nuraghi"). The car park can be seen from the road. If you go down to the sea on foot you will realize that, next to the wide, white beach there is an infinite number of little beaches. This is the coast which stretches from Magomadas to Tresnuraghes, inaccessible, studded with rocks and punctuated with little coves and sandy or pebbly beaches. The landscape is hilly, characterized by rias and volcanic slopes with terraces which slope down to the sea.

Porto Foghe

From Tresnuraghes, the largest inhabited center of Planargia, a road on the left, if you are coming from the north, will take you to a coast with many coves and eventually to the mouth of the Rio Mannu. The landscape is dark and volcanic, dropping into sudden cuestas, natural terracing in the soil. The beach of Porto Foghe (mouth) is an inlet, worn into the basaltic cliff by the centuries-old course of the river. The coast is wild and almost deserted and the craggy cliffs stretch as far as Cuglieri, the most picturesque village on Montiferru, the ancient volcanic cone which, millions of years ago, gave birth to the nature in these parts.

S'Aba Druche

About 4 km before Bosa you will find the sign S'Aba Druche (meaning "freshwater" in Sardinian dialect). The beach has some questionable facilities but is easy to get to and especially pleasant in less busy months, such as September. The beach, consisting of sand and pebbles from the river, is perhaps not the loveliest in the area, but the surrounding context merits a stopover for a relaxing swim.

CABRAS

S. Caterina di Pittinuri and S'Archittu

This is the seaside resort of Cuglieri, which you can get to from the road which leads from the village down to the sea. The coast is the dark and basaltic coast of Montiferru and the curving beach ends in a headland with the tower of Pittinuri, evidence of ancient Barbary raids. The real attraction is the nearby beach of S'Archittu, rather famous due to its splendid monumental arch, hollowed by the sea from limy rock. Here there is a break in the dark volcanic landscape of Montiferru: the coast becomes limy and dazzlingly white, the result of thousand year old seashell deposits. The rock is smooth and pleasant to the touch, the azure waters contained in circles of rock like natural harbors.

Is Arenas Beach

After the beach of Is Arenas, with its red sand, begins the Sinis peninsula which stretches as far as Marina di Torregrande, in the gulf of Oristano. With pools Is Benas, Sale Porcus and Cabras, the peninsula is ideal for boat-lovers. At sea you can appreciate the thousands of small coves with their high white limestone walls. To get to Is Arenas from Cuglieri just follow the signs on the SS 292 for S. Caterina di Pittinuri and then continue towards Oristano for about 3 km. Turn right onto a dirt road and it is another hundred meters or thereabouts.

Is Arutas Beach

This beach is on a low-lying, sandy stretch of coast several miles long. There are many ways to get to the sea and the shore is quite dazzling as there is no vegetation. Coming from the north, once you reach Riola Sardo on the SS 292, follow the signs for San Giovanni di Sinis. Long before you reach the village you will see signs for the beach which can be accessed from the B-road.

SASSARI

Argentiera Beach

You can get there from Alghero on the road of the "Due Mari" heading towards Porto Torres. After driving for about 20 km turn left for Argentiera and follow a lovely road into the interior pock-marked with mines like Palmadula. Follow the road until you reach the mining town of Argentiera, abandoned in the 1960s. Before you enter the town you will see a white sandy beach. On the right there are dunes which are as high as hills while on the left you can see the mining landscape. The village is a mining museum: houses, shafts, offices and machinery are still visible. On the other side of the village there is another beach with a deep blue sea. The sand is limey and quartzose and you will find yourself caught between the magic of the sea and the disquieting thought of the miners' centuries of toil.

Porto Ferro Beach

The inlet of Porto Ferro, which you will reach after leaving the headland of Capo dell'Argentiera behind you, has a large beach with a mixture of yellow and ruddy sand. At the end of the bay there are two imposing sentries: Torre Negra and Torre di Bantine Sale. If you are coming from Sassari you must follow the road for Porto Conte and turn at the fork for Porto Ferro. Once you get to the beach a half hour walk along the foreshore will be rewarded with the discovery of lovely deserted little coves. The nearby Lago Baratz, the only salt lake in Sardinia, is also worth a visit. It was formed by enormous dunes heaped by the wind which, in time, closed the sound.

ALGHERO
Cala Dragunara

This is a delightful rocky inlet where there is a bar and small jetty where you can catch a boat which will take you to the caves of Neptune in just a few, short minutes. You can get there from the coast road following the signs for Capo Caccia. The road forks in two directions: one leads to the cove while the other leads to Belvedere, the point from where you can admire Isola di Foradada with its stack.

BEACHES

Cala Viola

From the beach of Porticciolo, after a short hike which takes about 20 minutes, you will reach the splendid Cala Viola, where white limestone stands out against the mounds of collapsed earth which characterize it. The sandy beach is rather narrow while the rest is "comfortable rock". The purplish-blue sandstone of the Cala, dating back to sedimentary formations of the Triassic period are some of the oldest in Sardinia and in the whole of Italy. They amazed Alberto della Marmora, the first geographer of Sardinia, who described them as having the color of "wine dregs". An extremely interesting geological trail leads us in just a few, short minutes along the coast from Cala Viola to Guixera. Here abundant chalk intrusions have created a curious "lasagne" landscape.

Pineta Mugoni

Traveling about 15 km east along the coast road from Capo Caccia will get you to Pineta Mugoni, which stretches along the coast of the Parco di Porto Conte. It is both very popular and extremely long. The numerous points of access to areas where it is safe to swim enable you to reach various small beaches of sand and rock. Leave your car in front of the entrance to the pinewood.

X Beaches

Let's call these gorgeous stretches of sand which lie between Bombarde and Lazzaretto "X Beaches". Indeed, they do not have a name but it would be a pity to miss them. Sunken as though in the middle of a canyon which ends in the sea, they were practically deserted until a few years ago. This is no longer the case in the hottest months of the year but June and September are quiet. You can get there from the road to Porto Conte. Heading towards Bombarde turn right onto a small surfaced road which connects Bombarde with Lazzaretto. Along this road there are various ways to get to the sea. The area is entirely fenced off but you can still find narrow gaps. Leave your car on the road. The area is covered in maquis, but a five minute walk along a narrow escarpment between granite boulders guarantees you will be the only person on a small stretch of powdery sand with crystal-clear waters for swimming.

Lazzaretto Beach

About halfway between Porto Conte and Alghero lies Spiagga del Lazzaretto, fringed by a lovely and lush maquis with mastic and highly perfumed myrtle. Once you have left the car you can continue on foot to find other beautiful little beaches which are even more secluded. On the shore you can see the ruins of a quarantine station built in the 18th century, used to keep ships' crews thought to be carriers of infectious diseases in quarantine. Bombarde Beach is next. It is a fashionable place to go so it leaves a great deal to be desired in terms of peace and quiet. If you are interested you can get there from nearby Fertilia, driving for a little way along the coast road and turning left along small surfaced road.

Mariapia Beach

Near the town of Alghero there are some almost too famous beaches which still manage to be beautiful. Mariapia is

about 1 km from the town and can be reached from the road to Fertilia. This fine sandy beach stretches for about 2 km and is hidden by a tall dune topped with trees. Behind it there is a pinewood with a sign-posted nature trail. The beach is busy but behind it many dunes full of juniper shrubs provide secluded and sheltered spots.

Porticciolo Beach

Equipped with a good pair of walking shoes a day spent in the inlet of Porticciolo will be an unforgettable adventure. Lovely but a little awkward to walk on, the beach and foreshore are scattered with many rocks and detritus. On the right there is small hill with a Saracen tower, built by the Spanish. To get there from Sassari or Alghero head towards Porto Ferro and then follow the signs for Torre del Porticciolo. The road leads straight to the sea.

STINTINO

Cala S. Andrea (Asinara Island)

The western coast of Asinara Island, a National Park, is high and rocky while, in the east, the coastal landscape is intricate and colored with a variety of features: rias, isthmuses, cliffs, beaches. The most beautiful beach is Cala S. Andrea which you can get to from the sea or from the principal dirt road, the only one which crosses the island from south to north. The coast drops gently and the cove suddenly appears with its powdery white sand

and crystal-clear waters. The strong contrast with the dark scrub and the rugged rocks throws the picturesque landscape and shore into sharp relief. The feeling you get is that you are in touch with unspoiled and unique nature. Indeed, you can look but not touch. You cannot swim there as the cove is entirely protected by the National Park Authority of Asinara.

Lampianu Beach

From Porto Torres take the road to Stintino and continue towards Palmadula from the hamlet of Pozzo S. Nicola. You will get to the beach of Lampianu after the fork which leads to Villaggio Nurra. After 800 m you must turn onto a surfaced road and follow it until the end. Then turn left along 500 m of dirt road which ends in a large lay-by where you can leave your car. To get to the sea just go down the flight of steps.

Saline Beach

You can get to this rather busy beach from Sassari on the SS 131 "Carlo Felice" heading towards Porto Torres. At the entrance to the town leave the main road and continue towards Stintino, following the various signs which follow one another in both the industrial zone and along the B-road. Just before Stintino, near a villa and a little before a Spanish tower, you must turn right onto a recently surfaced road which leads straight to the beach. You will find yourself facing a long stretch of powdery white sand which is well worth the trip.

ASINARA ISLAND

YEAR OF FOUNDATION: 2002

PROVINCE: SASSARI

COMUNE: PORTO TORRES

SURFACE AREA: 10,732 HECTARES

TYPOLOGY: ISLAND WITH ROCKY COASTS AND SEABEDS WITH ROCK, SAND AND UNDERWATER MEADOWS.

MANAGEMENT:
NATIONAL PARK AUTHORITY OF ASINARA, VIA IOSTO 7, PORTO TORRES (SS), TEL. 079503388.

WWW.PARCOASINARA.IT

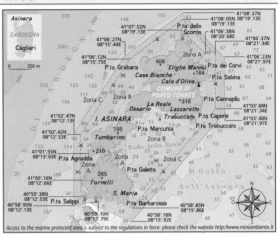

Access to the marine protected area is subject to the regulations in force: please check the website http://www.miniambiente.it

A penal colony, quarantine station, prison camp, jail and finally a park and protected marine area. These are the steps which led to the island eventually being handed back to the citizens. Separated from the coast

A sea just waiting to be discovered

The marine environment is characterized by the considerable integrity and diversity of its flora and fauna, by its exceptional beauty and by the cleanness of its waters. Like the surface, the seabeds too are

by a strait which hardly reaches 5 m in depth, Asinara runs into the western sea of Sardinia for about 18 km, its four small mountain ridges connected by an isthmus making it seem an archipelago.
The western coast is almost totally inaccessible due to the soaring cliffs which reach heights of up to 200 m, while the eastern coast is generally low-lying and rocky with beaches in the largest coves sheltered from the points.

different on either side of the island. The western coasts are characterized by steep walls which reach depths of 50 m just a short distance from the coast. Battered by strong currents and subject to intense wave phenomena due to the action of north-westerly and westerly winds, these seabeds are uneven, full of gullies, recesses and fissures and there is practically no sand. Low-lying coasts with stretches of sand are to be found instead in the east where, between Cala dell'Oliva and Punta Trabuccato, and in Rada della

Reale, there are large virgin meadows of posidonia which cover an area of over 15 km², reaching depths of up to 35-40 m thanks to the unpolluted waters. On the island researchers have detected species of particular interest, such as lithophyllum and red and calcareous algae able to form large concretions, giant limpets, pinnas (one of the largest bivalves in the world since it can reach a meter in length) and Rodriguez kelp, a cold and deep water brown alga, evidence of a Mediterranean sea which disappeared millions of years ago. Among the rocky recesses there are plentiful different species of fish such as dassies, sea-bass, scorpion fish, wrasse, corbinas, sea bream and dusky groupers which are generally found here in shallow water, unlike other parts of the Mediterranean where, in the past, they were continually disturbed by man.

CAPO CACCIA - ISOLA PIANA

YEAR OF FOUNDATION: 2002

PROVINCE: SASSARI

COMUNE: ALGHERO

SURFACE AREA: 2631 HECTARES

TYPOLOGY: ROCKY HEADLAND WITH NUMEROUS UNDERWATER CAVES AND A LARGE SANDY GULF.

MANAGEMENT: (TEMPORARY MANAGEMENT) COMUNE DI ALGHERO, VIA S. ANNA, TEL. 079997800.

WWW.COMUNE.ALGHERO.SS.IT

The inlet of Porto Conte, a natural harbor 6 km deep and 2 km wide, where the water remains calm during the most violent northwesters, is closed to the west and east by two majestic limestone ramparts: Punta del Giglio and Capo Caccia. The latter is a limestone peninsula with Monte Timidone (362 m) at its center and looks like an actual rock fortress which tapers towards the southern end, where a narrow isthmus joins the Cape, on which there is a lighthouse. In front of the towering cliffs of the headland is Foradada Island, a block of limestone severed from the coast while, further north, opposite Cala Barca, is Piana Island. Just after this the western coast rises at Punta Cristallo, where the Cape reaches a height of 326 m, overlooking the sea and creating a lofty panorama which takes your breath away. Here seabirds reign supreme, from precious peregrine falcons to extremely rare griffons, the large vultures which are slowly returning to reclaim the skies of the island once more.

Underwater caves and green meadows

In this area there are about twenty dive sites and though there is no lack of interesting things to see, such as wrecks, it is the caves which attract hundreds of scuba-divers together with their guides, indispensable for this type of experience, above all if the way is tortuous and tricky. The parts of the underwater cliff nearest to the surface are highly concretionary due to the presence of red algae and calcareous algae and especially lithophyllum. Deeper down there are colonies of red coral and vast walls covered in red and yellow sea fans and candelabra sponges. Inside the caves there is a dearth of vegetation, while there is no end of living creatures, above all sessile invertebrates (who are unable to move), depending on the light and the circulation of the water, making every expedition a novel and unique experience. It isn't unusual to encounter fair sized fish such as moray eels, conger eels, corbinas, sea bream, tadpole fish, groupers or lobster, crayfish and mantis-crab.

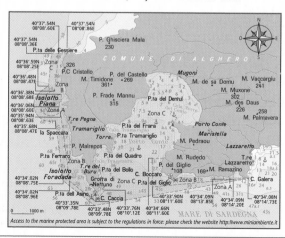

Access to the marine protected area is subject to the regulations in force: please check the website http://www.miniambiente.it

Córsica
(FRANCIA)

Bonifácio

I. Maddalena

Parco Nazionale
dell'Arcipélago
de la Maddalena

S. Teresa Gallura

I. Caprera

Palau

Parco Nazionale
dell'Asinara

I. Asinara

Golfo
dell'Asinara

Porto
Torres

Castelsardo

Témpio
Pausánia

Ólbia

Golfo Aranci

SÁSSARI

Lago del
Coghinas

Monti

Óschiri

Alghero

Mores

Ozieri

Siniscola

Valle dei Nuraghi

Bitti

Orosei

MAR DI

Bosa

Macomer

NÚORO

Dorgali

Golfo di
Orosei

Abbasanta

Lago
Omódeo

Parco Nazionale
del Golfo di Orosei
e del Gennargentu

Sórgono

MAR

Sinis

Stagno di
Cabras

Tirso

Monti d. ▲ 1829
Gennargentu

Árbatax

ORISTANO

Golfo di
Oristano

Parco Naturale
la Giara

Láconi

Lanusei

Tuili

SARDEGNA

Barúmini

Sárdara

Lago
Mulargia

Flumendosa

TIRRENO

Gúspini

Mannu

Dolianova

Muravera

Iglésias

Monastir

Quartu S. Élena

I. di S. Pietro

Stagno
di Cágliari

Sant'Antíoco

CÁGLIARI

Carbónia

I. di S. Antíoco

Golfo di
Cágliari

Teulada

Pula

MAR MEDITERRÁNEO

	HISTORICAL ITINERARIES
	CHILDREN
	PARKS
	BIKING ROUTES

From the historical past to the present evolving natural world, the following itineraries offer options for all interests. Nature lovers will find Sardinia the ideal place to discover rare flora and fauna in the mountains, caves and gorges of Parco del Gennargentu and Golfo di Orosei, two of the most beautiful and wildest protected nature areas in Italy. For something special, take the kids to see the last remaining wild horses in Europe, in the Giara di Gèsturi where the famous little horses can be viewed along the guided nature trails. Especially suited to the cyclist, Sardinia has well marked routes that weave through lush vegetation, ancient inland valleys, and along coastal byways of archaeological merit.

Itineraries & special interest

Highlights

- The basilica of S. Gavino in Porto Torres, S. Simplicio in Olbia, the basilica of S. Pietro in Torres, the castle of Serravalle in Bosa and S. Michele in Cagliari - just a few of the main examples of Sardinian Romanesque architecture
- The Trenino Verde from Arbatax crosses fascinating and otherwise inaccessible inland zones
- Five cycle tours through dense Mediterranean maquis passing the monumental millenary stones of the Nuraghic valley

Inside

THE GREAT ROMANESQUE PERIOD

There are two main periods in Sardinian history which set the local architecture: the long "Nuraghic" age, which saw the spread of seven thousand towers throughout the island, and the 'giudicale' period, during which the large Romanesque churches were built. The term 'giudicale" comes from the period between 1000 and the beginning of 1300 when Sardinia, by then already independent from Byzantine rule, was divided into four fairly autonomous regions governed by lords called "iudikes".

Despite the various bonds between the island and the "continent", particularly with the Maritime Republics of Pisa and Genoa through marriage and alliances with influential families on the mainland, but especially as of 1016 when the two powerful cities armed a large fleet to ward off an Arab invasion of the island, the "giudici" were the outright lords of the four dynasties and administered the whole island. Indeed, it was they who brought in the powerful religious orders that, in turn, built the most beautiful medieval churches on the stretches of land the "giudici" had given over to them. Some of these churches are located inside some of the largest towns or outlying towns, like the imposing S. Gavino di Porto Torres basilica, the forefather of the lords' Romanesque monuments located throughout the island. These monuments are characteristic, apart from their majesty,

for not having a frontal but two apses facing each other. Inside, the columns and capitals mostly come from the Roman city of Turris Libisonis; inside the crypt the three "Turritani" marters (Gavino, Proto and Gianuario), patrons of Turris and Sassari. The facade of S. Simplicio di Olbia has a mix of Lombard patterns that are drawn from Pisa architecture. One of the most beautiful examples of Romanesque architecture on the island is a group of churches located throughout the island and built high up dominating the surrounding countryside where monks, particularly Benedictine monks from Montecassino and Camaldoli, would pray and where they drained the land, administered farms and taught. Though the areas are now unpopulated the immense Romanesque constructions tend to strike tourists deep down.

Five of these masterpieces are to be found not far from each other in the north-west of the island and can be visited in a few hours. Though no one is really sure, it seems the basilica of SS. Trinità di Saccargia near Sassari was built in two periods by master builders from Pisa, initially between the end of the 11th century and 1116, then a few decades later. This basilica lies beside a former Camaldolesi monastery and is striking for the harmonious way the layers of white limestone and dark basaltic stone alternate around the main building, the bell tower and the front portal. Experts remind us that the basilica as it stands today underwent great renovations between the 19th and 20th centuries. In any case visitors will be awed by the harmony of the entire building. There is a set of frescoes inside, the only entire set remaining from the Sardinian medieval Romanesque period.

Going on towards Olbia (and S. Simplicio), we go by the church of S. Michele di Salvènero, which the Vallombrosani built at the beginning of the 12th century. Turning right we go towards Àrdara. The church of S. Maria del Regno, on the edge of the town, was the seat of the "giudici" of Torres; indeed, the church was the lords' palatine chapel. Built by Georgia, the sister of Gonnario-Comita 'giudice' of Torres and Arborèa,

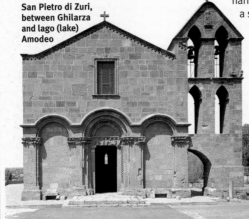
San Pietro di Zuri, between Ghilarza and lago (lake) Amodeo

The great Romanesque period

Sartène
Córsica
(FRÁNCIA)
Porto-Vécchio

Bonifácio

Parco Nazionale
dell'Arcipélago
de la Maddalena

Í. Maddalena
La Maddalena
Í. Caprera

S. Teresa Gallura
Palau
Báia Sardínia

Vignola Mare
Porto Cervo

Arzachena
Porto Rotondo

Í. Asinara
Parco
Nazionale
dell'Asinara
Golfo
dell'Asinara

Ísola Rossa
Luogosanto
Golfo Aranci

Stintino
Castelsardo
Témpio
Pausánia
Ólbia
S. SIMPLÍCIO
Í. Tavolara

Porto Torres
S. GAVINO
Monti
S. Teodoro

Argentiera
**S. Antíoco
di Bisárcio**
Budoni

S.S. TRINITÀ DI SACCÁRGIA
SÁSSARI
Ploaghe
Óschiri
S. ANTÍOCO
Alà d. Sardí

S. MICHELE DI SALVÉNERO
Ardara
Ózieri
Lodè
Siniscola

Porto
Conte
Ittiri
S. MARIA DEL REGNO
Bitti

Alghero
Mores
S. PIETRO DI SORRES

Bonorva
Bono
Orosei

CASTELLO DI
SERRAVALLE
Burgos
Dorgali

Bosa
Macomer
Ottana
NÚORO
Parco
Cala Gonone

S. Caterina
di Pittinuri
Abbasanta
Zuri
S. PIETRO
Mamoiada
Nazionale del
Golfo di
Orosei

Fonni
Golfo di Orosei
e del Gennargentu
MAR

MAR DI
Stagno di
Cabras
Sórgono
Baunei

Fordongianus
Aritzo
Árbatax

ORISTANO
S. Giusta
CATTEDRALE
Láconi
Séui
Lanusei
TIRRENO

Golfo di
Oristano
Jerzu

Arborea
Áles
Barúmini
Tertenía

SARDEGNA
Sárdara

Gúspini
Senorbì

Sanluri
Fluminimaggiore

Monastir
S. MARIA

S. PLATANO
Dolianova
Muravera

**Villa
Speciosa**
S. PANTALEO

Iglésias
Sibiola
S. Príamo

CATTEDRALE
DI S. CHIARA
Síliqua
Uta
CAST. DI S. MICHELE

Portoscuso
S. MARIA
Quartu S. Élena

Carloforte
Carbónia
CAGLIARI

Í. di S. Pietro
Tratalias
S. MARIA DI
MONSERRATO
Villasimius

Sant'Antíoco
Giba
Golfo di
Cágliari

Í. di S. Antíoco
Teulada
Pula

S. Margherita

MAR   MEDITERRÁNEO

Cathedral, Church

Castle

0   25 km

it was consecrated in 1107; is made entirely of dark Trachyte. One of the most beautiful retables on the island can be seen inside: an enormous alter table dating back to the beginning of the 16th century.

Further ahead, on the left of the main road SS 597 there is another masterpiece of Romanesque architecture, S. Antìoco di Bisarcio. This was the diocese's cathedral for many years before being transferred to Ozieri and rebuilt before 1000 A.D. having been damaged by a fire. It is believed the church was built according to the structural and decorative norms of Pisa architecture and the skilful hands of Lombard and Sardinian builders.

The fifth building of this group of Romanesque monuments is not too far

Malaspina castle in Bosa

from Àrdara, in the area of Borutta. Built between the 11th and 12th centuries the basilica of S. Pietro di Sorres was also the seat of the local diocese. The base of the basilica is made of layers of white limestone blocks, whereas the upper part repeats the two-colour bands used in the Trinità di Saccargia. A monastery was added to the basilica, where the Benedictine monks have now started to renovate books. High up on a projection of rock is S. Pietro di Sorres, the last Romanesque building in the north of the island. However, we have to mention two pieces of civil architecture: the Burgos castle, in Gocèano, built in the middle of the 12th century, and the Serravalle castle in Bosa, which was

started in the same period as the Malaspina family.

Even the centre-east of the island, the ancient lordship of Arborèa, has some very beautiful Romanesque churches, including the little church of S. Pietro di Zuri, near Ghilarza. Made of pink trachyte rock, it is lit up at dusk.

We know the name of the person who had it built, the "giudice" of Arborèa Mariano II. We even know who the architect was, a certain Anselmo from Como, who was by then already "projected towards gothic architecture" – wrote Roberto Coroneo, author of the book "Architettura romanica dalla metà del Mille al primo '300" (Romanesque architecture from the middle of 1000 to the beginning of 1300) – though he was still sensitive towards the ideas of Romanesque architecture.

Initially built between 1923 and 1925, it was dismantled stone by stone when the Omodeo dam was built in the Tirso valley and rebuilt in its current position, higher up. There is a very interesting cathedral near Oristano called S. Giusta, a magnificent church of "Pisa-Lombard-Sardinian" architecture built at the beginning of 1100.

The south of the island also boasts magnificent monuments, though the churches are somewhat smaller. There are, though, a few exceptions, like the cathedral in Iglesias, built by count Ugolino, and S. Pantaleo in Dolianova, mostly located inside the towns. However, it is this very difference that makes the area so fascinating and explains why visitors are so surprised to find authentic jewellery with refined architecture being sold on the edges of these farm towns. It is worth mentioning: S. Maria di Monserrato in Tratalìas, 1213; S. Platano in Villa Speciosa, built by the Vittorini di Marsiglia around 1144; S. Maria in Uta, also built by the Vittorini, a little earlier; S. Maria di Sibiola in Serdiana, also beginning 12th century.

The book by Coroneo mentions 169 Romanesque churches on the island, plus 9 castles, including the S. Michele castle which was built by Pisa architects in the 13th century, under the domination of Cagliari.

TRENINO VERDE

ÀRBATAX (OGLIASTRA)

FACILITIES: BARS, SELF-SERVICE CAFETERIAS, PICNIC AREAS, NURSERIES, PLAYGROUND. VISITORS ARE NOT ALLOWED TO BRING PETS OR GLASS CONTAINERS INTO THE PARK.

HOW TO GET THERE
BY CAR: SS 125 TO TORTOLÌ, THEN THE TURNING FOR ÀRBATAX.
BY TRAIN: ÀRBATAX TRAIN STATION.
BY BOAT: FERRY FOR CAGLIARI FROM CIVITAVECCHIA, FIUMINCINO AND OLBIA.

INFO: TRENINO VERDE, 08041 ÀRBATAX (OGLIASTRA), TEL. 800460220, E-MAIL: TRENINOV@TIN.IT, WEB: WWW.TRENINOVERDE.COM

TRAIN SCHEDULE
JUNE-SEPTEMBER (ÀRBATAX-MANDAS LINE).

TIMES: DEPARTURE FROM ÀRBATAX 8 A.M. AND 2:30 P.M.

ENTRANCE CHARGES
ÀRBATAX-LANUSEI DAY RETURN, FULL FARE EURO 19, HALF FARE (4-12 YEARS) EURO 9.50; 2 DAYS EURO 21, HALF FARE EURO 10.50.

The "Trenino verde" is a tourist train service run by the Sardinian Railways that crosses the most interesting inland areas of the island that are difficult to reach otherwise. The train can be rented (groups or associations); the whole train or as many coaches as you want –you can even choose the engine (steam or diesel). You can also take schedule trains along the various routes: Mandas-Àrbatax, Isili-Sorgono, Macomer-Bosa Marina, Tempio-Palau, Sassari-Tempio. The line that connects the coastal area of Àrbatax with the inland has been called "the most beautiful line in the world" and is 160 km long. You can travel the whole length and sleep overnight in one of the many towns along the way, or simple take a return trip to one of the towns and make good use of all the visits and excursions.

GIARA DI GÈSTURI

TUÌLI (MEDIO-CAMPIDANO)

HOW TO GET THERE
BY CAR: FROM CAGLIARI SS 131 TOWARDS SASSARI, AFTER THE ROAD 40.800 KM TURN RIGHT TOWARDS VILLAMAR-LAS PLASSAS THEN TUÌLI.

INFO: GIARA DI GÈSTURI, VIA G.B. TUVERI 16 (JARA COMPANY HQ), 09029 TUÌLI (MEDIO-CAMPIDANO), TEL. 0709364277/3482924983, E-MAIL: INFO@JARA.IT, WEB: WWW.JARA.IT

OPENING TIMES ALL YEAR.

ENTRANCE CHARGES
FARES ARE BASED ON NUMBER OF PEOPLE: FEWER THAN 4 PAYING EURO 30, TO BE DIVIDED; FROM 5 ADULTS UPWARDS EURO 6 PER PERSON; CHILDREN 5-12 YEARS EURO 3; FREE UP TO 5 YEARS OF AGE.

The Giara di Gèsturi high ground is a favourite place for nature walks with children, especially since you can see the famous little horses close by, the last remaining wild horses in Europe. Excursions are organised by the Jara di Tuìli company and last about 2 hours. They are not very difficult. Having met the guide you will proceed to the Giara along a tarred road which takes you 400 metres above sea level very quickly. From here you will move inland, into the woods with their oak trees, cork trees, shrubs, mastice trees, mock privet shrubs, arbutus and myrtle; fields with ferula, euphorbia, asphodel and helichrysum; the characteristic paulis (natural basins that fill with rainwater) and awesome blossoms. The guide will explain how to recognise the plants and tell you which ones are eaten, used as a local medicine or as a game, as well as some history of Sardinia and some archaeology featured.

GENNARGENTU AND GOLFO DI OROSEI

PROVINCE OF NÙORO

AREA
73.935 HECTARES. MOUNTAIN ROCK, DEEP FLUVIAL VALLEYS WITH CLIFFY COSTS, RICH IN CAVES AND GORGES.

HEADQUARTERS
TO BE DEFINED.

VISITORS' CENTERS
WWF SARDEGNA, VIALE DEI MILLE 13, 09127 CAGLIARI, TEL. 070670308,
E-MAIL: SARDEGNA@WWF.IT,
WEB: WWW.WWF.IT/SARDEGNA.

ENTE PROVINCIALE PER IL TURISMO, PIAZZA ITALIA 19, 08100 NÙORO,
TEL. 078432307/078430083,
WEB: WWW.ENTETURISMO.NÙORO.IT

View of the wild landscape of the Supramonte, part of the Parco del Gennargentu

Many people consider this the most beautiful and wildest nature reserve in Italy. The Parco del Gennargentu and Golfo di Orosei contain wonderful, almost untouched mountain terrain and costal land. It can be compared to a marvellous transatlantic ship ready to take to sea but that has been held up in the shipyard. Opened five years ago, forty-five years after the project was launched, this nature reserve is, to all intense and purposes, at a standstill, until the final authorisation from all the fighting factions is forthcoming and all the paperwork required to turn it into the fully fledged park it deserves to be has been completed.

An ever-changing landscape

Harsh and inaccessible, jealously guarded by the wild natural, the landscape in this part of Sardinia seems even lager and changeable.

Depending on the side or area you want to explore, you will come across mountains, grassland, rocks, canyons, valleys, forests, woods, beaches and cliffs. All this amazing variety of landscapes can be seen in the park area itself, with its massive Gennargentu rock facing south and east towards the deep valley of the Flumendosa river. This is the largest mountain range in the area; the highest points are Punta Paulinu (1,792 m), Bruncu Spina (1,829 m) and Punta La Marmora (1,834 m). On a clear day you can see as far as the furthest coast line. The protected area is closed off by the Barbagia and Supramonti mountains with their karstic features; then on, as far as the sea and the high, wild coastline of the Golfo di Orosei with its many caves and "codule", narrow valleys formed by rivers as they flow to the sea, the most famous being in Luna, Sisine and Fuili.

Characteristic fauna

Though it is still wild, the area of the Gennargentu shows clear signs of man's presence. The original thick, uninterrupted woods are today broken by grasslands and steppes, especially in the highest part of the region. Fortunately the woods have not disappeared; the holly undergrowth, yew and alder trees, especially by the streams as they cut there way through the undergrowth creating tunnels, alternate with holm oak woods surrounded by the most common Mediterranean brush, juniper, arbuto, mock privet and terebinth.

At an altitude of about 1,000 m, where oak trees once grew, there are till a few durmast oak and other species of oak tree sparse here and there, including the very rare oak quercus congesta.

As you can see from this very brief description, the reserve is an extremely important natural area from the botanical point of view thanks to the variety of plant life and species, clear proof of changing seasons. On the highest areas, fields of thyme and rare species of juniper (for example the Moris juniper), mountain shrubs like Prunus rostrata, Rosa serafinii, Astragalus genargenteus and ranno alpino. Along the coastal cliffs, where the climate is particularly warm, there is a strip of wild olive trees, mastic tree, carob trees and juniper. There are many native species of plant life and many of them get their names from the area, such as Euphrasia genargentea, Armeria sardoa genargentea, Ribes sardoum.

Rare and highly precious fauna

The isolated conditions so typical of an island have led to a number of species and sub-species of animal and insect life that can only be found in Sardinia. The Papilio hospiton butterfly, for example, is on the list of endangered Italian butterflies. There are a number of native species of reptiles and amphibious creatures such as the water reptile "natrice del Cetti", the "discoglosso sardo" and the bedriaga lizard. As far as mammals are concerned we must not forget the mufflon, the Sardinian deer, the Sardinian wildcat and the Sardinian fox. The island is also abundant in birdlife; there are over 100 species of nesting bids including a few very rare ones such as the golden eagle, a rare species of raven, hawk and sea gull.

The spectacular "Aguglia" (lofty mountain peaks) of Cala Goloritzè in the Golfo di Orosei, a natural monument

FOR CONNOISSEURS ONLY

From the wild to the garden and back: this seems to be the destiny of red and black currents, a natural shrub that grows best in cool, shady woody mountain areas. Cultivated for the bunches of slightly acid red and black berries, this shrub seems to be fleeing the fields of fruit growers back to the wild. One of the seven species of Italian currents has not been domesticated, nor has it been drawn away from the heart of the Parco del Gennargentu and Golfo di Orosei where it is the undisputed gem. Ribes sardoum is, in fact, an endemism; it is known to grow in a single area at an altitude of 1,100 m. Anyone wanting to grow this shrub should resign themselves to the fact that this shrub does not produce much fruit, a cause for concern over its survival.

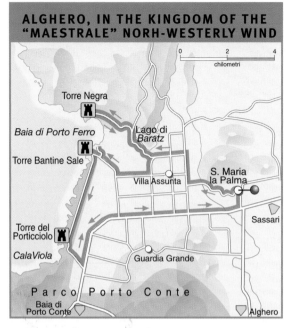

ALGHERO, IN THE KINGDOM OF THE "MAESTRALE" NORH-WESTERLY WIND

Key to symbols

- Point of departure and arrival
- Stop en route
- Tower
- Church
- Museum
- Viewpoint
- Ancient monuments, ruins
- Beach

Torre Negra

Baia di Porto Ferro

Lago di Baratz

Torre Bantine Sale

Villa Assunta

S. Maria la Palma

Sassari

Torre del Porticciolo

CalaViola

Guardia Grande

Parco Porto Conte

Baia di Porto Conte

Alghero

ROUTE 30 KM: SANTA MARIA LA PALMA - LAGO BARATZ (LAKE) - PORTO FERRO - CALA VIOLA - SANTA MARIA LA PALMA.

DIFFICULTY: THIS ROUTE IS ALMOST ALL ON TARRED ROADS, THOUGH THERE ARE A FEW STRETCHES OF DIRT ROAD THAT ARE, IN ANY CASE, NOT DIFFICULT TO CYCLE ALONG. THERE ARE NO DIFFICULT CLIMBS EXCEPT FOR THE STRETCH BETWEEN PORTO FERRO AND THE TOWER OF PORTICCIOLO, A HILLY AREA WHERE THE ROAD SURFACE IN SOME PARTS IS RATHER FULL OF HOLES.

BIKE SERVICE AND INFORMATION
MARIO AND PATRICIA OPPES VELOSPORT
TECHNICAL ASSISTENCE, VIA VITTORIO VENETO 90/92, SANTA MARIA LA PALMA, 07040 ALGHERO (SASSARI), TEL. 079977182.

TOURIST INFORMATION
AZIENDA SOGGIORNO E TURISMO, PIAZZA PORTA TERRA 9, SANTA MARIA LA PALMA, 07040 ALGHERO (SASSARI), TEL. 079979054.

Between Lago Baratz (lake) and Porto Ferro

This is a wonderful bike ride amongst the thick Mediterranean vegetation of the coral coast.
From the square in Santa Maria la Palma, with the church to your back, take the first on the right (one way). On leaving the town you ride along a road lined by eucalyptus trees. Continue for 2.4 km until you reach a T-junction: turn right. Go on for 1.2 km and then turn left and follow the signs for the lake "Lago di Baratz". After 1.4 km the road forks. Take the right fork and ride on until you reach the fenced parking area (1.1 km). You can see lake Baratz from the square, the only natural lake in Sardinia. A dirt road leaves the square between the left corner and the end of the square. This road runs along the right of the pinewood, ups and downs all the way, until you reach a tower called Torre Aragonese (1.7 km) overlooking the bay of Porto Ferro. Back to the square, take the tarred road for 800 m to the road on the right and down into the pinewood. You will meet the road

Alghero, cala Viola and the tower overlooking the bay

from the left fork later (1.3 km further on). Continue your ride until you reach a large junction (700 m). This time turn left and after 300 m you come to a tarred road near another junction. Turn right, and after a fast ride (400 m) you come to Porto Ferro. Following the tarred road back to the junction, you take the right road; another 50 m and you turn right and go on until you reach a large parking area and the Bantine Sale tower with its magnificent view over the golf of Porto Ferro. Now cycle back 400 m to the junction and turn right onto the wide dirt road that seems to cut the vegetation into two. This is a wild stretch of coast between Porto Ferro and the Porticciolo tower, ups and downs all the way. Many of the roads on the right lead to the sea. After 4.6 km the dirt road ends in front of a tarred T-junction: the road to the right takes you to a square (200 m) with its wonderful view over the Porticciolo tower and cala Viola (creek). If you take the road on the left go on until you reach a crossroads (700 m), turn left towards Sassari. After 600 m you turn right and cycle along the narrow tarred road among fields for 1.4 km until you come to a T-junction.

Now turn left and go on until you come to a junction in front of a fishmonger's shop; turn right and continue for 4.1 km until you reach a large tarred road. Turn left and go on to the traffic lights (1.9 km); go straight on until you come to the square in Santa Maria la Palma.

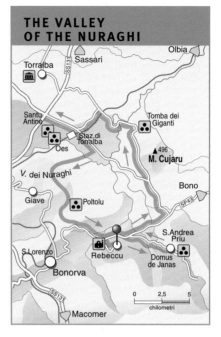

THE VALLEY OF THE NURAGHI

ROUTE 34.5 KM: REBECCU - TORRALBA STATION - NURAGHE SANTU ANTINE - REBECCU. YOU CAN GET TO THE STARTING POINT QUITE EASILY FROM BONORVA (5.5 KM).

DIFFICULTY: THIS IS AN EASY BIKE RIDE. HOWEVER, IN LATE SPRING AND SUMMER DO NOT RIDE IN THE MID-DAY SUN WHEN IT GETS VERY HOT. YOU WILL BE RIDING ALONG FLAT TARRED ROADS, WITH ONLY 3.2 KM OF DIRT ROAD WHICH, IN ANY CASE, ANY KIND OF BICYCLE CAN GO ALONG.

BIKE SERVICE AND INFORMATION:
SOCIETÀ CICLISTICA SANTA BARBARA, VIA A. MORO 28, BONORVA, 07010 SASSARI, TEL. 079 866272.

USEFUL CONTACTS AND TOURIST INFORMATION
AZIENDA AUTONOMA DI SOGGIORNO, VIA ROMA 62, 07100 SASSARI, TEL. 079231777.

From Rebeccu to Santu Antine

This ride through the inlands of Sardinia is a real trip through time, with its thousands-of-years-old rock monuments in the valley of the Nuraghi, between Bonorva, Sant'Andrea Priu and the heart of the nuraghi area.
Leaving from the square in Rebeccu you descend towards the main state road (1.2 km). At the main road turn right towards Bono and go on for 1.8 km until you come to a crossroads. The sign to the right points the way to the archaeological site of Domus de Janas di Sant'Andrea

Priu. After 2 km, near the small church of Santa Lucia, you ride along a smooth dirt road for 500 m to Sant'Andrea Priu. After a walk around the archaeological site continue along the same road to the main road SP 43, turn right and go on for 2.7 km until you come to a crossroads. Take the SP 21 on the right and follow the signs to Torralba and the SS 131. 3.1 km along this road and you have to turn right to Torralba, notice the volcano top of mount Cujaru. A little further on (2 km) and the road turns into a dirt road, though the surface is good enough even for a normal bike (1 km). Back onto the tarred road and, after 2.6 km, you are near the giant's tomb, "Tomba dei Giganti" (on the right) and 2 km further on a train crossing. Immediately after the train crossing (100 m) there is a dirt road on the left that goes to the Torralba train station (2.1 km). In front of the station, turn right and follow the signs towards the SS 131. On the right you will see the nuraghe di Oes, a rare example of a construction without a "tolos" covering. A short distance further on (1.1 km) and you come to nuraghe Santu Antine, which is really worth a visit; you can get a drink or have something to eat at the nearby bar. Now we return to the rail crossing. Cross the lines and, 1.4 km further on, turn left along a road that winds its way long the edge of the valley, below the town of Giave (high up on your right) and not far from a small hill (as the road curves sharply to the right) dominated by the nuraghe Poltolu (5.3 km). Continue along this road for 1 km until you come to a large crossroads. Turn left (back onto the main road SP 43) and ride on until you reach the turning for Rebeccu (2.7 km). The last kilometre is uphill. On the right you will see the 12th century Romanesque church of San Lorenzo well in view on the right. Taking a different road from the nuraghe Santu Antine you can ride to Torralba (4 km), where there is an interesting archaeological museum.

THE PENINSULAR OF THE SINIS 1

ROUTE 34 KM: SAN SALVATORE - IS ARUTAS - FUNTANA MEIGA - SAN GIOVANNI - THARROS - CAPO SAN MARCO - SAN GIOVANNI - SAN SALVATORE. YOU CAN GET TO THE STARTING POINT QUITE EASILY FROM CABRAS (ABOUT 4 KM).

DIFFICULTY: ANYONE CAN RIDE THIS ROUTE. IT IS MAINLY FLAT: 14.6 KM ON DIRT ROADS WITH LITTLE TRAFFIC.

BIKE SERVICE AND INFORMATION

F.LLI CEMEDDA, VIA THARROS 61/63, 07092 CABRAS (ORISTANO), TEL. 0783290804.

CICLOSPORT CABELLA, VIA BUSACHI 2, 09170 ORISTANO, TEL. 078372714.

TOURIST INFORMATION

GUIDE PENISOLA DEL SINIS, 07092 CABRAS (ORISTANO), TEL. 0783370019, 328 6973235.

ARCHAEOLOGICAL EXCURSIONS AND NATURE WALKS (INCLUDNG THE PROTECTED AREA OF PAULI AND SALI).

ENTE PROVINCIALE TURISMO DI ORISTANO, PIAZZA ELEONORA D'ARBORÈA 19, 07092 ORISTANO, TEL. 078336831.

ASSOCIAZIONE PRO LOCO ORISTANO, VIA VITTORIO EMANUELE 8, 07092 ORISTANO, TEL. 078370621.

Tharros and the quartz beaches

This cycle route runs in the southern part of the peninsular along good biking roads; the area is characteristic for its white quartz beaches.
Leave San Salvatore towards Is Arutas

along the main road SP 59. The road climbs slightly and goes over the hills of Su Pianu and, after 5.8 km, you will come to a parking area with a low wall all around, near the Is Arutas beach, a nice swimming area.

Now, facing the sea, you ride out of the parking area, turn sharp left and climb the dirt road and follow the wall with its wire fencing for 50m; then you turn right and follow the coastline. A little less than 5 km and you are riding by the right of the municipal park of Seu; the entrance is a little further on (6.2 km from Is Aruttas). Make sure you ride to the tower and the coast, going through wonderful Medittereanean vegation and a little group of crooked Aleppo pine trees. 1.4 km and you reach a crossroads: take the road on the right and descend among the little houses in Funtana Meiga and then onto the tarred road near the sea (T-junction).

Now turn left. 400 m and the road turns into a dirt road. Continue until it meets the main road. Turn right and, on the other side of San Giovanni (1 km) with its beautiful early Christian church, you come to Tharros and the ruins facing the sea. After the archaeological diggings continue along the dirt road leaving the San Giovanni tower on your right. You will be riding along the spine of the peninsular. The road climbs for a bit (250 m) but you will soon find yourself in the thick vegetation as far as the cape of San Marco (700 m).

On a beautiful jut of land nearby with a wonderful view there is a light house. Back to Tharros on the same road (1.7 km) you ride along a flat tarred road as far as San Giovanni (800 m); 2.4 km further on and the road turns right near the nuraghe Angioa Corruda and leads to a crossroads. Follow the signs for Putzu Idu and then on to San Salvatore.

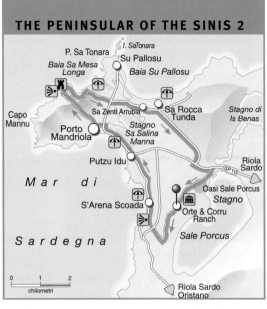

THE PENINSULAR OF THE SINIS 2

ROUTE 14.6 KM (10.6 KM ON DIRT ROADS, 4 KM ON TARRED ROADS): SAN VERO MILIS (OASI DI SALE PORCUS - ORTE & CORRU RANCH) - S'ARENA SCOADA - PUTZU IDU - SA SALINA MANNA - CAPO MANNU - SA MESA LONGA BEACH- SA ROCCA TUNDA - OASI DI SALE PORCUS. YOU CAN GET TO THE STARTING POINT QUITE EASILY FROM CABRAS OR RIOLA ALONG THE ROAD FOR "STAGNO DI SALE PORCUS" WHERE THERE ARE SIGNS FOR THE MUSEO DEL FENICOTTERO ROSA (PINK FLAMINGO MUSEUM).

DIFFICULTY: THE ONLY UNEVEN ROAD, THOUGH NOT VERY TROUBLESOME, IS THE CLIMB TO "CAPO MANNU". A MOUNTAIN BIKE IS SUGGESTED.

BIKE SERVICE AND INFORMATION:

F.LLI CEMEDDA, VIA THARROS 61/63, 07092 CABRAS (ORISTANO), TEL. 0783290804.

CICLOSPORT CABELLA, VIA BUSACHI 2, 09170 ORISTANO, TEL. 078372714.

TOURIST INFORMATION
GUIDE PENISOLA DEL SINIS, 07092 CABRAS (ORISTANO), TEL. 0783370019, 328 6973235.

ARCHAEOLOGICAL EXCURSIONS AND NATURE WALKS (INCLUDING THE NATURE RESERVE OF PAULI E' SALI).

ENTE PROVINCIALE TURISMO DI ORISTANO, PIAZZA ELEONORA D'ARBORÈA 19, 07092 ORISTANO, TEL. 078336831.

ASSOCIAZIONE PRO LOCO ORISTANO, VIA VITTORIO EMANUELE 8, 07092 ORISTANO, TEL. 078370621.

Towards the headland of Capo Mannu

Wide views along the coastline and an easy extraordinary ride among the little lakes in the marshland with their pink flamingo.

The beach in San Giovanni di Sinis

You leave Orte & Corru Ranch near the Oasi di Sale Porcus (horses and the pink flamingo museum) and follow the dirt road on the right for 1.1 km, through a field, until you come to a crossroads. Turn left then immediately right and skirt the eucalyptus wood. When you get back onto the tarred road turn right and, after 20 metres, left. When you reach a T-junction on the dirt road, turn right. Continue for 200 m and at the crossroads, turn right; another 200 m, another crossroads where you turn right, and then on until you come to some cliffs with some nice views (suggested starting point for the longer ride).

Now continue towards the S'Arena Scoada beach; 100 m and the road runs among the houses in S'Arena Scoada and then through the town of Putzu Idu. Back onto the tarred road and, at the T-junction, turn left and ride along the road between the beach and Sa Salina Manna marshland. After the turning for Mandriola you take the third 'white' crossroads on the left (1.1 km from the beginning of the tarred road) and cycle on until you come to a very wide stretch of road. Keep to the left and the road will meet another road which, in front of you, climbs up to the headland of Capo Mannu. On reaching the headland, 1.4 km, keep to the right until you reach the tower overlooking the bay of Sa Mesa Longa, the headland of Sa Tonara with its island of the same name and,

behind, the bay of Su Pallosu.

You are now in the most southerly point of the Sinis peninsular where, on a very clear day, you can see cape Caccia in the distance, 66 km away.

Ride down from the tower for 1.1 km along a track full of holes and with the Sa Salina Manna marshland in front of you. At the end of the descent continue straight along the main track towards the Sa Mesa Longa beach (200 m) keeping to the right (all signs to the left take you to the beach). Once you are back on the tarred road (600 m) there is a T-junction; turn right and ride on until you come to a crossroads (200 m) where you turn left onto a wide tarred road.

Continue for 400 m until you come to a crossroads. Turn right onto a road that goes by the agriturismo Sa Zenti Arrubia (holiday farm - 400 m), part of the own of Sa Rocca Tunda. On again for 800 m, take the tarred road on the right which, after 2 km, joins the main SP 10 road for Riola Sardo (on the left). Ride on for 600 m until the entrance to the Oasi di Sale Porcus which is near a very wide tarred road in front of the marshland.

Now continue along the centre road with its wood telephone pylons and the marshland on your left until you reach a fork (1 km). Keep to the left and follow the signs to the flamingo nature reserve Centro del Fenicottero Rosa e l'Orte & Corru Ranch (600 m).

THE "GIARA" NATURE RESERVE

ROUTE 5.5 KM: TUÌLI (MADAU PARKING AREA) - BRUNCU 'E SULAS - PAULI MAIORI - CRABILI ECCIU - ZEPPAREDDA. YOU CAN GET TO THE STARTING POINT QUITE EASILY FROM TUÌLI BY TAKING THE ROAD TOWARDS LA GIARA (5.5 KM).

DIFFICULTY: AN EASY RIDE, ALMOST COMPLETELY FLAT ON WELL BEATEN DIRT ROADS.

BIKE SERVICE AND TOURIST INFORMATION
CENTRO SERVIZI JARA, VIA G.B. TUVERI 16, 09029 TUÌLI (MEDIO-CAMPIDANO), TEL. 0709364277/ 3482924983, 3482924983 E-MAIL: INFO@JARA.IT WWW.JARA.IT.

BIKE RENTAL, GUIDED TOURS ON FOOT AND BY BIKE.
COOPERATIVA SA JARA MANNA, SS 197, KM 44, 09021 BARÙMINI (MEDIO-CAMPIDANO), TEL. 0709368170/070 9369116.

Between Pauli Maiori and Zepparedda

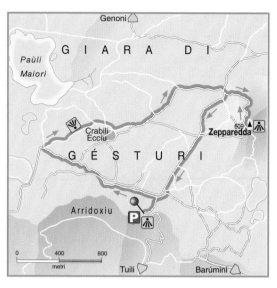

La Giara is an enormous plateau covered in basalt lava dating back two and a half million years that spewed out from the Zepparedda (609 m above sea level) and Zeppara Manna (580 m above sea level) craters. Today the craters are harmless mountains dominating the surrounding plain covered in arbus, mock privet, myrtle, mastic trees and rockrose. The area widens out near the paulis, the basins that fill with water in winter and are covered in white buttercups. Everywhere, wide expanses of the Sardinian flagship tree, the cork oaks, that cannot grow higher up because the "maestrale" north-westerly wind up here wants no hindrance and wants to blow free. Just like the little Giara horses, the last remaining wild horses in Europe and the symbol of this mysterious land, half way between land and sky.

You leave Tuìli from the Madau parking area along the flat dirt road. After a few metres turn right (if you turn left you can visit the church of Santa Luisa). Having crossed a wood with holm oaks you will come out onto an open flat piece of land with an old pylon and then on towards another wood, keeping to the right, with various low dry walls. The dirt road then goes through a narrow part of the wall on the right: on the other side of the wall turn left and follow the road by the wall until you come, 1.8 km, to a round courtyard, (Bruncu 'e Sulas). This courtyard was one used to round up horses. Now continue on the right until the road widens (500 m) and where you can see the Pauli Maiori marshland. There are two tracks on the right: the left-hand one goes by the marshland as far as the Salamessi spring (450 m), whereas our route continues on the right track. The track narrows

until it becomes a narrow footpath. When it becomes wide again keep to the right and, 30 m on, you come to another track that veers right towards Crabili Ecciu, with its hut called "masoni" and goat enclosures so typical of this area. Back to our main track now, (30 m back), continue for a few dozen metres until you come to a cart-road; turn left. At the first crossroads (150 m) turn right and follow the main track as far as a T-junction. Turn right towards the high ground of Zepparedda (500 m) crossing two junctions, the first on the left and the second on the right. Zepparedda is the volcanic crater that, two million years ago, spewed out the lava that today covers this plateau. Now you have to go back to the T-junction where, with your back to the high ground, you turn left. Ride on for 1 km along the main track until you reach a cork-oak wood not far from a crossroads. Turn left along the road to a wood gate which can be seen from the Madau parking area in Tuìli. More experienced bikers might like to extend the ride and descend from the high ground towards Genoni, on towards Nuragus, Gèsturi, Barùmini and then Tuìli. In this case the ride is 36 km long. However, it would be wise to ask for specific information.

Córsica
(FRÁNCIA)

Bonifácio

Í. Maddalena
Parco Nazionale
dell'Arcipélago
de la Maddalena

S. Teresa Gallura

Í. Caprera

Palaú

Parco Nazionale
dell'Asinara

Í. Asinará

Arzachena

Golfo
dell'Asinara

Castelsardo

Témpio
Pausánia

Ólbia

Golfo Aranci

Porto
Torres

Lago del
Coghinás

Monti

SÁSSARI

Óschiri

Ozieri

Siniscola

Alghero

Bonu

Bitti

Orosei

Bosa

Sindia

NÚORO

Dorgali

MAR DI

Macomer

Golfo di
Orosei

Ghilarza

Parco Nazionale
del Golfo di Orosei
e del Gennargentu

Abbasanta

Lago
Omodeo

Stagno di
Cabras

Sórgono

Monti d. 1829
Gennargentu

MAR

Cabras

ORISTANO

Tortolì

SARDEGNA

Golfo di
Oristano

Láconi

Lanusei

Tuili

Barúmini

TIRRENO

Sárdara

Lago
Mulargia

Flumendosa

Donori

Dolianova

Villasor

Muravera

Iglésias

Monástir

Serdiana

CÁGLIARI

Í. di S. Pietro

Carbónia

Quartu
S. Elena

Sant'Antíoco

Golfo di
Cágliari

Í. di S. Antíoco

Teulada

Pula

MAR MEDITERRÁNEO

Steeped in centuries of tradition, the food and flavors of Sardinia are surprising and uncommon. Although Sardinia is an island, most specialties are not primarily from the sea. The vast inland areas provide the fertile ground for an outstanding bounty of products ranging from the famous Pecorino Sardo and Fiore Sardo

PASTA   **OIL**

HAMS AND SALAMI   **WINE**

CHEESE   **CAKES**

Food

cheese to olive oils, hams, unusual pastas, honey, wine, liqueurs and, of course, sweets. The best way to experience the taste and heritage of Sardinia's typical food products is to attend one of the many regional food and wine festivals held through the year.

Highlights

- Prized mullet roe is the typical topping chosen to give an exceptional flavor to Sardinia's traditional pasta
- Fiore sardo DOP, a cheese that has been made for centuries in the countryside, is cited in 18th-century chronicles
- Vermentino, exported as a high-quality product, is the true symbol of Sardinia's wine industry. Other winning choices are Cannonau and Monica
- Many of the island's typical sweets are made out of oranges, almonds, lemon zest and honey

Inside

In 1929, a Touring Club of Italy correspondent wrote, "Whoever travels across this island, even if only briefly, will take away lasting impressions and memories of a way of life that is unique in all senses because Sardinians are proud of their heritage and have kept it intact for centuries...". At the beginning of the third millennium, things have not changed a great deal. This carefully guarded pride in origins remains in the local cuisine, which is simple but not boring, because various ingredients could only be obtained at a cost from across the sea. It is also still evident in the independent way people live and think.

Almonds give a special flavor to amarettos

An island with a pastoral soul

Mention an island and one thinks of the sea and, in terms of food, of fish. As such, Sardinia is unusual as it is not solely an island of fishermen. There are, of course, some places noted for seafood, such as the tuna of Carloforte or the lobster of Alghero (interestingly, these places have strong Ligurian and Catalan ties, respectively), but the inland dominates the island's cuisine. There, the relatively small fertile plains provide vegetables, fruit and cereal crops, and the extensive hilly areas are ideal for vines and olives, and for farming animals, especially sheep and goats. In fact, animal breeding is the outstanding economic resource of the island. Sardinia has a real heritage of indigenous breeding animals, although the presence of Charolaise and Limousine cattle is notable. The dairy and meat industries are also important. In addition, every type of Sardinian production has the added value of the exceptional quality of an environment – from the scents of the Mediterranean maquis to the rough tastes of the Gennargentu area – like very few others in Italy.

The most typical flavors are from inland

What has been said above also applies to the traditional gastronomy, which is strongly influenced by farming and animal breeding. There are plenty of different types of pasta and soup: small semolina dumplings that are often known as "malloreddus", sheep cheese ravioli called in different ways, such as "angiulottus" and "culurgiones", and "pane frattau", a flatbread in broth flavored with cheese. Next on the list is meat, especially white lamb and goat meat. There is also plenty of pork and, notably, the wonderful "porceddu", a suckling pig that is simply cooked on the grill or spit with abundant myrtle and other herbs. In autumn, the rustic nature of the island's cuisine is further reinforced with the addition of game and mushrooms. Of course, one should definitely not forget the seafood dishes that thrive on the abundance of raw materials, ranging from crustaceans to tuna. The true highlight is probably the mullet roe, collected by the coastal fishermen. In terms of places to eat, the general trend is somewhat reversed since the massive influx of tourists means there are far more coastal than inland restaurants. Still, although the seaside places are more famous and busier, the inland ones are more "natural" and full of surprises.

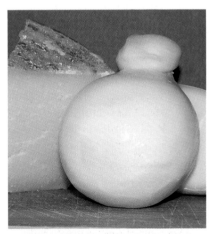

Despite being the home of Pecorino, Sardinia has many cow cheeses as well

PASTA

Sardinian cuisine is based on simple, tasty dishes that are linked to ancient traditions which have survived the passage of time. Preparing food on this island has an almost ritualistic quality, as can be clearly seen in the way the numerous types of bread are made for the most important festivals. Sardinian dishes, never overly elaborate, reveal their pastoral and peasant origins in both the ingredients and the preparation methods. The pasta is a definite example of this: "culurgiones, fregula, maccarones" and the famous "malloreddus", like the other pasta dishes, combine the consistent texture of the island's famous grain with typical products from the land, especially the excellent cheese. The inland areas generally prefer to combine the pasta with lamb, mutton or game meat sauces, normally flavored with a touch of pecorino or ricotta cheese; the coastal zones are well-known for their sauces based on fish and shellfish, especially clams, lobster and the excellent mullet roe. An unusual aspect of Sardinian pasta is the addition of saffron to the mix, giving it a clearly identifiable aroma.

Cashcà (cascà, couscous)

Cashcà is a variation of North African couscous. It is a traditional dish on the island of Tabarka and a typical part of Carloforte cuisine (Isola di San Pietro).

Culurgiones

This semi-circular ravioli, also known as "angiulottus", is made with egg pasta and filled with vegetables and cheese. It is normally made for festivities and is from Ogliastra. The dough is cut into circles, which are then made into little sacks, and the flaps are decorated like ears of wheat. Elsewhere, you can find "culurgiones de casu", filled with fresh (ricotta) cheese with beets (culurgiones de era) or spinach, or even flavored with lemon and orange rind or juice.

Fregola (fregula)

This simple pasta, similar to Sicilian "cùscusu", comes from Campidano of Cagliari and Oristano. Named from the Latin word "fricare" (to chop or to crumble), it consists of little balls of semolina kneaded with egg yolk and water with saffron. In the coastal areas, "fregola" is usually eaten in a shellfish broth (especially clams). Around Cagliari, you can try "fregula cun cocciula" (fregola with small clams) while further inland, it is not only served in broth, but also with a tomato and sausage sauce (su succu).

Fiuritti

A type of Lasagna made with semolina or egg pasta. It is typical of the Gallura area.

Impanadas (sas panadas)

These are not unlike small calzone pizzas, but are served fried. The mix is made of flour, lard and salt, and the filling has pork, beef or game (wild boar, partridge or hare), vegetables and mild or strong cheese. There is a lighter version with fish or shellfish.

Malloreddus

'Malloreddus' (literally, calves) are tiny dumplings of semolina and water, with the occasional addition of saffron. This is a typical Sardinian pasta and is also known as "gnocchetti sardi". Two of the best sauces for "malloreddus" are "campidanese", with tomato, sausage and pecorino cheese, and "oristanese", with spinach, chards, egg and cream.

Maccarones de busa (maccarones a ferritu)

The Sardinian version of "ferretto pasta". The semolina dough is cut into little rods and then pressed against a knitting-needle (ferretto in Italian) until you get a type of macaroni. It goes with many different sauces: lamb, veal or wild boar meat sauce, fresh cheese, dried tomatoes or walnut sauce.

FOOD

The pleasure of a ritual dish: su filindeu

Marraconese de 'rmathadura, Marraconese de patata

These are gnocchi that have been cut into pieces and pressed against a "palineddu" (basket made with asphodel), giving them a furrowed appearance. It is eaten with cheese and tomato sauce. The "marraconese de patata" are made by adding potato and egg to the dough.

Pillus

Thin strips of pasta cooked in sheep broth and served with pecorino cheese. At Giba, in the Sulcis area, there is a variant that is almost wide lasagna made with wild fennel and cooked in the oven with a tomato or meat sauce and cheese.

Ravioli di melanzane

Egg pasta filled with a mix of eggplant, ricotta cheese, parsley, basil, nut kernels, pecorino cheese and egg.

Su filindeu

A special soup made in Barbagia di Nùoro for the Feast of St Francis of Lula. It consists of a 'net' made of thin, dried semolina pasta that is cut into pieces and cooked in sheep broth. It is served with sharp pecorino cheese.

Taddharini

"Taglierini pasta". This word is used in the Gallura area and describes thin, small strips of semolina or egg pasta lasagna.

CAGLIARI

ASSEMINI
Pastificio I Cagliaritani
Truncu Is Follas, tel. 070948100
www.icagliaritani.com
This pasta shop makes homemade pasta with semolina and water, including typical Sardinian pasta, such as, "malloreddus, trifide, orecchiette, strozzapreti" and "macaronis".

PIRRI
Pastificio F.lli Mascia
Via dei Tigli 12, tel. 070521070
This pasta shop makes fresh homemade pasta that is sold loose, in packs and frozen. The specialties are handmade ravioli with ricotta, potato or vegetables and egg pasta, like tagliatelle, tortellini, cappelletti and gnocchetti. Some wonderful local cakes.

QUARTU SANT'ELENA
Pastificio Atzeni
Via Armando Diaz 31, tel. 070883455
This pasta shop has two branches (in Quartu and Ninnai) and makes homemade pasta with durum wheat, semolina, egg and ricotta cheese, which they also make. The pasta is both fresh and handmade (for the ravioli, "sebadas", baked pasta), and dry and made with a pasta machine (for the gnocchetti sardi and fregola).

CARBONIA-IGLESIAS

SANTADI
Antica Tradizione
Piazza Guglielmo Marconi 20
tel. 0781954064
This pastry and pasta house makes local products and handmade fresh pasta, such as "sebadas" (filled with cheese), "sappueddus" (maltagliati pasta with whole-wheat flour), tagliatelle and fried

ravioli filled with ricotta cheese. The ravioli and gnocchetti are made with a pasta machine.

MEDIO-CAMPIDANO

SAN GAVINO MONREALE
Pastificio S. Lucia
Via Giacomo Matteotti 68
tel. 0709339208
www.grupposantalucia.com
The pasta here is homemade and the ingredients are durum wheat, bread flour and fresh eggs. The ravioli, "malloreddus", tagliatelle and "fregola" are all made with a pasta machine and can be bought either fresh or dried.

NÙORO

Pastificio Artigiano Di Cutali
Via Piemonte 11, tel. 0782622156
This small pasta shop makes homemade fresh and dried pasta with local flour and semolina. Extensive range: the "culurgiones", including variants filled with mushrooms or eggplant, classic ravioli and gnocchetti are finished by hand; spaghetti, tagliatelle, various types of tagliolini, potato gnocchi, filled panzarotti and tortellini are made with pasta machines.

ORISTANO

Punto & Pasta
Via Gialeto 76, tel. 078378070
This pasta shop makes homemade fresh pasta with flour, semolina, eggs and dairy products. Their products include three-color "malloreddus" from Oristano, tagliatelle, ravioli and tortellini as well as some local cakes.

MARRUBIU
Pastificio Maccaronis
Via Napoli 122, tel. 0783858287
www.maccaronis.com
This pasta shop makes homemade fresh pasta with semolina. The "sebadas" and "culurgiones" are both handmade while the "malloreddus" are made using a pasta machine.

SASSARI

Specialità Pasta Fresca di Onali snc
Via Mercato 42, tel. 079232310
This pasta and pastry house makes homemade typical Sardinian pasta. The handmade products include "culurgiones", cannelloni with ricotta cheese, baked pasta and "spianata sarda" bread. The potato gnocchi, "malloreddus" and ravioli are made with a pasta machine.

FOOD

MULLET ROE

For most people, roe has only become well-known in recent years; however, true gourmets have enthused about it for numerous centuries. At the head of this list is Bartolomeo Scappi, Pope Pius V's personal chef, who wrote at length about the superior quality of mullet and bass roe. One of the best varieties is made in August and September by the fishermen of the Stagno di Cabras (pond near Oristano). There, mullet abounds and the egg sacks can be prepared the moment they are taken from the water. After these sacks are removed from the fish, taking care not to damage them in any way, they are salted and placed on an inclined plane to drip dry; in addition, light pressure is applied to ensure most of the pond water drains away. When this first stage is complete, they are left to dry for a further few days before being allowed to mature for 60 - 90 days in a dry, well-ventilated room. When buying mullet roe, the color should be uniform, tending to brown and there should be no marks or speckles. It should be firm and compact when cut and the membrane of the sack should stick to the dried eggs.

With its crystal clear sea, powerful winds and arid inland mountains, Sardinia is an island with a distinct and imposing character. The local products, seemingly preserved by the island's untamed nature, maintain their original, genuine flavors rooted in the farming and pastoral world where the simple, rustic means of preparation bring taste to the ancient recipes. The traditions have remained in an unbroken continuum and the shepherds still prepare the sheep fillet and ham, while the hunters provide the raw materials to make the wild boar ham and cured cheek fat in Ogliastra and Barbagia. The suckling pig, "porceddu", is often used in the rich minestrones of cabbage – flavored with the trotters, skin and lard – or broad beans with trotters, ribs, pancetta, sausage and crushed lard. These, and other thick soups, are enjoyed with strong, refined red wines like Cannonau, Girò and Monica.

Filetto di pecora

This typical Sardinian product is produced in limited quantities using sheep fillets. The meat is boned and any fat and nerves are removed. Then, in a special room, it is seasoned with salt, pepper, red chili and various other spices. After 4 days of seasoning, it is left to dry in the open for 2 more days. The fillet is then placed on a piece of linen for a few days. Finally, the individual pieces are tightly tied together in bundles of four.

Grandula

This is a type of cured pig's cheek, or "guanciale", from Gennargentu. It is made using the cheek, cheek fat and neck of a free-range pig. The cheek, cured with a mixture of salt and pepper, is left to season for 7-15 days, then pressed and smoked or allowed to mature naturally. After all this, it is allowed to season for a further month or two.

Guanciale di cinghiale

This cured meat is made with the fresh cheek of a Sardinian wild boar. First, it is cleaned, and then it is placed in a specific fridge where it is covered in salt and pepper, and cured for 20 days. Then, it is brushed and dried for 6 days. Next, it is smoked in a specific room using wood and myrtle leaf smoke before being allowed to age for about 2 months.

Mustela

This pure, lean pork sausage is made using the neck and loin of pigs reared in Sardinia or, sometimes, elsewhere in Italy. The meat is cured dry with a mixture of salt, aniseed and the herbs found in Mediterranean maquis. During these 15 days, the "mustela" is massaged until the flavors have been uniformly absorbed. Next, it is washed and stuffed into gut casings before finally being placed in an appropriate location or room to season for 2 months.

Gennargentu's particular climate allows the Prosciutto di Desulo to get the right seasoning. This raw ham is aromatic and strong-flavored

Prosciutto di Desulo

This raw ham is produced in limited quantities in Desulo, a small village near Gennargentu, between Lanusei and Fonni. It is made using the leg or shoulders of free-range pigs. These parts are soaked in a brine solution with pepper, garlic and vinegar. The ham, after draining, is then left to dry in the open air before being covered in a paste of pig fat, salt and pepper. It is then moved and allowed to season for several months in a warm place before being left to mature in a cellar for at least a year.

Now produced only in small quantities in Gallura, "sa supressada" is made of pure pork

Prosciutto di pecora

This raw ham is made in limited quantities using the legs of Sardinian sheep that have just finished lactating. After the animal is butchered, the legs are prepared and the fat and nerves are carefully removed. Part of the skin is also taken off before it is cured dry with a mixture of salt, pepper and Mediterranean herbs. After 20 days, the ham is placed in a fridge for a week and then left to season, in an appropriate room, for somewhere between 3 and 5 months.

Sa supressada

This pure pork sausage, produced in limited amounts, comes from Gallura (in the province of Sassari). It is made with prime cuts and lard chopped into small pieces. It is cured with salt, pepper and herbs before being stuffed into ventricle or rectum casings and pressed for about 7 days. This sausage is then left to dry in the kitchen before being placed in an airy room for a further 30 days.

Salame di Tergu

This cured sausage is made in limited quantities with good quality lean meat cut from the legs. It is cut by hand to ensure it includes a percentage of firm fat and then cured with salt and pepper before being stuffed into a natural casing. It is then left to mature for 7 days in a place of moderate temperature. During this stage, some butchers burn resinous wood on small grills to give the sausage a distinctive smoked flavor. It is then seasoned for 3 months before being eaten or placed in terracotta bowls and covered in ash.

Salsiccia fresca di Irgoli

Also known as "cannaca", this fresh sausage is from the Nùoro area and is made with lean and fatty pork from Italian-bred animals. The ingredients are minced and then cured with salt, pepper, fennel seeds and spices. The mix is then stuffed into a gut casing that has been washed with Vernaccia wine or vinegar. The sausages are normally half a meter long.

Salsiccia sarda stagionata

This seasoned sausage is made using both lean and fatty pork from pigs reared on the island. The ingredients are flavored with salt, pepper, fennel seeds and herbs. The mixture is then stuffed into a gut casing that has been rinsed either in vinegar or wine. The final sausage is normally half a meter long and is tied up with string such that the ends are joined and the final shape is something like an elongated donut.

Testa in cassetta

This cured meat comes from the province of Sassari and is produced in limited amounts. It is made using the freshly boned head of a pig that has been cut in pieces, the tongue and other pork or wild boar cuts. Everything is cured with salt, pepper, spices, local herbs, Vermentino wine and a small amount of Marsala. The mixture is then placed in a fridge and left for a week. Finally, it is divided into portions, wrapped in sheepskin and boiled.

CAGLIARI

Piras Carni
Via Pessina 95, tel. 070303272
Located in the heart of Cagliari, this shop sells traditional cured meats made by hand.

FOOD

115

MARACALAGONIS
Salumificio Su Sirboni
Via Fani 11, tel. 070789535
www.susirboni.com
The wild boars used are, literally, wild. Try the fillet, especially as a starter flavored with herbs and dry tomatoes.

MONASTIR
Salumificio Campidanese Su Sartizzu
tel. 0709177056, www.susartizzu.com
Centered on the "salsiccia campidanese", this family-run shop has transformed into a modern business, but keeping in mind traditional methods and recipes.

Sweet and slightly peppered Mustela is made with particularly lean meat

MEDIO-CAMPIDANO

GONNOSFANÀDIGA
Macelleria Salumeria Eredi Giovanna Pinna
Via Porro Bonelli 104, tel. 0709799467
The meat comes from an indigenous black pig that is actually a cross with a wild boar. These free-range animals are reared at the foot of Mt Linas. This butchery uses traditional methods, with no additives or seasoning rooms.

VILLACIDRO
Salumificio Monte Linas
Zona Industriale - Strada C2bis
tel. 0709311180, www.montelinas.it
In the inland areas of Sardinia, pork is a central part of the cuisine. As such, this meat deli, at the foot of Mt Linas, sells sausages that are made using local pork.

NÙORO

IRGOLI
Salumificio Murru
Via Marconi 66, tel. 078497053

www.salumificiomurru.it
Combining tradition with modernization, this shop has superb Sardinian sausages.

OLIENA
Salumificio Puddu
Orbuddai, tel. 0784288457
Located at the foot of Supramonte, this is an ideal place for rearing pigs and curing meats. The land is also good for growing vines.

ORISTANO

LACONI
Salumificio Santa Lucia Laconi srl
Santa Sofia, tel. 0782869784
This flagship for Sardinian pork butchers even supplies meat to the Papal kitchen.

MARRUBIU
Salumificio La Magica
Is Bangius, Via Case Sparse 3
tel. 078386478, www.salumimontearci.it
These cured meats, made using pork from the area, are flavored with myrtle and are infused with the aroma of the Mediterranean maquis on Mt Arci.

SASSARI

Salumeria Alberti Mario
Via Roma 23, tel. 079236659
This traditional shop has wooden furnishings reminiscent of the 1920s, the decade in which it was founded. This long experience makes it possible for them to choose the best local products to sell.

Satta e Murgia
Zona Industriale - Strada 18
Via Predda Niedda, tel. 0792679004
This company sells products from many small producers and carries out checks throughout the production process. It also sells some of the cured meats under its own name.

PLOAGHE
La Genuina di Pintus Maria
Corso G. Spano 306, tel. 079449223
This shop only sells meat from Sardinian breeds. It makes its own sausages, including some flavored with myrtle, using traditional methods and their own special technique.

CHEESE

Sardinia is surrounded by a truly gorgeous sea. The 1.850 km of coastline encloses a proud land that is solitary yet hospitable as it sits amid the granite rocks, the sheer, bare mountain slopes and the intense fragrances coming from the Mediterranean maquis. It is not fish, but meat and cheese that truly define Sardinian cuisine. Animal rearing and cheese production are the real heart of the island. Fiore Sardo, a lightly smoked pecorino cheese aged in mountain caves, dates from prehistoric times. A bronze statue now in the Archeology Museum of Cagliari depicts a shepherd with a ram across his shoulders, which was the icon of daily life during the prehistoric period. Ancient customs are still preserved in the traditions, while at the same time new methods are successfully experimented with. The Animal Husbandry Institute of Olmedo, in the province of Sassari, develops tasty new sheep and goat cheeses. On the table, "culurgiones", "sebadas" filled with "casu spiattatu", potato and goat cheese ravioli are all interpretations of this wondrous ingredient.

Bonassai

This rectangular or square cheese is made with Sardinian sheep's milk and has a firm, white texture. It tastes slightly sharp, with traces of fermented sheep's milk. The exterior is covered in potato flour. For every kilo of cheese, it is soaked in brine for an hour and then aged for 20 to 30 days.

Casizolu

It is made using full cream milk from pasture cows. The texture is compact and elastic, or hard when aged. Mild when young, the taste becomes stronger as it ages. After the stringing of the curd, it is placed for 6 to 8 hours/kg in saturated brine.

Casizolu di pecora Pirittas (Pirittas sheep Casizolu)

A typical of Goceano (in province of Nùoro), this strung cheese is made Sardinian pasture sheep's milk. The strung curd is soaked in brine for 5 hours/kg, then tied in twos and hung up to dry.

Casu axedu

The regional product has many names: "frua merca", "fruhe" and "frughe". The smell is distinctly sheep, while the taste is sharp when fresh and spicy, salted when aged. Normally, it is eaten fresh, after being lightly dry salted, but it can be aged for months in brine. In Ogliastra, the aged cheese is called "Fiscidu" or "Vìscidu" and it is used in minestrones or the typical potato ravioli of the area.

Dolcesardo

Typical of Arborèa (in the province of Oristano), it is cylindrical, white and soft with some air holes. It has no rind; the taste is mild and the smell delicate.

FOOD

Farming in Sardinia: bound to the past, fascinated by future

It is made with unprocessed, pasteurized cow's milk from Sardinian dairies.

Fiore Sardo DOP

This is the Sardinian cheese mentioned in 18th-century chronicles and is the symbol of the oldest pastoral traditions in central Sardinia. It is made from full cream sheep's milk and processed with lamb rennet into wheel shapes. It is aged for 3 to 6 months and the rind changes from deep yellow to dark brown. The texture is compact and the taste full and strong. It is sometimes lightly smoked using wood from shrubs in the Mediterranean maquis.

Fiore sardo Dop

Formaggio di colostro ovino

After pressing, the shaped curds are salted in brine for a day. The cheese is eaten fresh and the whey is used to make superb ricotta. Beestings (colostro) is the thick milk secreted just after parturition and has nutritional value and a pleasant taste; however, it can only be milked for 4 or 5 days after the birth of a lamb.
It is often drunk by babies and old people alike, and used in dairy products.

Fresa

Although found in the whole region, it is linked to Maghine, Planargia and Montiferru (Nùoro and Oristano provinces). Normally like a compacted cylinder, it can be square with rounded corners. It has a soft texture, a buttery smell and a sharp taste. It is made with cow's milk from the end of lactation, with peaks of production in autumn (Fresa de attunzu). The name comes from Latin (fresus, squeezed) and the cheese probably has Roman origins, but is now Sardinian.

Gioddu

It is fermented sheep's and goat's milk from Sardinian breeds. It is creamy with a sharp taste. After boiling and pasteurization, 2% of "Gioddu" (made during a previous production cycle) and milk enzymes obtained from the same

product are added. This is then thoroughly stirred and kept at 40°C/100°F until it coagulates. It is eaten cold.

Pecorino di Osilo

This cheese is cylindrical in shape and can be soft or hard. The taste is mild or savory, becoming slightly spicy if aged for over 6 months. It made from sheep's milk collected in two milking sessions. The curd is cooked, pressed and then salted both by hand and in brine. While the cheese is aging, it is washed with water and brine.

Pecorino Romano DOP

Born across the Tyrrhenian Sea, it was adopted by Sardinians and is mainly made in the provinces of Sassari and Nùoro.

Pecorino Sardo DOP

Produced exclusively on the island, it is made from fresh sheep's milk. DOP recognition encompasses two types: mild Pecorino Sardo, shaped like a wheel weighing 1 to 2.3 kg, ready to be eaten after 20 to 60 days, with a minimum fat percentage of 40%; mature Pecorino Sardo, shaped like a wheel weighing 1.7 to 4 kg, destined for long aging, with a minimum fat percentage of 35%. The rind is smooth and thin, ranging from white to brown. The texture is soft and compact, initially with a mild aromatic or slightly sharp taste, then becoming spicy.

Provoletta di latte vaccino Sardo

This soft cheese with a thin rind has a delicate taste that is slightly aromatic. It is made from raw, pasteurized cow's milk. The shaped curds are soaked in a saturated brine solution. Initially, it is kept for 7 days at 4° C/10°F (95% humidity) and for 48 hours in a special aging room at 16° C/40°F (70% humidity).

Ricotta di colostro ovino

A fresh cheese that is eaten right away. It is made from the whey produced when making sheep's beestings cheese.

Ricotta di pecora o di capra lavorata

Found mainly in the Basso Sulcis, at Teulada, Santadi and Giba, this processed sheep or goat ricotta cheese is very creamy and spicy. The ricotta is fermented for at least 30 days. It is made in summer and eaten in late fall and in early winter, normally spread on toast. There is also a mild version.

Ricotta fresca ovina

This fresh sheep ricotta is shaped like a truncated cone and wrapped in vegetable parchment. It is white, with a delicate smell and a mild flavor. It is produced from the whey of milk from Sardinian sheep.

Ricotta moliterna

This ricotta is produced with the whey from the milk of Sardinian sheep. It has a truncated cone shape and is semi-hard with a delicate smell and a savory flavor. It is lightly pressed and dry salted with two layers of salt. It is aged for 15 to 20 days and is then vacuum packed with shrink wrap.

Soft, square-shaped Bonassai excels among Pecorini

Ricotta mustia

This ricotta is made with whey from the milk of Sardinian sheep. It is sold in various shapes: cylindrical, with a flat top and bottom, and vertical sides, and "like a squashed loaf". It has a slightly amber color without a rind. The texture is soft and smell is smoky. It is smoked with herbs.

Ricotta testa di morto

A Greek ricotta made with whey from Sardinian sheep's milk. It is round with a delicate smell and savory taste. The shaped curds are pressed and salted with fine salt, then aged for 20 to 30 days.

Ricotta toscanella

Made from Sardinian sheep's milk, it is cylindrical in shape with a semi-hard texture, delicate smell and savory taste. It is pressed and, after being salted once or twice with fine salt, it is left to age for 15 to 30 days.

Treccia

A typical product of the Comunità Montana del Montiferru. This strung cheese is shaped by hand and made using milk from the Sardo-Modicana cow, which is reared in the wild. After soaking in brine for 24 hours, it is dried on a cloth, wood or a trellis. It must be eaten within 3 days.

CAGLIARI

Bonu - Cose Buone dalla Sardegna
Viale Diaz 162, tel. 070306453
www.bonu.it
This shop sells many Sardinian cheeses, like Fiore Sardo, variously aged pecorino, caprino and mixed goat-sheep cheeses. It stocks other local products, such as cured meats, mullet and tuna roe, "carasau" flatbread, cakes and wine. They make international deliveries.

Industria Lattiero Casearia F. Podda
Sestu, Viale S. Avendrace 345
tel. 070281988, www.cheese.it
Pecorino Sardo and Pecorino Romano, Fiore Sardo, Bello di Sardegna, Caprino, Pecora Smeralda, Perette, Mature Classico Misto and Semimature Rigato Misto. The company only uses milk from Sardinian breeds.

DONORI
Caseificio Aresu
SS 387, tel. 070981177
Fresh and aged goat and sheep cheeses. It has more than 50 years of history; the guided tours are worth booking.

NÙORO

Formaggi Tuffu
Prato Sardo 121, tel. 0784294063
Variously aged sheep cheeses. Small cheeses: half-cooked, "toscanello", fresh and salted ricotta, "frue" or "merca" (curds).

FOOD

SINDIA

Salis Pasquale e Figli
Nuragh'elighe, tel. 078571761
Organic products: from sheep and cows, beef and cheese ("Tamuli" Fiore Sardo, "Norax" pecorino, "Shardana" salted ricotta). The wide open spaces of the Campede plateau have large pastures interspersed with sporadic cork groves. This is where the first organic farm was set up. Excellent cheeses, especially the delicate pecorino and the special salted sheep ricotta.

OLBIA-TEMPIO

BÈRCHIDDA
Nuova Casearia
Via Umberto 37, tel. 079704101
Organic products: fresh and aged sheep cheeses, ricotta.

OSCHIRI
Casearia Fogu
Zona artigianale S'Utturu
tel. 079734149, www.fogucaseario.com
Variously aged Pecorino Sardo, including with pepper or chili, cow's milk "peretta" cheese, mixed cheeses and caprino, cream cheese and butter. All of the produce, including the Rio Coghinas, is guaranteed as organic. The company produces a wide range of typical Sardinian cheeses and offers tasting for potential buyers during tours (booking necessary).

ORISTANO

Caseificio Marcello Cuozzo
Via Cagliari 25, tel. 0783212441
Young, mild and aged pecorino cheese, provoletta, caprino, mozzarella, and an Oristano dessert made from cow's milk, and fresh and salted ricotta. This family-run business was established in 1959 and is now well-known: their products are also sold in Via Costa at the Mercato Civico. Visits only by booking.

CUGLIERI
Pievi
Corso Umberto I 172
tel. 078536147

www.pecorino.it
Pecorino Sardo and caprino. Products from the dairy, but also olive oil, wine, liqueurs and local desserts and cakes. The shop has the best of the island's gastronomy, with all the products being guaranteed and made using traditional Sardinian methods.

SASSARI

ALGHERO
Casa del Formaggio
Via Mazzini 43, tel. 0799733067
Located in the centre, it has offered numerous delicacies for 30 years. Free tasting for potential buyers.

MORES
Coop. Allevatori Mores
Via Risorgimento 4, tel. 079706002
Pecorino Romano and Pecorino di Monte Acuto, semi-cooked cheese from Osilo, Moro del Logudoro, caciotta cheese, fresh and smoked ricotta. It has produced good cheese for 50 years and even exports to the US. Guided tours by booking and tasting for potential buyers.

OZIERI
In.Ca.S.
Piazza S. Sebastiano 3, tel. 079787681
Pecorino Sardo and Pecorino Romano (DOP), ordinary pecorino and ricotta.

PORTO TORRES
La Bottega Salumeria Formaggeria
Piazza XX Settembre 1, tel. 079514834
Many Sardinian cheeses, cured meats, roe, products preserved in oil, wine and liqueurs, "carasau" flatbread and cakes. The organic section is 25 years old.

VILLANOVA MONTELEONE
Coop. Allevatori Villanovesi
Via Su Laccheddu 51
tel. 079960576
www.coopvillanova.it
Pecorino Romano (DOP), semi-cooked pecorino and caciotta cheese. During visits (booking necessary), they offer tasting for potential buyers.

OIL

From the splendid coastline to the rough and mountainous interior, olive trees are the essence of the Sardinian landscape and are used to make high quality products that have received the highest forms of recognition. Despite the different climatic zones of the island, the olive tree has taken root all over, making this one of Italy's most promising oil producing regions. In short, this is a specialized sector that is growing fast. During the 1999-2000 olive season, roughly 38,000 hectares were cultivated and over 10,000 tons of pressed oil were produced. This figure is well above the average of the previous four years. These positive results in terms of producing good quality oil have led to a rethink in how the land is cultivated, the use of machines, the processing cycle and how oil is promoted and marketed.

Each province has some olive growing districts

In the province of Cagliari, the area is around Dolianova, where Tonda di Cagliari and Pizz'e Carroga olives are used to make high quality oil with a refined and distinct aroma. To the north, in the Sassari zone, especially the area from the west of the city to the coast, the oil has a strong aroma but the taste is often milder with hints of vegetables and grass. The typical cultivar of this area is the Bosana (known locally as Tonda del Sassarese), which has medium-sized olives with a high oil yield. This variety produces many olives and is resistant to the cold and pests. The best olive groves in the province of Oristano, where the Bosana cultivar dominates, are found from the foot of Mt Ferru (north of Oristano) up to 500 m above sea level. In the Nùoro area, the olive groves tend to be in the eastern sector, with the main centers being Oliena, Dorgali, Orosei and the mouth of the Cedrino.

Sardinia at the table

Olive oil, used both raw and cooked, greatly enhances the flavors of Sardinian food. The apex of the culinary tradition in the interior is roast meat that has been softened and scented with oil and local herbs. Young goats or pigs and lambs are roasted whole on the spit over a fire of scented wood or, following an ancient tradition, by placing them in a hole in the ground covered with stones, above which a fire is lit to cook the meat slowly and produce a special flavor. Along the coast, by contrast, fish is popular and found in numerous varieties: there are many crustaceans, including tasty lobsters; the tuna roe is excellent, but the mullet one is even more highly prized; the day's catch can be eaten fried, grilled or prepared using a local recipe. In any case, olive oil is used to enhance and season the dish, which is completed with many fresh or cooked vegetables that also go well with extra virgin olive oil.

FOOD

CAGLIARI

Agriser srl
   Via dell'Artigianato 6, tel. 0702116300
Aureu - Consorzio prod. Olio extravergine di oliva di Qualità della Sardegna
   Via Lungo Saline 27, tel. 070383070
Bardi Teobaldo
   Largo Gennari 4, tel. 07042907

DOLIANOVA

C.O.PAR - Coop. Olivicoltori del Parteolla
   Via E. Lussu 43, tel 070741329
   www.diocopar.it
Fattoria Enrico Loddo
   Corso Repubblica 81,
   tel. 070740715
   www.diodolia.com
Locci Francesco
   Viale Europa 18, tel. 070740651
   www.diodeltempio.com

DONORI

Frantoio Corona di Luigi e Lucia Corona & C. sas
   Via Sa Defenza 28, tel. 0709818616

QUARTUCCIU
Casu Isidoro
Su Camp'e Sa Pira, tel. 070845657

SERDIANA
Argiolas spa
Via Roma 28, tel. 070740606
www.cantine-argiolas.it

SINNAI
Oleificio F.lli Serreli di Serreli I. & C. sas
Via F. Sotgiu 11, tel. 070785146

UTA
Azienda Agricola Giovanni Sarais
Via S. Giusta 35, tel. 070968897

VALLERMOSA
Oleificio Valle Hermosa Di Lai e Pinna snc
SS 293 - Zona Industriale, tel. 078179175

VILLASOR
Consorzio Interprov. per la Frutticoltura
SS Villasor - km 14.250, tel. 070964411

CARBONIA-IGLESIAS

IGLESIAS
La Valle dei Lecci srl
Via Corsica 17/U, tel. 070247385

SANTADI
Frantoio olearia di Rubiu Nicoletta M. sas
Via Balia 18, tel. 0781941006

MEDIO-CAMPIDANO

ARBUS
Caddeo Angelo Salvatore
Via E. D'Arborea 68, tel. 0709758749
Floris Maria
Via Mentana 28, tel. 0709758524

GONNOSFANÀDIGA
Azienda Agricola Bruno Cabras
Spadula, tel. 070971289
Coop. Olearia Santa Barbara srl
Via Pabillonis 1, tel. 0709799092
Eredi Foddi Fiorenzo
Via Mameli 14, tel. 0709799208
Fattorie del Maestrale srl
Viale Kennedy corner Via Rossini
tel. 0709797126
Franco e Roberto Lisci
Zona P.I.P. - lotto 11
tel. 0709799194

SIDDI
Matta Isaia
Via V. Emanuele III 22, tel. 070939805

TUÌLI
Porcu & Pinna snc
Via Roma 13, tel 0709364415

USSARAMANNA
Oleificio Podda di Podda Aurelio & C. sas
Zona P.I.P. - lotto 4, tel. 078395414

VILLACIDRO
Azienda Agricola 3D di Gianpaolo Deidda
Via Nazionale 316, tel. 0709314957
Oleificio f.lli Cabriolu Felice e Francesco
Zona Industriale, tel. 0709311390
Campo Molas sas
Via V. Emanuele 93, tel. 070932274
Concas Angelo
Via Azuni 3, tel. 0709315103
Enolearia Monte Linas Soc. Coop. arl
Villacidro - S. Gavino - km 5
tel. 0709311210
Frantoio Oleario F.lli Serra Di A. e L. snc
Zona Industriale – strada C4
tel. 0709311199
Mocci Efisio Fausto
Via N. Bixio 19, tel. 070932645
Frantoio oleario di Pittau snc
Zona Industriale, tel. 0709311405

SASSARI

Nuovo Oleificio San Pasquale s.n.c.
Zona Industriale Predda Niedda -
strada 48 Caniga, tel. 079260280
Oleificio Cooperativo di Sassari
Via Predda Niedda 4/D, tel. 079261054

ALGHERO
Accademia Olearia di Fois Giuseppe
Via De Muro 13, tel. 079980394-
079970954
Antica Compagnia Olearia Sarda
di A.G. Fois
Via V. Emanuele 225, tel. 079951597
www.anticacompagniaolearia.it
Domenico Manca s.p.a
Via Carrabuffas c.p. 56
tel. 079977215
www.sangiuliano.it

ITTIRI
Azienda Agricola F.lli Pinna
Via Umberto 133, tel. 079441100
www.oliopinna.com

WINE

The pristine rural environment and an age-old tradition of quality are the strengths of the new Sardinian wine industry. With the Vermentino DOCG at the helm, tourism is likely to be the catalyst for real growth in this industry. In 1392, Eleonora, Queen of the Giudicato di Arborèa, passed the "Carta de Logu", the act which imposed the planting of vines on uncultivated land. At that stage, vine-growing already had a long history on the island, but her initiative caused its expansion and, thus laid the foundations for today's success.

An island attached to its traditions

Dry whites with great character, a unique range of dessert wines, rapidly improving reds – this is a snapshot of Sardinia's wine industry. Although certain vines are found across the region, the industry can be divided into three districts. To the south is the sizeable zone around Cagliari, which includes the Campidano area and the neighboring mountainous districts of Iglesiente and Sarrabus. The central area runs from the planes of Alto Campidano and Sinis, near Oristano, to the Arborèa and Mandrolisai mountains in the Nùoro area. The northern section includes the expanses of Nurra, near Alghero, the hilly landscape of Logudoro, south of Sassari, and the rough, wind-carved landscape of Gallura, near Olbia. By looking at the statistics, you get the idea that this is a "traditional wine region". The vines are predominantly indigenous, with the white Nuragus (22.1%) and the red Cannonau (20.8%) and Monica (17.8%) taking up the top spots. These, together with Pascale di Cagliari, Vermentino Bianco and Carignano, account for more than 88% of the wines. The remainder consists of local wines such as Malvasia di Sardegna, Vernaccia di Oristano and Girò. The only continental "intruders", so to speak, are Sangiovese and Trebbiano. In terms of distribution, some grapes are now grown quite far from their places of origin. The most telling examples of this are the Cannonau, Monica and Moscato, but recently Vermentino has boldly crossed over the borders of the Gallura region.

A wine industry that is on the rise again

Production has decreased sharply from 2.5 million hectoliters in the decade from 1970-80, to the current figure of 700-800 thousand. This clearly discernable trend can be explained by the European Union incentives for uprooting plants – this scheme was part of the policy to reduce agricultural surpluses – and, especially, by the droughts that led many vineyards to be abandoned. Nowadays, with the substantial demand and the higher quality, Sardinia is facing a grave shortage of raw materials. Over 90% of production is consumed on the island, but this only meets 50-60% of demand. To counteract this problem, indigenous grapes are being planted, although some imported vines are also planted since they can improve production and increase variety. In terms of regulations, Sardinia has made great strides and now has a DOCG wine, namely Vermentino di Gallura, 19 DOC wines and 15 with the Italian IGT (Typical Geographic Indication) recognition. DOC wines account for more than 10% of the regional total, which is notably higher than the average in central and southern Italy. The DOC system is designed to encourage the production of wines made from a single grape – traditional or imported – while the Vino da Tavola (table wine) categorization favors the creativity of wine-makers using a variety of grapes. An indication of the future of the industry is Vermentino, which is exported as a top quality product.

FOOD

Vines near Oliena, upon the background of the Supramonte

Wine categories

Three labels define Italian wines according to quality. IGT (Typical Geographic Indication) guarantees vine cultivation according to certain regulations. DOC (Controlled Origin Denomination) indicates conformity to regulations on area of origin, and production and maturation procedures. The top label is DOCG (Guaranteed and Controlled Origin Denomination); there are around 20 DOCG wines in Italy, 6 in Tuscany. VDT (Table wine with an alcoholic content of at least 10 per cent).

Cannonau

Recorded as early as 1612, it is probably a variety of the Granacha grape that the Spanish brought to the island. The wine is ruby red, of greater or less intensity, becoming slightly orange when aged. It has a unique aroma and a dry, slightly bitter taste.

Malvasia di Sardegna

Originally a Greek vine, it arrived in Byzantine times and is now grown across the island, although the best comes from Bosa (in the province of Nùoro). The wine has a high alcohol percentage and the intensity of the color can vary. The aroma is refined and strong, while the taste ranges from sweet to dry, depending on the processing, with an almond aftertaste.

Vats for ageing wine

Monica

This grape of Iberian origin probably dates from 11th century when the Camaldolese monks introduced vine cultivation on their lands. The wine has a clear ruby color, becoming amaranth with ageing. The aroma is strong and the taste is dry, but pleasant, with a peculiar aftertaste.

Vermentino Bianco

Originating in Spain, this vine sailed the sea to Sardinia and Liguria. It is one of the island's top wines and holds the prestigious DOCG status in Gallura.

The wine is clear, hay yellow with touches of green. The aroma is subtle but intense and the taste is alcoholic but soft with a slightly bitter aftertaste.

Vernaccia di Oristano

Some people say this grape, now grown in the southern Tirso Valley, was introduced by the Phoenicians of ancient Tharros, while other claim it was the Spanish. The wine is a golden or amber yellow, the aroma is delicate and flowery, and the taste is smooth and warm with an almond aftertaste.

CAGLIARI

CASTIADAS
Cantina Sociale di Castiadas
Olia Speciosa, tel. 0709949004

DOLIANOVA
Dolianova
Sant'Esu, SS 387 - km 17.150
tel. 070744101, www.cantinedolianova.it
● *Cannonau di Sardegna - Doc*
● *Monica di Sardegna - Doc*
○ *Vermentino di Sardegna Naeli - Doc*
○ *Moscato di Cagliari - Doc*

MONSERRATO
Cantina Sociale di Monserrato
Via G. Cesare 2, tel. 070560301

SENORBÌ
Cantina Trexenta
Viale Piemonte 40, tel. 0709808863
www.cantinatrexenta.it
● *Cannonau di Sardegna Baione - Doc*
● *Tanca Su Conti Isola dei Nuraghi Rosso - Igt*
○ *Nuragus di Cagliari Tenute San Mauro - Doc*
○ *Vermentino di Sardegna Tanca Sa Contissa - Doc*
◑ *Monica di Sardegna Duca di Mandas - Doc*

SERDIANA

Argiolas spa
> Via Roma 28, tel. 070740606
> www.cantine-argiolas.it
> ● Cannonau di Sardegna Costera - Doc
> ● Korem Isola dei Nuraghi - Igt
> ● Turriga Isola dei Nuraghi - Igt
> ○ Vermentino di Sardegna Costamolino
>   - Doc
> ◗ Monica di Sardegna Perdera – Doc

Fratelli Pala
> Via Verdi 7, tel. 070740284, www.pala.it
> ● Cannonau di Sardegna Triente - Doc
> ● Monica di Sardegna Elima - Doc
> ○ Nuragus di Cagliari Sàlnico - Doc

SETTIMO SAN PIETRO

Ferruccio Deiana e C. sas
> Su-Leonaxi, tel. 070749117
> www.ferrucciodeiana.it

CARBONIA-IGLESIAS

SANTADI

Cantina Santadi
> Via Cagliari 78, tel. 0781950127
> www.cantinadisantadi.it
> ● Carignano del Sulcis Riserva Rocca
>   Rubia - Doc
> ● Carignano del Sulcis Superiore Terre
>   Brune - Doc
> ○ Vermentino di Sardegna Villa Solais -
>   Doc
> ○ Villa di Chiesa Valli di Porto Pino
>   Bianco - Igt
> ◗ Latinia Valli di Porto Pino Nasco
>   Vendemmia Tardiva - Igt

NÙORO

Perda Rubia
> Via Asproni 29, tel. 078432832
> www.perdarubia.it

DORGALI

Cantina Sociale di Dorgali
> Via Piemonte 11
> tel. 078496143
> www.csdorgali.com
> ● Cannonau di Sardegna
>   Vigna di Isalle - Doc
> ● Fùili Rosso dei Baroni
>   Provincia di Nùoro - Igt
> ● Noriolo Provincia di
>   Nùoro - Igt
> ○ Calaluna - Igt

OGLIASTRA

CARDEDU

Vitivinicola Alberto Loi
> SS 125 - km 124.2, tel. 070240866
> www.cantina.it/albertoloi
> ● Tuvara Isola dei Nuraghi Rosso - Igt
> ● Loi Corona - Igt
> ○ Leila - Igt

JERZU

**Vitivinicola Antichi Poderi Jerzu soc.
coop. agricola**
> Via Umberto I 1, tel. 078270028
> www.jerzuantichipoderi.it
> ● Cannonau di Sardegna Marghìa - Doc
> ● Cannonau di Sardegna Riserva
>   Chuerra - Doc
> ● Cannonau di Sardegna Riserva Jostu
>   Miglior - Doc

OLBIA-TEMPIO

ARZACHENA

Capichera
> SS Arzachena - S.Antonio - km 6
> tel. 078980612,
> www.capichera.it
> ● Capichera Assajè - Vdt
> ● Capichera Mantènghja - Vdt
> ○ Capichera Classico - Vdt
> ○ Capichera Vendemmia Tardiva - Vdt
> ○ Capichera Vigna 'Ngena - Vdt

BÈRCHIDDA

Cantina del Giogantinu
> Via Milano 30, tel. 079704163
> www.giogantinu.it
> ● Terra Mala Vigne Storiche Colli
>   del Limbara Rosso - Igt
> ○ Karenzia - Docg

MONTI

Cantina Sociale del Vermentino
> Via S. Paolo 2, tel. 078944012
> www.vermentinomonti.it
> ○ Vermentino di Gallura
>   Superiore Aghiloia -
>   Docg
> ○ Vermentino di Gallura
>   Funtanaliras - Docg
> ○ Vermentino di Gallura
>   S'Eleme - Docg
> ○ Vermentino di Gallura
>   Arakena - Docg, late
>   vintage

WINE LEGEND

Wines are listed with
symbols which indicate
their type
● red
○ white
● rosé
◗ sweet or dessert

FOOD

OLBIA
Cantina delle Vigne
Cala Saccaia, tel. 078950717
www.pieromancini.it
- Cannonau di Sardegna - Doc
○ Vermentino di Gallura Cucaione - Docg
○ Vermentino di Gallura Saraina - Docg

TELTI
Pedra Majore
Andrieddu, tel. 078943185
○ Vermentino di Gallura Hyonj - Docg
○ Vermentino di Gallura I Graniti - Docg
○ Vermentino di Sardegna Le Conche - Doc

TEMPIO PAUSANIA
Cantina Sociale Gallura
Via Val di Cossu 9, tel. 079631241
- Dolmen Rosso Colli del Limbara - Igt
○ Vermentino di Gallura Gemellae - Docg
○ Balajana Bianco Colli del Limbara - Igt

ORISTANO

Cantina Sociale Cooperativa
della Vernaccia
Rimedio, Via Oristano 6/A
tel. 078333155

CABRAS
Azienda Vinicola Contini
Attilio
Via Genova 48, tel. 0783290806
www.vinicontini.it
- Cannonau di Sardegna Riserva
  - Doc
- Nieddera Rosso della Valle del Tirso
  - Igt
○ Vernaccia di Oristano Antico Gregori
  - Doc
○ Vernaccia di Oristano Riserva Speciale
  - Doc
◑ Karmis Vernaccia della Valle del Tirso - Igt

MOGORO
Cantina Sociale Il Nuraghe soc. coop.
SS 131 - km 62, tel. 0783990285
www.inuraghe.it
- Cannonau di Sardegna Vigna Ruja - Doc
- Monica di Sardegna Superiore Nabui
  - Doc
○ Vermentino di Sardegna Dongiovanni
  - Doc

SAN VERO MILIS
Cantina Puddu
Via S. Lussorio 1, tel. 078353329

www.cantinapuddu.it
- Cannonau di Sardegna Antares - Doc
- Monica di Sardegna Torremora - Doc
○ Vermentino di Sardegna Marìs - Doc
◑ Vernaccia di Oristano Riserva - Doc

SASSARI

Enoteca Regionale della Sardegna
Museo del Vino (wine museum)
tel. 079299131

ALGHERO
Cantina Santa Maria La Palma soc. coop.
Santa Maria La Palma, tel. 079999008
www.santamarialapalma.it
- Alghero Cagnulari - Doc
- Cannonau di Sardegna - Doc
○ Vermentino di Sardegna I Papiri - Doc
○ Vermentino di Sardegna Palmador
  - Doc Barrique
Tenute Sella & Mosca
I Piani, tel. 079997700
www.sellaemosca.com
- Alghero Marchese di Villamarina - Doc
- Cannonau di Sardegna Riserva - Doc
  ○ Vermentino di Gallura Monteoro
    - Doc
  ○ Vermentino di Sardegna
    La Cala - Doc
  ◑ Alghero Monteluce - Doc

FLORINAS
Tenute Soletta
Via Sassari 77, tel. 079438160
www.tenutesoletta.it
- Cannonau di Sardegna Riserva
  - Doc
○ Vermentino di Sardegna Prestizu - Doc
○ Vermentino di Sardegna Soletta - Doc

SENNORI
Tenute Dettori
Badde Nigolosu, SP 29 - km 10
tel. 079514711
www.tenutedettori.it
- Dettori Romangia Rosso - Igt
- Tenores Romangia Rosso - Igt
- Tuderi Romangia Rosso - Igt
◑ Moscadeddu - Vdt

USINI
Azienda vinicola Cherchi Giovanni Maria
Sa-Pala e Sa Chessa, tel. 079380273
- Cannonau di Sardegna - Doc
- Cagnulari Isola dei Nuraghi Rosso - Igt
○ Vermentino di Sardegna Tuvaoes - Doc

LIQUEURS

Sardinia has a well developed tradition of liqueurs and they tend to be based on the local plants and herbs. These exquisitely simple liqueurs have unmistakable tastes and aromas. They also have unusual names, which often refer to the type of plant used to make them. One of the best loved is a type of aqua vitae called "fil'e ferru", made from the rape of very carefully selected grapes.

Fil'e ferru
The name comes from the piece of iron wire that was used at the beginning of the 20th century to find alcohol that had been buried underground by the producers to avoid the heavy taxes.

Liquore di Cardo
The primary ingredient in this liqueur is the blessed thistle, it has a bitter taste.

Mirto di Sardegna tradizionale
This ancient red liqueur is made by mixing myrtle berries, sugar and/or honey in a solution of alcohol and water. It helps digestion.

Villacidro Murgia
This semi-sweet liqueur has a deep yellow color. It is flavored with 25 herbs.

Villacidro Murgia Bianco
A semi-sweet liqueur with an aniseed taste, it is colorless and flavored with 20 herbs.

CAGLIARI

Agri.Sar spa
Via dei Passeri 3, tel. 070662302

QUARTU SANT'ELENA
Ditta Eredi di Luigi Poscia e C. s.a.s.
Via Catalani 49, tel. 070884869

SELARGIUS
Ditta Giovanni Pacini
Viale Trieste, tel. 070842663

SINNAI
Liquorificio Artigianale di A. Bruno
Via Pio XII, tel. 070782266

MEDIO-CAMPIDANO

VILLACIDRO
Ditta Comm. Gennaro Murgia s.a.s.
Via Parrocchia 29, tel. 070932014

NÙORO

Prase Dolciaria Sarda s.n.c.
Prato Sardo 32-33, tel. 0784294051

OGLIASTRA

TORTOLÌ
DIOS s.r.l. – DistillerieaOrientale Sarda
Via Baccasera – km 18
tel. 0782624133

OLBIA-TEMPIO

OLBIA
Cantina Delle Vigne di Piero Mancini
Cala Saccaia, tel. 078950717

MONTI
Cantina Sociale del Vermentino Soc. Cop.
Via S. Paolo 1, tel. 078944012

ORISTANO

CABRAS
Azienda Vinicola Attilio Contini spa
Via Genova 48/50, tel. 0783290806

FLUSSIO
Cantina Sociale della Planargia
Via Nuova 8, tel. 078534886

MOGORO
Mulino 900 s.r.l.
Via Gramsci 246, tel. 0783 991571

SASSARI

F.lli Rau S.n.c. di Rau Giovanni Mario & C.
Predda Niedda Sud - Strada 15
tel. 079261905, www.rau.it

ALGHERO
Zedda Piras spa
I Piani, tel. 079997777

FOOD

CAKES

Sardinian cakes are essentially out of three ingredients: ricotta, especially the rich and tasty one made from sheep's milk; almonds, easily available and of good quality; and honey, which is found in an unparalleled variety of flavors, from the Mediterranean maquis to the woods of Gennargentu. Of course, the combinations in which they are used differ and other local products are added, such as oranges, lemons, raisins and cooked wine. Still, the essence remains the same. The island's cake production is so closely linked to the rural traditions that, even in the cities, there has never been the desire to do something different or more creative.

S'aranzada

This cake is made with oranges, almonds and honey. Although this is an age-old recipe, it was an artisan from Nùoro, Battista Guiso, who patented it in 1886 and brought it to the world's attention. It is still the cake chosen for important festivities.

Amaretto or Amarettos de mendula

This sweet cookies with ground sweet and bitter almonds come in various forms. The mix is shaped into ovals or circles.

The caschettas are shaped into auspicious objects

Biscotto di Fonni or Pistoccu

These are similar to the classic Savoy biscuits, although larger. Soft and crumbly, with a golden color.

Candelaus or Pastissus

A delicious, age-old cake: a very thin layer of almond paste covers a soft fresh almond mix flavored with orange-flower water.

Carapigna

A truly white lemon sorbet with a texture like fresh snow.

Caschettas or Tiliccas

Layers of pastry filled with honey, saffron and almonds. It is shaped like a horse-shoe, an ellipse, a half moon or a heart, with a crumbly white exterior.

Copuletas or Copuletta

An almond cake covered with frosting. It is white and crumby with a truncated dome shape.

Corikeddos or Cuoricini

A traditional gift given to the bride by her mother-in-law. Nine large "coros" are surrounded by many little hearts called "sos corikeddos". The number of hearts is always odd and is related to the standing of the family.

Culingiones Dolci or Culingionis de mendula

Typical carnival sweets, these square ravioli are made with a mix of honey and chopped almonds, and flavored with lemon rind and orange-flower water. They are fried and then served sprinkled with vanilla sugar.

Frittelle lunghe or Frisjoli longhi or Frisjolas

These are cylindrical and spongy. The dough is fried in special containers that determine the length. They should be eaten immediately with melted bitter honey.

Gallettine or Pistoccheddus grussus or Gallettinas

These elongated oval cookies are covered in sugar. Crumbly, light and golden, they have a strong taste and a clear lemon aroma.

Gateau or Su gattò de mendula

Almond toffee that is sometimes flavored with lemon rind. After being cooked, it is placed on a flat surface and cut into diamonds. The shapes are then decorated with tiny confetti and placed in cupcake holders. This traditional dessert even gets mentioned in Grazia Deledda's novels.

Gueffus

A small, spherical dessert made with almonds, egg whites and lemon rind. After it is cooked, the dough is shaped into balls, rolled in sugar and wrapped 'like sweets' in small pieces of colored paper.

Mandagadas or Trizzas or Acciuleddhi

A braid-shaped sweet that is made with semolina and Sardinian honey. The braids are fried in oil and then dipped in boiling honey. They are kept in glass or terracotta containers.

Mostazzolos

These cookies, typical of the Oristano area, are made with concentrated must and wheat flour. Their rhomboidal shape is, according to some experts, a stylized representation of the Mediterranean Mother Goddess. They are one of the oldest Sardinian sweets, and a must at festivals and other traditional events.

Orilletas

This typical carnival sweet is made with the classic ingredients: eggs, durum wheat flour, lard, water and Sardinian honey. The mix is pressed into a thin layer from which strips are cut and then fried in oil. Finally, they are dipped in honey.

Pabassinas or Papassinos

This sweet is well-known outside of Sardinia. The name comes from the Sardinian word "papassa", meaning raisin. The ingredients include sultanas, cooked wine and almonds.

Pani 'e saba or Pani 'e sapa

This cake is typical of Campidano di Cagliari and the Nùoro area. The shape varies, but the color is the dark brown of cooked wine and the fragrance is intense. This ancient rural dessert is one of the first 'transformations' of bread into a cake. It is normally associated with All Saints Day and Christmas.

Pardulas or Formagelle

An Easter dessert: they are small 'baskets' of fried pastry filled with fresh ricotta or pecorino cheese. In Sassari, raisins are also used. In the Nùoro area, "casu" cheese replaces the ricotta, and the sweets are called "Casadinas".

Pirikitos

This flattened, round cake is covered in frosting and has a smooth texture. The mix is divided into portions and, when the cooking is done, the "pirikitos" are plunged into frosting and then placed in the oven to dry.

Pompìa intréa

Normally associated with Siniscola (in the province of Nùoro), this rounded, squashed cake is compact and has

FOOD

ICE CREAM PARLORS

Ice cream is one of the most famous Italian foods and is well known throughout the world. Homemade ice cream and sorbets are created by combining experience with excellent ingredients.

Pula (CAGLIARI)
Su Nuraghe
Via Nora 57, tel. 0709209144
Excellent desserts and ice cream, ranging from classic flavors to those that are more Sardinian, like "fico morisca" (prickly pear).

Mamoiada (NÙORO)
Francesco Cardenia
Via Verdi 4, tel. 078456405
They make classic and Sardinian cakes and pastries. Ice cream parlor as well.

Tortolì (OGLIASTRA)
Drago Rosso
Via Umberto I 133
tel. 0782623579
A modern, double-storey establishment with a veranda for summer. Upstairs, above the bar, the pastry house has handmade cakes, fruit, yoghurt and chocolate tarts, "fritelle" (for carnival) and homemade ice cream in summer.

La Maddalena (OLBIA-TEMPIO)
Gelatissimo
Via Amendola 46
tel. 0789739070
Numerous different flavors of ice cream.

Santa Teresa di Gallura (OLBIA-TEMPIO)
Il Capriccio
Via Carlo Alberto 40
tel. 0789754716
An ice cream parlor that also makes, especially for carnival, local cakes and pastries, like "frati fritti" and "frittelle".

Ghilarza (ORISTANO)
Vaniglia
Via Carlo Alberto 41
tel. 078554664
This shop sells the classic and traditional homemade Sardinian cakes and pastries.
The ice cream parlor in Corso Umberto 250/C is run by the same people and specializes in fridge desserts.

Sassari
Gelateria Artigianale Slurp
Piazza Castello 4/b
tel. 079236075

a citrus flavor, with a touch of almond. The ingredients include 'Pompìa's fruits' (a type of citron that is endemic to the Baronie area) and Millefiori honey.

S'azza de casu o Còccias de casu

These sweet ravioli are filled with fresh, sour goat's cheese. They are diamond or square shaped, with an opening on the sides, and have a sweet taste. The filling is based on a slightly sharp, but fresh goat's cheese.

Culingioneddus de melairanni

These sweet ravioli are filled with quince. They are rectangular, crunchy on the outside and soft inside. The peeled fruit is boiled with sugar until a red cream is obtained. This cream is then placed in small portions on the sheet of pastry and, using a wheel cutter, the shapes are cut and then fried.

The famous pabassinas: good and good-looking

Seadas or Sebadas

Starting with a sheet of egg and durum wheat pastry, "seadas" are filled with a cheese based stuffing and then covered in honey frosting. These large, round ravioli are the most famous dessert coming from the island's pastoral tradition. The name comes from a dialect word, "seu", meaning tallow, which is a reference to the greasy shine of this dessert.

Sos pinos

Usually spherical in shape, these sweets are prepared using semolina and then cut into large, pine-nut-shaped pieces (hence the name), before being fried. They are traditional wedding sweets.

Sospiri di Ozieri or Suspirus

Among the oldest sweets in Ozieri, these pastries are now easy to find across the whole region. Round, very small and frosted on the outsides, they are made with chopped almonds. In a more modern version, they are covered in chocolate and flavored with the mirto liqueur. They are sold in colored paper.

Torrone di mandorle or Su turroni

This semi-soft type of nougat has two types: sweet honey (Millefiori) and bitter

honey (from the strawberry tree, which is the more typical and prized, or eucalyptus). Almonds and lemon rind are added to the original mixture. When it is still hot from cooking, the mix is placed in moulds lined with wafers.

CAGLIARI

Caffè Royal
Via G. Manno 40, tel. 070651121
A superb selection of coffee, cappuccino, tea and herbals teas. There are also many fresh classic cakes: "sacher", "millefoglie", strudel and "semifreddi" (fridge desserts).
Durke
Via Napoli 66
tel. 070666782
www.durke.com
Traditional pastries and cakes on sale.
Pasticceria Piemontese
Via Cocco Ortu 39
tel. 07041365
Many master bakers think of this place as the cake school. Chocolate cakes and pastries are the specialties.
Pasticceria di Piazza Yenne
Piazza Yenne 13/14, tel. 070290159
They make and sell classic and local cakes and pastries.

MONASTIR
Dolcissimi
Via Michelangelo 15, tel. 0709177864
Production and wholesale of local traditional cakes.

MURAVENA
Dolci Sardi
Via Sardegna, tel. 0709930148
As the name suggests, local cakes are favored but there are some classic one and pastries for tea.
Il Fornaio
Via Roma 200, tel. 0709931290
This typical shop makes its own traditional cakes and sells them directly to the public

QUARTUCCIU
Zia Peppina
Via Rosselli 12, tel. 070881576
They specialize in and sell numerous traditional Sardinian cakes.

SAN SPERATE
Biscottificio di Corronca Rita
Via Cagliari 101, tel. 0709600252
This pastry house sells typical local cakes that are made on site.

SILIQUA
La Dolceria di Serra e Bachis
Corso Repubblica 50, tel. 078177030
Classic cakes, pastries for tea and traditional Sardinian cakes and pastries.

CARBONIA-IGLESIAS

IGLESIAS
San Pio X di Atzeni Giovanni
Corso C. Colombo 30, tel. 078142186
Local and classic cakes as well as pastries for tea. Everything is made on site.

NÙORO

Luisa Monne
Via Rubeddu 8
tel. 078435542
The Sardinian cakes and tea pastries sold here are made on site.

ONIFERI
Caterina Brau
Via Garibaldi 6/A
tel. 0784709011
The attached pastry kitchen makes traditional Sardinian cakes and desserts.

Symbolic and auspicious Easter sweets

TONARA
Torronificio Gianni Pili
Via Vittorio Emanuele 5, tel. 078463445
www.torronpili.it
Sardinian honey makes the Torrone di Tonara especially tasty.
Torronificio Pruneddu
Via Ing. Porru 5, tel. 078463805
Even beyond the shores of the island, Tonara is well-known for its torrone.

OGLIASTRA

LANUSEI
Salvatore Marci
Via Roma 26, tel. 078241576
They make, exhibit and sell traditional Sardinian cakes and desserts.

OLBIA-TEMPIO

LURAS
Antica Dolceria
Via Ariosto 11, tel. 079647764
The production in this pastry house is inspired by all that is local. Direct sale of items.

OLBIA
Loi & Figli Dolci Sardi
Centro Commerciale Terranova
tel. 078953450
Production and sale of local desserts, cakes and fresh pasta. There is another shop in Via Caen (Sa Minda Noa zone).
Caselli Cesarina
Viale A. Moro 297, tel. 078957980
This pastry house makes classic and Sardinian cakes and desserts, as well as ice-cream in season.

OSCHIRI
Dolce Mania
Via Umberto 36, tel. 079733799
"Origliettas" and "sospiri": traditional Sardinian cakes are inspired by what is genuine and based on superb raw materials.

SANT'ANTONIO DI GALLURA
Da Stefania
Via Calangianus 36, tel. 079669298
Sardinian desserts and cakes are handmade in this shop: "acciuleddi", "cucciuleddi" and "formaggelle".

SANTA TERESA DI GALLURA
Conti
Via Regina Margherita 2, tel. 0789754271
Good coffee and cappuccino, interesting range of cakes and desserts. Everything is homemade.

ORISTANO

Crem Rose
Via Cagliari 424, tel. 078374186
Pastry and coffee house. A good range of snacks, cakes and desserts, all made using traditional recipes.

BARESSA
Ignazio Cabras
Via A. Moro 20, tel. 0783930128
They make and sell traditional local

FOOD

131

desserts and cakes.

Il Forno Sardo
Via Milano, tel. 0783930013
The name, Sardinian Oven, tells all: island specialties are made and sold here.

GHILARZA

La Dolce Vita
Corso Umberto 259, tel. 078553311
A lovely shop where you can taste a few items. The selection ranges from Sardinian cakes to pastries for tea.

MARRUBIU

Magie di Sardegna
Via Rinascita, tel. 078386330
They exhibit and sell typical Sardinian cakes and desserts.

SIMAXIS

Mostaccioli Oristano di Mattu A.
Via Gialeto 7, tel. 0783405579
As the name suggests, they sell the "mostaccioli" (or mustazzolus) biscuits from the Oristano area.

SASSARI

Artigiana Pasticceria Vanali
Via Ettore Mura 20, tel. 079398841
www.vanali.it
There are two parts, the pastry house and the chocolate factory, where they make classic and traditional desserts and cakes: "papassine" and "formagelle", "torrone" and small chocolates.

L. & G. Fratelli Rau
Via Gorizia 7, tel. 079292264
This shop has a large kitchen where you can watch what is happening through a big window. Specialties: little "torrone" (from a recipe developed in 1926),

"papassine", "tiricche" and "copulette".

Livio Masia
Via Esperson 8, tel. 079232497
A pleasant shop divided into sectors: cakes and little pastries; the coffee bar, which has wonderful Sardinian cakes and desserts, ranging from biscuits to warm pastries.

Puggioni
Via M. Zanfarino 54, tel. 079276497
They make classic and local cakes and pastries, as well as "torrone", little chocolates and formagelle.

CHIARAMONTI

Ziccheddu Cossu & C.
Via Carmelo 6, tel. 079569066
They make classic cakes, homemade pralines and fridge desserts. The house specialty is "tiricche".

ITTIRI

Dolci Sardi
Via IV Novembre 87, tel. 079442199
Display and sale of products. The cakes are the traditional ones from the area.

Manunta
Via Spano 21, tel. 079440410
Numerous forms and packages of "torrone" and chocolate as well as "chiacchiere" and typical Sardinian biscuits.

OZIERI

Officina del Cioccolato
Via Stazione 1, tel. 079771114
This chocolate factory produces homemade pralines as well as chocolate bars, slabs and eggs.

THIESI

Pasticceria del Corso
Via Vittorio Emanuele 33, tel. 079886744
This bar and pastry house makes its own classic and local cakes.

SARDINIAN HONEY

An archeology site not far from Oliena (Nùoro province) is known as Sa Idda e su medde, 'the village of honey'. There, a bronze figure of Aristaeus, the Greek god who taught man to farm, was found with his body covered in bees. This indicates that honey was already a prized food.
The amazing thing in Sardinia is the enormous variety of flavors: orange, mild yet sharp; strawberry tree, strong and bitter; thyme, penetrating and aromatic; heather, strong and red; rock rose, slightly salty. Even the Millefiori honey is something special, with the decisive and characteristic taste of the thistle or asphodel version being common, but the rosemary and wild lavender being more delicate. Of course, there is also eucalyptus, another widespread tree, which is used to make a balsamic honey.

Food and Wine Festivals

JANUARY

↘ January-February
**LU BOGAMARÌ
(SEA-URCHIN)**
Alghero (SASSARI)
*Azienda Autonoma
di Soggiorno e Turismo*
tel. 079979054
For a whole month, all the
restaurants in Alghero offer
a special menu based on sea-
urchins. Don't miss the raw
eggs with bread or pasta.

↘ Easter (Easter weekend)
SAGRA DEL TORRONE
Tonara (NÙORO)
Pro Loco tel. 078463448
The true Sardinian torrone,
made exclusively from
Sardinian honey, is available
at a height of 1000 m in the
west side of Barbagia. Don't
miss the bitter cane apple
honey torrone. Tastings of
other local products and
Mandrolisai wines.

MAY

↘ May
**CANTINE APERTE
IN DIVERSI PAESI**
*Consorzio Vini D.O.C.
Sardegna tel. 070658989*
Get a taste of typical
products, traditional art
and cuisine in cellars
through the whole region.

**SAGRA DEL COUS COUS
CARLOFORTINO**
*Carloforte (CARBONIA-
IGLESIAS)*
Pro Loco tel. 0781854009
In a small island off the
southwest coast, taste
the fish couscous from
Carloforte, a tradition going
back to the times when
the locals lived in Tabarka,
a tiny island facing Tunis.

↘ Late May/early June
**SAGRA DEL TONNO
DI CARLOFORTE**
*Carloforte (CARBONIA-
IGLESIAS)*
Pro Loco tel. 0781854009
Taste the typical tuna dishes
from a place called 'Tuna

Island': "tunnina", "cassuli"
and "curzetti" served
in crock pots with white
wine, all at a very
reasonable price.

JUNE

↘ June
**SAGRA DELLE CILIEGIE E
DELLE CASCHETTAS**
Belvì (NÙORO)
Comune tel. 0784629216
On the western side
of Gennargentu, try the
delicious local cherries
and the sweet "caschettas",
thin layers of puff-pastry
filled with thick grape must.

AUGUST

↘ First weekend of august
SAGRA DEL VINO
Jerzu (OGLIASTRA)
Pro Loco tel. 078271311
In the heart of Ogliastra,
taste local
products from
the tradition, and
don't miss the
famous Cannonau
di Jerzu wine,
robust and
aromatic.

↘ First Sunday of August
SAGRA DELLA LUMACA
Senis (ORISTANO)
*Pro Loco Senis
tel. 3407981833*
In the historical center get
a taste of exquisite snails
cooked by the town's skilled
housewives following
traditional recipes. Everybody
is welcome to try, and don't
miss the collateral events
(exhibits, music, etc.).

↘ Summer
SAGRA DEL GATTULIS
Villagrande (OGLIASTRA)
Pro Loco tel. 078232779
On the west side of
Gennargentu. 'Gattulis' are
deep fried croquettes made
of potatoes, pickled fresh
cheese and lard.
This specialty is available
exclusively in Villagrande.

SAGRA DEL PROSCIUTTO
Talana (OGLIASTRA)
Pro Loco tel. 0782646862
The pigs of this area are
small, slim and spotted,
and live on berries, roots and
acorns. They are used to
produce the typical, strong-

flavored Sardinian raw ham.
After being salted, peppered
and pickled in red wine,
it is aged in the cool breezes
of Ogliastra.

SEPTEMBER

↘ September
SANTA GRECA
Decimo Mannu (CAGLIARI)
Comune tel. 070966701
This important town festival
features many kiosks where
you can try simple but tasty
dishes: roasted mullet, meat
on the spit, "malloreddus"
with sauce.

OCTOBER

↘ Mid-October
SAGRA DELLA LUMACA
Gesico (CAGLIARI)
tel. 070987043
Tasting of traditional recipes
based on snails: stewed,
au gratin and roasted.

↘ Last weekend of October
SAGRA DELLE CASTAGNE
Aritzo (NÙORO)
Comune tel. 0784629223
Wine and roasted chestnut
tasting in the woods of
Gennargentu. You can also
purchase local products.

NOVEMBER

↘ November
NOVELLO D'ORO
Arzana (OGLIASTRA)
Pro loco tel. 078237290
A tasty journey through the
scents of Sardinia. On the
Green Train from Cagliari to
Arzana, four stops for novello
wines and delicious dishes.

**RASSEGNA DEI VINI
NOVELLI**
Milis (ORISTANO)
Pro Loco tel. 078351168
Regional novello wines fair,
with tasting of local
products.

↘ Autumn
PORCINO D'ORO
Arzana (OGLIASTRA)
*Local Tourist Board
tel. 078237290*
All the restaurants in Arzana
offer a special menu based on
porcini mushrooms. Meetings
and seminars, excursions
and a culinary contest.

FOOD

Córsica
(FRÁNCIA)

Bonifácio

Í. Maddalena
Parco Nazionale
dell'Arcipélago
de la Maddalena
Í. Caprera

S. Teresa
Gallura

Palaú

Parco Nazionale
dell'Asinara

Í. Asinará

Golfo
dell'Asinara

Témpio
Pausánia

Ólbia

Golfo Aranci

Porto
Torres

Castelsardo

Monti

Sénnori

Lago del
Coghinas

SASSARI

Óschiri

Ozieri

Siniscola

Alghero

Bitti

Orosei

Bosa

NÚORO

Dorgali

Macomer

Golfo di
Orosei

MAR DI

Parco Nazionale
del Golfo di Orosei
e del Gennargentu

Abbasanta

Lago
Omódeo

Sórgono

MAR

Cabras

Stagno di
Cabras

Monti d. 1829
Gennargentu

Tortolì

ORISTANO

Láconi

Barbagia

Lanusei

Golfo di
Oristano

SARDEGNA

Barúmini

Gúspini

Lago
Mulargiá

TIRRENO

Iglésias

Monástir

Selargius

Muravera

Villamassárgia

CÁGLIARI

Í. di S. Pietro

Carbónia

Quartu
S. Elena

Sant'Antíoco

Í. di S. Antíoco

Teulada

Pula

Golfo di
Cágliari

MAR MEDITERRÁNEO

Legend

CERAMICS	
WOVEN BASKETWARE	
GOLDSMITHERY	
FABRICS AND EMBROIDERY	
WOOD	

Shopping in Sardinia is an opportunity to discover the techniques of ancient crafts that cannot be found anywhere else in the world. Centuries-old methods and traditions are passed down from generation to generation keeping the indigenous spirit alive in handcraft items such as baskets, tapestries, household furniture and chests carved from chestnut and cork, masks, gold filigree jewelry, and the famous Pattadese knives with ram horn handles. Visit the local markets for antiques as well as modern objects that are characteristic of the region including carpets from Samugheo, Aggius and Nule. And don't forget the local food stalls where you can purchase Sardinian specialties to enjoy on the spot.

Highlights

- You often still see women sitting at their doorways weaving mats and baskets

- Chestnut and cork are the woods most commonly employed to make traditional utensils and chests. The Mamuthones masks are masterpieces of folk art and the work of master carvers

- Rugs and tapestries, in splendid colors and designs, and gold-work, filigree in particular, are the island's most popular souvenirs

- Don't miss the fascinating Museo del Coltello Sardo (Sardinian knife museum) in Arbus

Inside

ARTS AND CRAFTS

When we look at the world of Sardinia's arts and crafts we could be led to believe that one of the most favourable conditions for this sector's livelihood is isolation. Indeed, nowhere in Italy are traditional arts and crafts more widespread and part of the local social fabric than in Sardinia, traditions that still today conform to the particular technical and aesthetic doctrines that have made their mark on the island ever since they appeared. Sardinia simply exudes with arts and crafts, from ceramics to wood carving, goldsmiths, fabric weaving, all local activities that started and evolved on the island without any external influence except for the adoption of a few aesthetic norms, mostly Spanish, that are clearly visible in some traditional filigree jewellery. The final seal on this indigenous evolution is given by the decorative objects that seem to have been passed on from one sort to another, the only difference being in the techniques used. Thus, wherever you look there are geometrical spiral patterns, Greek frets, diamond and round shapes, all of which undoubtedly stem from the original braided objects, or even shapes styled on nature. It is quite extraordinary how two different art forms can meld into the very same decorative context, thereby giving rise to artistic effects that simply cannot be found anywhere outside Sardinia.

Finely embroidered shawls are an unmistakable feature of the typical Sardinian costumes

Basket and rug weaving

It is still very easy to see people making woven rugs and baskets in the streets of the little towns around the wide expanses of water in the province of Oristano. We can date rug and basket weaving with the Nuraghic age, though the techniques developed along different lines due to the raw materials available in a given area. In the marshy area they used bundles of rushes to make the "fassonis", the traditional fishermen's boats used on the small lakes near the towns of Cabras and Santa Giusta that are still used in the traditional regatta that takes place in the Santa Giusta lake. Inland, on the other hand, (particularly in the towns of Flussio and Tinnura located between the two large towns of Macomer and Bosa) and in Barbagia (especially in Olzai, Ollolai and Nuorese) they use the asphodel shrubs, which are abundant in this area. However, people's inventiveness has no limits: in the towns of Castelsardo, Sennori and Sorso along the coast of Sassari the locals use the strong fibre obtained from the "palma nana" (dwarf palm tree). This fibre is suitable to make highly functional baskets that people use in the field and at home.

Wood

Chestnut and Cork Oak, these two trees dominate the Sardinian landscape; the local craftsmen use them to make most of their objects. Apart from traditional tools and the objects made of cork, this wood is mainly used to make the finely carved fronts of chests, a very important piece of furniture in Sardinian. There are basically two sorts of chest: the low, long chest is typical of Montiferru, whereas the higher chest is specific to Barbagia. The area around Nùoro is particularly well known for chest making, particularly the towns of Tonara, Orani and Orosei where, apart from chests, they make solid wood furniture suits, straw-stuffed chairs and wardrobes. Apart from household objects, wood is also used to make some of the more traditional objects, first and foremost the Mamuthones and Merdules masks and the Su Bundu masks. These masks are real masterpieces of popular artwork made by master carvers in the area around Nùoro. The masks are a mainstay of anthropic culture where the techniques, materials and aesthetic norms come together in a single fascinating object. All the masks are made of pear, chestnut or cork wood and depict devils and animals.

Weaving

Sardinian weaving began thousands of years ago alongside sheep farming. It was a household activity and the products were specifically used in the home and in the country. This is why the patterns and designs traditionally found on woollen garments depict imaginary and legendary objects, symbols and myths that stem from a mysterious world of happiness and solitude. You only have to look at the tapestries and carpets with all their dancers, flowers, geometric symmetry, horses and fallow deer, doves, fantastic garlands. You will understand that a product has become an artwork, alive and lively, that it depicts an independent world, an isolated world, religious, that the immense value is a true hallmark in a never-ending poetic context. Weavers around the area of Nùoro make carpets with geometric patterns or designs based on nature that have been made quite unique by the wool dyeing technique: vegetable dyes and often secret methods. Just as in the

area around Goceano (Nule, Benetutti and Bono, in the province of Sassari) and in many other towns around Barbagia, weavers use traditional vertical looms, much less used than horizontal looms with pedals, typical of the other areas of the island. Among the most significant products, the carpets made in the area of Logudoro (Ittiri, Villanova Monteleone, Ploaghe and Bonorva) in the province of Sassari and in Gallura (especially in Aggius and Calangianus), and the blankets from Pozzomaggiore cannot but be mentioned. However, the products are lively wherever they come from in Sardinia, and are distinct for the various aesthetics and sort of product: from carpets to blankets to tapestries.

Goldsmiths

The birth of craft techniques is often bound to the availability of raw materials. This was not so for the goldsmith's art in Sardinia even though gold was mined on the island as far back as one can go. It is believed the first gold objects were made in the Middle Ages, though the oldest jewels found date back to the 18th century. However, this long incubation period seems to have had positive repercussions, given the lively objects made in the past few centuries with their very personal styles. Among the most traditional jewels we can find some religion ones (rosary beads, pendants and crucifixes) as well as items to be used on clothing: buttons made with very fine decorations using filigree and often set with hard stones.

Another gold item that is widespread throughout the island is the "lasu", a gold butterfly-shaped pendent of Spanish origins. The butterfly is made by perforating a piece of flat gold and then enhancing it by decorating it in beads. To end our journey through traditional Sardinian jewellery we must mention the classical "fede sarda", a must-have souvenir for anyone visiting the island; it has intricate filigree decoration on the top surface.

Shop with woven baskets and cork trays

Wooden chest with carved front

CAGLIARI

❋ **CERAMICS**
Cristina Di Martino
  Scalette Santa Teresa 2, tel. 070653898
  The art of ceramics
Kernos Ceramiche snc
  Via Cimarosa 31/33, tel. 070401471
  The art of ceramics
❋ **GOLDSMITH**
Gianni Murgia
  Via Rossini 46/f, tel. 070493339
  Sardinian filigree work
Giancarlo Tocco
  Via Università 7, tel. 070669469
Orfevre
  Corso Vittorio Emanuele 84
  tel. 070653325
❋ **FABRICS AND EMBROIDERY**
Dibai Ataolah
  Corso V. Emanuele 80, tel. 070664404
  Weaving

QUARTU SANT'ELENA
❋ **CERAMICS**
Massimo Boi
  Flumini di Quarto, Via delle Pandoree
  27, tel. 070807456
  The art of ceramics
❋ **GOLDSMITH**
Glauco Creazioni
  Via Gorizia 85
  tel. 070827436
  Jewels in filigree work

SELARGIUS
❋ **WOOD**
Legno e Ingegno
  Via Copernico 22
  tel. 070845475
  Wooden goods

CARBONIA-IGLESIAS

VILLAMASSARGIA
❋ **FABRICS AND EMBROIDERY**
Angioletta Peddio
  Via Carbonia 19, tel. 078174115
  Carpets and fabrics
Maria Giuseppa Ferreli
  Via Argiolas 11, tel. 078174665

MEDIO-CAMPIDANO

VILLACIDRO
❋ **GOLDSMITH**
Arte Gioielli
  Via Nazionale 247, tel. 0709310032
Fabbrica Orafa Artigiana del Gioiello
  Via Nazionale 254, tel. 0709310010
Marrocu Gioielli
  Via Roma 79, tel. 070932385

NÙORO

❋ **CERAMICS**
Rosaura Sanna Ceramiche
  Prato Sardo, lotto 71, tel. 0784294035
  The art of ceramics

BITTI
❋ **CERAMICS**
Ceramiche Artistiche Terra Pintada
  Via Brigata Sassari 74
  tel. 0784414072
  The art of ceramics

GAVOI
❋ **WOOD**
Falegnameria Artigiana D. Cugusi
  Via Roma 33, tel. 3497868837
  www.falegnameriacagusi.it
  Wooden objects

Antique filigree jewellery and intricate lace work are the pride of traditional costumes

OLBIA-TEMPIO

GOLFO ARANCI
✳ GOLDSMITH
Creazioni Antonello
Via Concas Caddinas 54
tel. 078946874

SANTA TERESA DI GALLURA
✳ GOLDSMITH
L'Angolo del Corallo
Porto Pozzo, Via Aldo
Moro, tel. 079371163

ORISTANO

✳ CERAMICS
Cooperativa Artigiana Ceramisti
Via Cagliari cover
Via del Porto
tel. 0783358103

BOSA
✳ GOLDSMITHS

Gioielleria Vadilonga
Piazza IV Novembre 23, tel. 0785373406

SASSARI

A traditional Sardinian wedding ring

✳ FABRICS AND EMBROIDERY
Espressioni Sarde
Via Roth 35, tel. 079293537
Weaving

ALGHERO
✳ GOLDSMITH
Galleria Arteorafa Sara Marogna
Piazza Civica 34, tel. 079984814

BUDDI
✳ CERAMICS
Franco Scassellati
Strada Buddi Buddi 134, tel. 079316711

SENNORI
✳ FABRICS AND EMBROIDERY
Gian Massimo Piana
Nigra 16, tel. 079361379
Carpets

SARDINIAN KNIFE MUSEUM

Paolo Pusceddu learned the fine art of jack-knife making from his father Mario, a master blacksmith and cutler. At the end of the 1970s, after his apprenticeship, Paolo opened his own knife shop in Arbus called Coltelleria Arburesa. Initially he only made knives that were traditional of the area, the so-called "coltello a pancia", a traditional knife with a horn handle and "laurel-leaf shaped" blade. However, he improved the quality of the blade using stainless steel (martinsetic), a highly successful knife in trade fairs and exhibitions. The array of knives made by Coltelleria Arburesa is vast, ranging from simple kitchen knives to artistic knives for collectors. Some of the knives can even be considered works of art, almost precious, such as the knives with horn handles of all shapes and colour, inlayed, carved to look like deer, boar, moufflon, eagles and the Sardinian fauna all enhanced with steel and bronze in the blade and the blade collars. In 1996 Paolo Pusceddu managed to carefully renovate an old house and turned it into a museum with all the objects he had collected over the years. The first room contains the oldest knives, the 16th century knives stand out, while the second room has the more modern traditional Sardinian knives. The last room is a reconstruction of an old blacksmith's workshop with 19th century tools: bellows, a "flywheel drill", a pedal grinder an antique anvil. Some curious objects: the largest knife in the world (weighing 80 kilograms, 3.35 metres long), in the Guinness Book of records since 1986.
Opening times: Mon-Fri 9 a.m. to 12 a.m. and 4 p.m. to 8 p.m.; Saturdays 9 a.m. to 12 a.m.; Saturday afternoons and Sundays open on appointment; guided tours on request. Via Roma 15, Arbus (Medio-Campidano), tel. 0709759220, www.museodelcoltello.it.

SHOPPING

139

MARKETS

Sardinia has a number of markets in the towns and cities, both large and small. Throughout the year local craftsmen put their wares on sale in the little characteristic markets alongside antiques and modern collectors art works. As such you can find sculptures, carpets and old traditional knives as well as prints, stamps, mirrors, picture frames, Liberty-style chandeliers, period chairs and, of course, silverware, old books and religious gifts.

CAGLIARI

Cagliari antique fair
First Sunday of the month
A market fair in the town centre where you can buy antiques and collectors items, local craftwork as well as modern art collectors pieces. Information: tel. 800016058, www.comune.cagliari.it

PULA
Artifolk
August
This exhibition is held in the cultural offices "Casa Frau" and includes a trade fair with things like ceramics and vases made by some of the best Sardinian craftsmen. You can actually watch objects being made. Information: tel. 0709245250, www.prolocopula.it

CARBONIA-IGLESIAS

IGLESIAS
Iglesias trade fair
First half of July
A ten-day trade fair in the town centre where some 50 exhibitors show off their best craftsmanship: gold, silver, ceramics, wooden objects, wrought iron, baskets, knives, fabrics and embroidery. There are also Sardinian food products. Information: tel. 078131170, www.prolocoiglesias.it

VILLAMASSARGIA
Artistic craftwork fair
End of July
The town's streets are full of some 50 exhibitors showing their local wares: traditional carpets, wooden sculptures, ceramics, vases, baskets, knives and collectors' items. Information: tel. 078175801, www.comune.villamassargia.ca.it

MEDIO-CAMPIDANO

GUSPINI
Arresojas – Biennale of Sardinian knives
End July to beginning August, every two even years
This exhibition is held inside the building of the mining headquarters near an old mine that is today under Unesco protection. There are hundreds of knives and blades on show manufactured over the years in Sardinia. Other exhibitions are organised by subject such as metal working and local agricultural equipment. Information: tel. 070972537, www.arresojas.net

NÙORO

DORGALI
Festa di Ferragosto
Bank-holiday week
Dorgali celebrates the week with civil and religious events. Market stalls where you can taste traditional Sardinian food. During the fair, singing and traditional dancing in local costumes, games. In the bank-holiday evening, a firework show. Information: tel. 078493696.

OLBIA-TEMPIO

AGGIUS
Aggese carpet exhibition
Beginning July to end September
Aggius has a long tradition in carpet making and is today one of the few towns where this antique art still exists. The show highlights craftwork and the farmers' traditions thereby allowing thousands of tourists to view and buy the best of Aggese carpets. Information: tel. 079620306, www.aggius.net

Hand woven carpets with wonderful colours and designs

BUDDUSÒ

International sculpture symposium
June-July
Artists from the world over come to sculpture granite and wood, turning the whole town into an open-air museum. Theatrical shows and stalls with traditional Sardinian products are dotted throughout the town's streets. Information: tel. 079715308.

ORISTANO

FORDONGIANUS

Sculpture contest using trachyte rock
End July to beginning August
This international contest is held within the spa archaeological area. The contest attracts Italian and foreign sculptors who meld together for a week to sculpture trachyte stone, a light-red heavy volcanic rock from the area. Information: tel. 078360123, www.comunefordongianus.it

Craftwork exhibition
Mid-July to mid-August
This trade fair is held inside the 15th C. Casa Aragonese. It includes local craftwork such as: carpets, Sardinian tapestries and fabrics, ceramics, stoneware, jewels, gold filigree work and local food. Information: tel. 078360157, www.forumtraiani.it

SAMUGHEO

Craftwork from the centre of Sardinia
Second half of August
This is one of Sardinia's main exhibitions; the island's best craftsmen are present. Some 30 exhibitors show off their wares in the town centre: fabric products, wood, glass and iron. Among the various items, the following are of importance: Samugheo carpets and fabrics, all decorated in traditional geometric, floral and religious designs. Information: tel. 078364023.

SASSARI

Sassari art and antique exhibition
April-May
This large trade fair has a great deal of antiques on offer. Some 30 Sardinian antique dealers exhibit their precious wares: rare carpets, period furniture, paintings, jewels, ethnical items to prints and old books. Information: tel. 079291572.

BONO

Olive-oil meeting
End of May
A meeting to promote the awareness of olive oil and Sardinian food. There is a market fair with wonderful cheeses, olives and quality olive oil, jodhu (a local sheep-milk yogurt) and traditional cakes. Information: tel. 0797916900.

NULE

Nule carpet show
August
For almost a month characteristic carpets, tapestries, blankets and other local fabrics are on show. Information: tel. 079798025.

PATTADA

Knife exhibition
August, every two years
One of the most widely known local products is put on show for a whole month, Pattadese knives, the "resolza", with their typical moufflon and ram horn handles. The best Pattadese knives are on show and you can buy these craftwork objects. Information: tel. 079755157.

One of the most intriguing aspects of Sardinia is its rich tradition of musical folklore and history. The musical instruments, such as the launeddas and double reed style lutes, are made only on the island and the sounds of Sardinia are best experienced in one of the many festivals and musical events held throughout the year. Religious festivals, parades and carnivals are also important events

Events

that epitomize the complex cultural history of the island. Springtime and Holy Week are filled with festivals and processions across the land, and in January, massive bonfires mark the start of festivities held in honor of Sant'Antonio Abate.

Highlights

- Bonfires are built almost all over the island on 17 January in honor of Sant'Antonio Abate who, according to Sardinian legend, stole fire to give it to humankind
- The traditional carnivals bear many affinities with similar rituals held in the Balkans, the Alps and the Pyrenees
- Festival Internazionale Sardegna Musical in Cagliari
- Festival "Ai confini tra Sardegna e Jazz" in Sant'Anna Arresi
- Festival Internazionale Rocce Rosse in Santa Maria Navarra

Inside

143

MUSIC

An island with an age-old heart, dotted with thousands of Nuraghi, that has conserved traces of Phoenicians, Carthaginians, Romans, Vandals, Byzantines, Pisans, Aragonese, Ligurians, Catalans and Spanish right down to the Savoys and the Kingdom of Italy. Despite all the clichés, Sardinia is not just a bleak land of shepherds shut away in their world of unusual traditions; it is a multifaceted reality that has conserved its culture and its art – a store of original and distinctive expressions now being rediscovered and maximised. The music of Sardinia has solid roots and forms a major part of the sturdy Mediterranean heritage. Many of the island's music events are played out against a background of religious celebrations, on which Spanish rule – which here lasted from 1316 to the early 18th century – left a permanent impression. After an Austrian interlude, the most significant turning point in the history of Sardinian music came with the arrival of the Savoys in 1718. From that moment on, musical activities, already present in the largest of the island's cities – Cagliari and Sassari – and in smaller but equally vibrant ones such as Alghero, slowly spread all over the region, although not until more recently do we see a radical change in the habits of the other two cities that later became provincial capitals: Nùoro and Oristano.

San Saturno, the oldest Basilica in Sardinia

CAGLIARI

Festival Internazionale Sardegna Musical

June-September

Every year, the Roman amphitheatre hosts a number of famous, great musicals drawn from repertoires both old and contemporary and staged by national and international companies. Sardinia's International Musical Festival is promoted by Soul & Mare Promotion. For further information: tel.0706848512, www.soulemare.it

Festival Spaziomusica

October-December

An international festival of contemporary classical music that has been held for more than 20 years. Cagliari and nearby Uta are the hubs of the event, the main and most beautiful settings of which the crypt of San Domenico and Exmà. Mostly Sardinian artists and musicians perform at the festival. For further information: tel. 070400844

Teatro Comunale

The Opera House was inaugurated in 1993 with a concert by the Chorus and Orchestra of Cagliari's Istituzione dei Concerti and Teatro Lirico. This extremely modern structure is 18,000 square metres in size and has a volume of 120,000 cubic metres; the stalls and two rows of boxes contain 1600 seats. Today, it is the home of the Fondazione Teatro Lirico di Cagliari, one of 13 national opera organisations. Via S. Alenixedda, tel. 0704082230

Anfiteatro Romano

This was constructed in the 2nd and 3rd centuries AD. The arena is excavated in the rock overlooking the Golfo degli Angeli and conserves the pits for the wild beasts, the cavea with dividing enclosures, the subterranean underpasses and three sets of tiered seats, offering a total capacity of nearly 6000. It has been the venue for many musical events since the end of WWII and is today principally used for the summer seasons of Cagliari's Fondazione Teatro Lirico (opera). Viale S. Ignazio da Laconi I, tel. 070669255

Conservatorio di Musica G. Pierluigi da Palestrina

One of the most important conservatories in Italy, it dates from 1921 when City of Cagliari decided to found a music school, known as the Istituto Musicale Cagliaritano and, later (in 1923) named the Istituto Musicale Mario de Candia, in honour of the famous Sardinian tenor. Today, it is an important point of reference for the artistic activities of Cagliari and the whole island thanks to its constant production of concerts, conferences and research projects. Piazza E. Porrino, tel. 0704520031

Teatro Alfieri

Originally a cinema, this was converted to a theatre in the 1980s and used for prose, classical music concerts, operetta and musicals. Via della Pineta 209, tel. 070302299

Chiesa di Santa Chiara

The church hosts the Festival di Musica Antica and concert seasons organised by the Amici della Musica (Friends of Music), as well as those of other city associations. Via Santa Chiara, tel. 070669245

Basilica di San Saturno

The oldest early-Christian church in Sardinia now hosts important religious music concerts and choir performances. Piazza San Cosimo, tel. 0702010316

The Roman Amphitheatre in Cagliari during a summer show

Exmà

Cagliari's former Mattatoio (abattoir) is now a multipurpose cultural centre, hosting the temporary exhibitions and concerts of many city associations and of the Conservatorio di Musica G. Pierluigi da Palestrina. Via San Lucifero 71, tel. 070666399

ASSEMINI

Festival Internazionale "Is Pariglias"

Last week in July

Three days of encounters held in the municipal amphitheatre that alternate performances, exhibitions and concerts by artists from several continents plus Sardinia. For further information: tel. 070941788

QUARTU SANT'ELENA

Sciampitta – Festa di etnie internazionali

July

An international folklore festival held over the second ten days of July every year since 1985. The square between the Town Hall and the Market is the hub of the event and comes alive for five evenings with ethnic evenings, music, dancing and entertainment. For further information: tel.070822725, web.tiscali.it/folkcittaquarto

CARBONIA-IGLESIAS

SANT'ANNA ARRESI

Festival "Ai confini tra Sardegna e Jazz"

August-September

Piazza del Nuraghe is the venue for seminars, concerts, encounters and workshops focusing on the national and international jazz culture and with the participation of leading artists from all over the world. Its renown has travelled to five continents since 1985. For further information: tel. 0781966102, www.santannarresijazz.it

NÙORO

Auditorium dell'Istituto Etnografico

A hall used for temporary exhibitions and an auditorium that hosts conferences, concerts, and theatre performances. Via A. Mereu 56, tel. 0784242900

Ente Musicale di Nùoro

This music body has offered a classical music programme (spring-December) for many years. Performances are held in the auditorium of the Istituto Etnografico. The programme includes jazz seminars that have made a name for themselves in the world of European jazz music. Via Convento 12, tel. 078436156

CALAGONONE (DORGALI)

Calagonone Jazz
July
An international jazz festival with numerous performers, photographic exhibitions and documentary showings held in the Auditorium Villa Ticca di Calagonone. Cagliari's L'Intramezzo cultural association is responsible for its organization and artistic direction. For further information: tel. 0784232539

OGLIASTRA

SANTA MARIA NAVARRESE

Festival Internazionale Rocce Rosse
July-September
Held every year, principally in the amphitheatre of S. Maria Navarra, this is named after the red rocks at Àrbatax, where the first festivals were held. Musicians of international fame as well as cabaret artists perform at it.
For further information: special rate tel. 800505077, www.turinforma.it

OLBIA-TEMPIO

OLBIA

Festival di Portorotondo
June-August
A music festival with a cast of renowned national and international artists held annually in summer, offering live concerts with a wide variety of repertoires. The performances are held in the loveliest parts of the village: the church of San Lorenzo, the theatre and the delightful setting of Piazza San Marco. For further information: tel.078934114

PALAU

Festival Internazionale di Musica, Teatro e Arti Visive
September

The "Isole che parlano" (talking islands) event focuses on artistic expressions that are half folk tradition, half innovation. The centre of the village is at the heart of the project with concerts, performances, encounters and exhibitions. For further information: tel. 3475987754, www.isolecheparlano.it

SAN TEODORO

"Uanciu....Free San Teodoro Jazz"
June-July
San Teodoro encounters signature jazz in a programme given entirely over to jazz composers with family or sentimental links with Sardinia. The event offers conferences, painting exhibitions, itinerant performances throughout the town and workshops involving the public. For further information: tel. 3387993809

A performance at the Auditorium in the Luigi Canepa Conservatory

TEMPIO PAUSANIA

Teatro del Carmine
Originally a church, this was later turned into a theatre. The building was sold to the municipality in 1991.
Piazza del Carmine, tel. 079630377

ORISTANO

TADASUNI

Raccolta di Strumenti Musicali Don Giovanni Dore
Searches dating back dozens of years and conducted by a priest, Don Dore, have produced this magnificent collection of traditional Sardinian instruments. The outstanding collection

Inside the Teatro Civico in Alghero

includes the oldest instruments in the island's repertoire. The house-museum contains more than 400 instruments. Via Adua 7, tel. 078550113

SASSARI

Conservatorio Luigi Canepa
In the late 19th century, the composer Luigi Canepa created the city's first public music school, the Istituto Musicale, which took the name Liceo Musicale Luigi Canepa and later became a conservatory. Piazzale Cappuccini, tel. 079296447, www.conservatorio.sassari.it

Teatro Verdi
Today, this theatre hosts the Ente de Carolis opera season and several concert programmes. The Ente Concerti Marialisa de Carolis is named after its founder and is one of the Teatri di Tradizione Italiani (traditional Italian theatres). Via Politeama, tel. 079239479, www.comune.sassari.it

ALGHERO

Estate Musicale Internazionale
July-September
Classical music concerts conducted and performed by musicians of international fame are held in the cloister of San Francesco and offer evenings with both classical and folk repertoires. For further information: tel. 07043621

Teatro Civico
Alghero's 19th-century theatre, reopened after lengthy and extremely interesting conservation-restoration, mainly offers a summer music programme. Piazza del Teatro, tel. 079997800

TRADITIONAL MUSIC

The oldest form of Sardinian music is that of the *launeddas*, an instrument with three pipes that players manage to play without interruption, using their cheeks as a "wind bag". It is used to accompany religious ceremonies and more often to provide the rhythm for the *ballo tondo* and other local dances, performed by men and women wearing multicoloured celebration costumes. The dance was and still is also led by the singing of a "tenor choir", which also originated very early in the Sardinian culture. It consists in four male voices that – in the case of the dance – execute short poetic texts of an amorous and often erotic nature, plus others of various kinds. Some religious festivals continue the tradition of *gosos*, praising the saints of remote Spanish origin. These, the bases of Sardinian music, have been supplemented over the years with others e.g. the dance is led by a diatonic organ, of which the island boasts excellent players; and some "tenor choirs", e.g. that of Bitti, have experimented in collaboration with players of modern music, rock in particular.

FOLKLORE

Sardinia's folk traditions conserve traces of an extremely complex cultural history. It is perhaps an exaggeration to see the island's folklore ceremonies as "surviving" from pre-Christian times but the daredevil acrobatics on horseback, typical of many Sardinian festivals, may date from the Nuraghic period. The old carnivals, such as those of Ottana and Mamoiada, have an old early-European cultural stratum and present analogies with similar rituals, seen principally in the Alps, the Balkans and the Pyrenees. Byzantine rule lasted until the 7th century and can be linked to the popular worship of certain saints of the Greek Church not recognized by the Latin one, e.g. St Constantine. The Spanish influence is particularly strong – also linguistically speaking – thanks to the Spanish rule that lasted until the early 18th century. The city of Alghero conserves the Catalan dialect of its colonizers. The selection of Sardinian festivals listed here must necessarily be arbitrary as the presence of traditional rituals remains strong all over the island. The moving celebrations for Holy Week still see profound participation in large cities and small villages alike. Bonfires are built all over the island for 17 January, with countless variations in honour of Sant'Antonio Abate who according to Sardinian legend – a Christian version of the myth of Prometheus – took fire away from the demons of the Inferno to give it to Man.

CAGLIARI

Pellegrinaggio di Sant'Efisio
1 - 4 May
The origins of this procession, which is held over a period of four days over a route of than 80 km, date from a vow made by the city in 1657 in exchange for the cessation of a plague. Honouring St Efisio the Martyr, it returns to the legendary locations of the saint's lifetime and martyrdom. For further information: tel. 070669255

SELARGIUS
Antico Sposalizio Selargino
Second Sunday in September
This is a re-enactment of the traditional local marriage rites. The groom goes to the bride's home on their wedding day. Here, they form a procession to the church, which they enter to the sound of the organ and the *launeddas*, the old pipe instrument peculiar to Sardinian tradition. When they leave the church, the groom puts the first link of a chain onto the little finger of his left hand and he encircles the bride's waist with it; the couple leads the procession to the nuptial house where the two mothers are waiting. The bride and groom kneel before them to receive the blessing of the two women, each holding a plate containing wheat, salt and coins that are scattered over the couple's heads. For further information: tel. 07085921

NÙORO

LULA
Novena di San Francesco d'Assisi
1 - 9 May
The "novena" is a pilgrimage that centres on a baroque church on the slopes of Mt Albo, 2 km outside the town. According to legend, the church was constructed by a bandit accused of murder who made a votive promise to St Francis of Assisi that he would build it if he managed to prove his innocence, which he did. The sanctuary remains closed and deserted until the next May. For further information: tel. 0784416615

MAMOIADA
Sfilata dei Mamuthones
Shrove Tuesday
One of the most interesting archaic carnivals in Europe focuses on two groups of masked men, the *Mamuthones* (twelve) and the *Issokadores* (eight). The former are disguised with a wooden mask, a beret and a dark kerchief; the

Two 'Mamuthones' with the typical fur coats and bells

Finely refined wooden masks for the 'Boes' of Ottana

Issokadores are unmasked but wear a coloured costume. During the procession, the *Mamuthones* advance at a slow pace, ringing bells. The *Issokadores* circle around the *Mamuthones* and "lasso" members of the public with ropes. For further information: tel. 078456023, www.mamuthonesmamoiada.it

OTTANA
Sant'Antonio
17 January
A huge bonfire is built on the square and it is set alight when the bells of the church of Sant'Antonio ring out. Children crowd around the fire and blacken each other's faces with the remains of burnt branches. In the afternoon, the procession – led by a group of women in costume with baskets of bread on their heads and a statue of the saint carried by men called Antonio – circles the bonfire three times. When the priest blesses the fire, masked groups appear, the *Merdules* and the *Boes*, heralding the start of the Carnival, which starts on 17 January, with their bells. For further information: tel. 078475830
Carnevale
Shrove Tuesday and Sunday
This is one of the most

interesting carnivals in Sardinia. The principal figures are the *Boes*, who wear a cow's mask with long horns, dozens of cowbells and a sheepskin jacket. The *Boes* are kept on a leash by *Merdules* wearing dark masks with grimacing expressions. The disturbing mask of Sa *Hilonzana*, the spinner, moves forward alone repeating the act of spinning wool and cutting the yarn with large scissors hanging from her neck. The masks move through the town with the *Merdules* frequently capturing a man in the crowd, dragging him into an inn and forcing him to buy drinks. The festivities culminate with a dance to the accompaniment of a *fuente*, the embossed brass plate used for church collections, on which the rhythm is beat with a large key. In the early hours of the night, the Carnival then takes on a very different nature with small masked groups knocking at the doors of houses. Once inside, the owners must guess the identity of the guests, but they are often unsuccessful. For further information: tel. 078475830

ORISTANO

Sa Sartiglia
Sunday and Shrove Tuesday
The ceremony is marked by its ritual and

A highlight of the Sartiglia in Oristano: the clothing of the 'Componidori'

extremely serious nature. The origin of the Sartiglia, after the Spanish *sortija* (ring), lies in the old tournaments during which galloping knights had to put their lance through a ring hanging from a rope. The Sartiglia has a leader called *Componidori*, chosen by the representatives of the trade guilds. He is invested in public then mounts on his horse. The aim of the competition is to manage to put a lance through a small hole in the centre of a

is busy enjoying herself. Towards evening, the masks disappear and are replaced by the Gioldzi mask, impersonated by a large number of people. At this point, the celebrations cease to differentiate between the public and the masks. The simple disguise consists in blackening the face, and wearing a pillowcase as a hood. For further information: tel. 0785376107, www.bosa.net

Hundreds of barefoot young men run down harsh and dusty streets in Cabras, while carrying the statue of San Salvatore

6-pointed metal star, hanging from a rope along the course, and detach it. The *Componidori* is the first to make an attempt. The number of successful attempts provide predictions on the results of the farming year. For further information: tel. 078370621

BOSA
Carnevale
Shrove Tuesday
Masked groups visit the homes of influential local figures singing satirical songs to them. The masters of the house offer sausages, wine and sweetmeats in exchange. Shrove Tuesday is dedicated to the masks of the *Attittadoras* (funeral lamenters). These are men with their faces dirtied black wearing the old mourning suits. The masks carry a doll or a live animal and improvise funeral laments directed at the doll (i.e. Carnival), which is dying, abandoned by its mother who

CABRAS
Corsa degli Scalzi
First Sunday in September
The statue of San Salvatore is taken from the parish church nine days before the festival begins and carried to the church of San Giovanni di Sinis. It is returned to the parish church on the first Sunday in September by young people wearing white habits. The route is 6 km long and completed running without interruption, with the barefooted runners constantly passing the statue around. The ritual apparently commemorates an episod e dating from the times of the Saracen forays. For further information: tel. 0783397308

SEDILO
S'Ardia
6 - 7 July
The name of the festival means the guard and it centres on a horserace

held on the afternoon of 6 July and repeated at dawn on 7 July. The event is held in honour of St Constantine, venerated as a saint here, and of the holy Cross. It is not a true race but a display of courage and skill. The race leader is known as *sa pandela madzore* (the main standard), after the standard entrusted to him by the parish priest. The race leader chooses another two riders, who in turn select an escort. The escorts must stop the other participants from overtaking *sa pandela madzore* in the race. Along the way, with the crowd on two sides, riflemen shoot blanks to excite the horses. After arriving at the church, the riders circle the building several times. The race is then on again upwards to reach *sa muredda*, a stone enclosure with a cross, which the riders also circle several times before returning to the church, amid an enthusiastic crowd. For further information: tel. 078559028

One of the nine candles used in the procession in Sassari

(cobblers), *Sarti* (tailors), *Muratori* (masons), *Viandanti* (travellers), *Contadini* (peasants) and *Massai* (farmers). The huge traditional candles have been replaced with wooden pillars fixed to a base with poles for the eight bearers. Each candle-bearer wears an image of the patron saint of that particular guild. Multicoloured ribbons are fixed to the pillar and held taut by children. The candle-bearers' "descent" starts in Piazza Castello, passes the City Hall and ends at the church of S. Maria di Betlem. The candle-bearers walk to the rhythm of a pipe and drum, making their load sway in a sort of dance. The *gremi* of the *Massai*, once the most important economic class, have a special function in the ceremony: they meet the mayor who gives them the flag of the guild along with that of the city. They are then the first to enter the church of S. Maria for the offering to Our Lady. For further information: tel. 079233534

SASSARI

Cavalcata Sarda
Penultimate Sunday in May
The festival consists in an impressive parade passing through the city centre with more than 3000 players on foot and on horseback, representing the whole of Sardinia. It is a unique opportunity to admire the island's extraordinary variety of traditional male and female costumes.
On the eve, there is a race with horsemen in costume at a gallop. Several groups perform traditional songs and dancing. For further information: tel. 079233534

I Candelieri
14 August
This festival originated as a votive offering to Our Lady of the Assumption for the end of a plague on 14 August 1580. It consists in a procession of nine candle-bearers representing the *gremi*, the old trade guilds: *Piccapietre* (stonemasons), *Falegnami* (carpenters), *Ortolani* (greengrocers), *Calzolai*

The horsemen of Sedilo gallop into town

Córsica
(FRÀNCIA)

Bonifácio

Pàrco Nazionale
dell'Arcipélago
de la Maddalena

Ì. Maddalena
S. Teresa Gallura
Palau
I. Caprera

Parco Nazionale
dell'Asinara
Baia Sardinia
Porto Cervo

Ì. Asinara

Golfo
dell'Asinara
Témpio
Pausánia
Ólbia
Golfo Aranci

Porto
Torres
Castelsardo

Lago del
Coghinas

SÁSSARI
Monti

Óschiri

Alghero
Ozieri
Siniscola

Terme di
S. Saturnino
Bitti

Terme
Aurora
Orosei

Bosa
Macomer
Dorgali

NUORO

MAR DI

Abbasanta

Parco Nazionale
del Golfo di Orosei
e del Gennargentu

Golfo di
Orosei

Stagno di
Cabras
Lago
Omodeo
Sórgono
MAR

Monti d. 1829
Gennargentu

Fordongiánus
ORISTANO
Tortolì

Golfo di
Oristano
Láconi
Lanusei

SARDEGNA
Barúmini

Lago
Mulargia

Gúspini
Terme
Sárdara
TIRRENO

Iglésias

Monastir
Muravera

Maracalagonis

Ì. di S. Pietro
Carbónia
CÁGLIARI

Quartu
S. Elena

Sant'Antíoco

Ì. di S. Antíoco
Teulada
Pula

Golfo di
Cágliari

MAR MEDITERRÁNEO

Waters rich in minerals have been
known for their beneficial properties
since Roman times, and Sardinia offers
a world-class selection of spas and
wellness centers where you can partake
in a variety of beauty and therapeutic
massage treatments. The use of wild
Mediterranean herbs in aromatherapy pools
is a delightful way to soothe away stress and aid
in the treatment of many respiratory ailments.

THERMAL SPA

HEALTH
CENTER

Wellness

Sardinia's many indoor
and outdoor facilities provide
beautiful surroundings
for "taking the waters"
or more modern therapeutic
services such as reflexology,
shiatsu, Rolfing, kinesiology,
seaweed therapy and
personalized diets.

Highlights

- The Sardara spa, with its bicarbonate and iodine waters, is ideal for inhalant, balneo-therapeutic and a vast range of cosmetic skin treatments
- Fordongianus: the beneficial properties of the sodium chloride, bicarbonate and fluoride in its waters were already known in Roman times
- Terme Aurora: its spa basin has surfacing waters rich in sodium chloride, sodium iodide and bromine at 41°C/105°F, beneficial for the treatment of skin, locomotory and respiratory complaints

Inside

There are many reasons to visit Sardinia - delightful beaches, a crystal-clear sea, fine food, folklore and handicrafts, but this stunning island also offers opportunities for health holidays. Its spas – an old solution to the desire for good health and mental and physical wellness – were popular from Roman times thanks to the abundance and benefits of waters rich in sodium chloride, sodium iodide and bromine. Fine examples of architecture can often also be admired close to the spas, which treat skin complaints and locomotory and respiratory problems. Spa treatments typically include aerosols, therapeutic bathing, nasal and other douches, and mud applications. Wellness centers also offer facial and body beauty treatments and a wide range of massages.

BAIA SARDINIA (OLBIA-TEMPIO) 🏃

Residenza Le Querce
Via Vaddi di Jatta, tel. 078999248
www.lequerce.com
Closed November-Easter
An old Gallurian sheep-farming complex surrounded by the verdant Mediterranean maquis in a park covering 30,000 square m where guests have their own garden with veranda. The wellness center developed from long experience in the use of wild Mediterranean herbs. It offers aromatherapy pools excavated in the rock, relaxation activities, massage room, a spa mud area and meditation areas. In summer, experts offer manipulation and therapeutic techniques (connective tissue massage, Rolfing, lymphatic drainage, deep massage, rebalancing, Samurai massage, Californian massage, cranial-sacral therapy, reflexology, shiatsu, postural rehabilitation, osteopathy), beauty treatments (facial and body, dietary rehabilitation) plus yoga, aromatherapy, relaxation techniques and meditation, and rebirthing for mental and physical wellness.
The "deep massage", a technique developed through the experience of the Canadian physiotherapist Thérèse Pfrimmer, is practiced here as well; it consists in a slow and continuous stretching that reactivates contracted or insensitive muscles.

FORDONGIANUS (ORISTANO) ⚕

Remains of Roman baths in Fordongianus

Terme Sardegna
SP 48, tel. 078360037
www.termesardegna.it
Fordongianus, a small town on the River Tirso 26 km from Oristano, is the descendant of the Roman town of Forum Traiani. The name replaced that of Aquae Hypsitanae – linked to the mineral springs by the river – in the 1st century. A spa complex in ruin – dating from the Imperial age – features a first building used for treatments and a second construction that was used for seaside pleasures, following the characteristic Roman pattern, with a number of rooms at different temperatures (frigidarium, tepidarium and calidarium). Today, it boasts a modern spa complex. The Fordongianus spring water is 50°C/122°F, with a medium mineral content of sodium chloride and fluoride; it is used to treat circulatory, locomotory, respiratory and gynecological complaints. The spa treatments offered are aerosols, therapeutic bathing, nasal and therapeutic douches, mud applications, humage, hot and cold inhalations, insufflation, nasal and vaginal irrigations, nebulisation and pulmonary ventilation. Other treatments include kinesitherapy, beauty treatments, fitness, respiratory gymnastics, hydro kinesitherapy, massage, beauty medicine, anti-stress programs, rehabilitation and physical therapies.

MARACALAGONIS (CAGLIARI)

Calaserena Village ★☆★
Geremeas, tel. 0707870000
www.bluserenahotels.it
Closed September
The complex lies on a private beach, surrounded by vegetation. Guests may use the tennis courts, basketball and volleyball courts, archery and bowls grounds and practice sailing, canoeing, windsurfing and diving.
The wellness center has in-house medical assistance and offers numerous services, with specialized areas for health, beauty and wellness treatments that tone, relax and regenerate the body. The several treatments include aromatherapy, mental and physical wellness, manipulation and therapeutic (massotherapy, thalassotherapy, mud therapy, limotherapy, seaweed therapy) and beauty (facial and body treatments, thalasso beauty) treatments.

PORTO CERVO (OLBIA-TEMPIO)

Cervo Hotel & Conference Center ★★
Porto Cervo, tel. 0789931111
www.sheraton.com/cervo
Closed November-February
An elegant complex situated in the small Porto Cervo square featuring low buildings set around a patio. The rooms overlook the patio, marina, garden and

Self-massage is a muscle-relaxing technique of gentle gymnastics

swimming pool. Guests may use the reading room, concert room, private beach, an indoor and two open-air swimming pools, a babysitting service, a gym and a tennis club.
The wellness center, run by Dr Perletto, is open to all guests and has a weights-fitness gym, gentle and postural gymnastics room, sauna, Turkish bath and Jacuzzi. It offers facial and body beauty, manipulation and therapeutic (shiatsu, Thai massage) treatments and hydro-aromatherapy for mental and physical wellness.

The swimming pool at the Cervo Hotel & Conference Center

PULA (CAGLIARI)

Forte Village Resort
S. Margherita, SS 195 di Pula - km 39.600, tel. 07092171
www.fortevillageresort.com
The Forte Village Resort consists in 7 hotels offering numerous services: travel desk, car rental, medical center, mini-club and babysitting service, go-kart track, bowling and the Millennium discotheque.
The Thermae wellness center boasts the experienced Dr Angelo Cerina's medical team. Facilities include one of the internationally most renowned thalasso-therapy centers, which includes pools with water at different temperatures. The cornerstone of integrated thalassotherapy is sea oil, natural seawater with a high concentration of magnesium, which favors the elimination of liquids. The treatment ends with a sauna and Turkish bath.
Manipulation and therapeutic treatments offered are high saline-density integrated thalassotherapy, shiatsu, Ayurvedic and salt massage, waterfeeling, osteopathy, chiropratice, cranial-sacral therapy, acupuncture, moxibustion, lymphatic-drainage, sports, therapeutic and Thai massage; psammotherapy and aromatherapy for mental and physical wellness; beauty treatments include gommage, peeling, firming crio treatment with sea oils, anti-stress and anti-ageing massage, seaweed and mud treatments, hydromassage, and hydro-electric rebalance using marine and phyto-talassotherapy elements, anti-cellulite and firming massages.

TERME AURORA (SASSARI)

Aurora Terme
San Saturnino, Sa Mandra Noa tel. 079796871, www.termeaurora.it
Benetutti – situated in the heart of the island, 87 km from Sassari and 28 from Nùoro – is an agricultural and shepherding town in the upper Tirso Valley, overlooking the Goceano mountain range. It attracts little mass tourism but is by no means uninteresting. Indeed, it is one of the richest areas of prehistoric finds with a comprehensive array of megalithic monuments. The spa basin consists in surfacing water rich in sodium chloride, sodium iodide and bromine at 41°C/105.8°F on the plain known as San Saturnino, where the modern spa amenities stand – part of the Aurora Terme – surrounded by a vast park with a spa pool, children's playground, solarium and tennis court. The spa doctor plus rheumatology, ear, nose and throat and physiotherapy specialists work in the treatment areas treating skin, locomotory and respiratory complaints; spa treatments are aerosols, therapeutic bathing, nasal and therapeutic douches, mud applications, humage, hydromassage, hot and cold inhalations, insufflations, spa pool, Politzer creno therapy. Kinesitherapy, fitness, massage, anti-stress programs and physical therapies are also available.

The swimming pool at Terme Aurora

TERME DI SAN SATURNINO (SASSARI) 🛁

Terme San Saturnino
Tel. 079791081
Bultei extends from the east side of the Goceano mountain range to the Tirso plain, where the San Saturnino spa zone is situated. The river follows an ancient road diagonal between Olbia and Oristano that favored human settlement from prehistoric times, as demonstrated by the Nurchidda nuraghe.
The spa, also known as Angioi, stands on the spot known to the Romans as Aquae Lusitanae, as revealed by the remains of a calidarium and other architectural finds. The spa, which stands beside the Terme Aurora of Benetutti, is a period construction but this by no means reduces its attraction, as demonstrated by the number of visitors.
The water flows at 43°C/109.4°F and is rich in sodium chloride, sodium iodide and bromine; it is good for treating skin, locomotory and respiratory complaints. Spa treatments include aerosols, therapeutic bathing, therapeutic douches, hydromassage, hot and cold inhalations and nebulisation. Guests can relax with pleasant massages.

TERME DI SARDARA (MEDIO-CAMPIDANO) 🤽 🛁

Those crossing the Campidano di Oristano see Sardara perched on a rocky spur – first a Nuraghic and then a Roman site. The most interesting monument is the Nuraghic pit temple found near the church of S. Anastasia, close to a curative water spring and evidence of the religious cult attributed to it around the 10th century BC. The road leaving the village to the west goes to the old Sardara spa, now in ruin, beside the medieval sanctuary of S. Maria de is Acquas. The hospitality amenities are on the edge of the archaeological site.

Terme di Sardara: tubs in the old spa

Antiche Terme di Sardara ★★★
Santa Maria Acquas, tel. 0709387200
www.termedisardara.it
Open all year round
The spa, set in a huge park with swimming pools and sports grounds, offers all mud, balneo-therapeutic, inhalatory and mineral water treatments and employs Fonte della Meraviglia cosmetic products. The water flows at 60°C/140°F and is rich in bicarbonate and iodine.
The wellness center has an open-air swimming pool, Jacuzzi, spa pool and Turkish bath. The center employs a strictly qualified medical staff supervising beauty and curative treatments using the bicarbonate-alkaline and thermal waters that flow from a nearby spring.
The manipulation and therapeutic treatments offered include massotherapy, connective tissue and Ayurvedic massage, Rolfing, Thai massage, lymphatic-drainage, kinesiology, shiatsu, postural rehabilitation, reflexology, cervical traction. As well as facial and body spa beauty treatments there are toning and firming massages and personalized diets.

WELLNESS

157

GETTING TO SARDINIA

By plane

ALGHERO – Fertilia
For information tel. 079935124, www.algheroairport.it.
Sogeaal lost luggage, tel. 079935282; SIBA luggage protection, tel. 095223638.
Coach links:
to the city of Alghero operated by: Ferrovie della Sardegna (FdS, tel. 079950458) and Deplanu-Redentours (tel. 078430325), with a terminus in Piazza della Mercede;
to Cagliari: Logudoro Tours (tel. 079281730);
to Nùoro: Autolinea Nùoro APT (tel. 078430325);
to Sassari by: Azienda Regionale Sarda Trasporti (ARST, tel. 800865042, 0704098327, www. arst.sardegna.it);
to Santa Teresa di Gallura by: DIGITUR - Autolinee e Turismo (tel. 079270756).

CAGLIARI – Mario Mameli a Elmas. Run by SOGAER, tel. 070211211, www.sogaer.it
From Cagliari: 7 km from the center, the airport can be reached in approximately 10-15 minutes from Piazza Matteotti, next to the railway station, by means of the shuttle bus which belongs to the company ARST (tel. 800865042, 0704098327, www.arst.sardegna.it).
From Sassari and Oristano: coach service Pani Trasporti (tel. 070652326, www.organizzazionepani.it).

OLBIA - Costa Smeralda. Run by GEASAR, tel. 0789563444, www.geasar.it
Services from and to Olbia are provided by the public transport company ASPO (tel. 0789553856, www.aspo.it).

By boat

The following shipping companies operate routes to and from Sardinia.

GRIMALDI FERRIES, operates routes: Genova-Olbia and Genova-Porto-Torres. For information tel. 081496444, www.grimaldi-ferries.com

LINEA GOLFI, operates routes: Livorno-Olbia and Piombino-Olbia. For information tel. 0565222300, www.lloydsardegna.it

MEDMAR, operates routes: Napoli-Palau, Corsica-Sardegna. For information tel. 0815513352, www.medmargroup.it

MOBY LINES, operates routes: Civitavecchia-Olbia, Genova-Olbia, Livorno-Olbia.
For information tel. 199303040, www.mobylines.it

SARDINIA FERRIES, operates routes Civitavecchia-Golfo Aranci and Livorno-Golfo Aranci. For information tel. 899929206, www.corsicaferries.com

SAREMAR, operates routes between Corsica and Sardegna. For information tel. 199123199, www.saremar.it

SNCM, operates the following international shipping routes: Marsiglia-Porto Torres; Tolone-Porto Torres; Corsica-Sardegna. For information tel. 825888088, www.sncm.fr

TIRRENIA, operates routes from and to Civitavecchia (Cagliari, Olbia), from and to Genova (Àrbatax, Olbia, Porto Torres; from and to Fiumicino (Àrbatax, Golfo Aranci); from and to Sicily (Palermo - Cagliari; Trapani - Cagliari). Also operates the international route Tunisi-Trapani-Cagliari. Other links: Napoli-Cagliari, Cagliari-Àrbatax, Olbia-Àrbatax. For information: tel. 199123199, www.tirrenia.it

TOURIST INFORMATION

Regione Sardegna web-site: www.regione.sardegna.it
Sardinian islands: www.allsardinia.it/isole_sardegna.htm

TRANSPORT WITHIN SARDINIA

Train

TRENITALIA, serves the whole of Sardinia. For information: tel. 892021, every day from 7 to 21 only from Italy; tickets by phone 199166177, every day from 7 to 21 and www.trenitalia.com

FERROVIE DELLA SARDEGNA, lines Cagliari-Isili, Macomer-Nùoro, Sassari-Nulvi, Sassari-Sorso, Sassari-Alghero. For information tel. 800460220, www.ferroviesardegna.it

TRENINO VERDE, lines Mandas-Àrbatax, Isili-Sòrgono, Macomer-Bosa Marina, Sassari-Tempio Pausania, Tempio Pausania-Palau Marina. For information tel. 800 460220, www.treninoverde.com (trains run from 15/06 to 15/09; from 15/09 to 15/06 you may only hire whole trains).

Coach

ARST, serves the whole of Sardinia. For information tel. 800865042, arst.sardegna.it

FdS, serves the whole of Sardinia, except the south-west. For information: tel. 800460220, www.ferroviesardegna.it

FMS (Ferrovie Meridionali Sarde), serves the south-west and Cagliari. For information tel. 800044553, www.ferroviemeridionalisarde.it

NICOS GROUP, serves the north of the island. For information www.nicosgroup.it

PANI TRASPORTI, operates the Cagliari-Sassari-Porto Torres route. For information tel. 070652326, www.organizzazionepani.it

REDEN TOURS, serves the center-north, north-west (Nùoro, Alghero). For information tel. 078430325.

SUN LINES, serves the north (Gallura, Costa Smeralda, Sassarese). For information tel. 078950885.

TURMO TRAVEL, serves the north, Cagliari e Oristano. For information tel. 078921487, www.turmotravel.it

Boat

Links to the Sardinian islands:
PALAU-MADDALENA, companies which operate ferry services: Saremar (one crossing every hour, tel. 1991231999, www.saremar.it), Enemar (tel. 899200001, www.enemar.it), Delcomar (tel. 0789731094), Tremar (tel. 0789730032);

CALASETTA-CARLOFORTE, companies which operate ferry services: Saremar, Delcomar (tel.0781857123);

PORTOVESME-CARLOFORTE, companies which operate ferry services: Saremar;

STINTINO-ASINARA, companies which operate ferry services: Timone d'Ogliastra (tel.

CLIMATE

The climate of Sardinia is mild and warm due to its being an island, no part of which is ever far from the sea. Generally, summers are hot and dry while winters are wet and cool. Average annual temperature is 17°C/62°F while, during winter, temperatures usually hover around 10°C/50°F in coastal towns, tending to be a little lower in the interior. During summer temperatures can exceed 30°C/86°F. Sardinia is beset all year round by winds blowing from every direction. Rains, scattered and thundery, are few and far between. Most rain falls at the end of autumn and at the beginning of spring.

PRINCIPAL DIVING CENTERS

Alghero: Adventure & Diving, Via Aggius 14, tel. 079 952930
Diving Center Porto Conte, c/o Porto Conte Marina km 48, tel. 079942122
Àrbatax: Mediterranea D.C., Via Lungomare 46, tel. 0782667880
Venta Diving Club Telis, Via Capri 487/b, tel. 0782667790
Cagliari: Diving Sella del Diavolo, Marina Piccola, tel. 3398428891; Diving Club, Via Martini 22, tel. 070651919
Golfo Aranci (Olbia): Atlantica Scuba Club Yachting Club Porto Marana, Golfo di Marinella, tel. 0789321862
La Maddalena: Aquapro Scuba Center, Villaggio di Porto Massimo, tel. 0789735385
Santa Maria Navarrese: Società Nautica, Via Monte Oili 3, Porticciolo Turistico, tel. 0782615555
San Teodoro: Aqua Diving Centers Puntaldia, tel. 0784864390; Atmosphere Diving Center & Sea Store, Via Sardegna 38, tel. 0784865130

079525377), for further information contact Parco Asinara (tel. 800561166, www.parcoasinara.it).

Car hire

You will find all the major car hire companies in Sardinia with an efficient network of agencies

AVIS
Booking center 199100133, www.avisnoleggio.it
Alghero: Fertilia airport, tel. 079935064
Cagliari: Elmas airport, tel. 070240081
Nùoro: Via Dessanay 97, tel. 0784263063
Olbia: Costa Smeralda airport, tel. 078969540

HERTZ
Booking center 199112211, www.hertz.it
Alghero: Fertilia airport, tel. 079925054
Cagliari: Elmas airport, tel. 070240037

Olbia: Costa Smeralda airport, tel. 078966024
Porto Cervo: Alba Ruja, Liscia di Vacca, tel. 0789900040

EUROPCAR
Booking center 800014410, www.europcar.it
Alghero: Fertilia airport, tel. 079935032
Cagliari: Elmas airport, tel. 070240126
Olbia: Costa Smeralda airport, tel. 078969548
Sassari: Via Predda Niedda 6, tel. 0792675118

MAGGIORE
Booking center 848867067, www.maggiore.it
Alghero: Fertilia airport, tel. 079935045
Cagliari: Elmas airport, tel. 070240069
Olbia: Costa Smeralda airport, tel. 078969457
Sassari: Piazza Santa Maria 6, tel. 079235507

Inside

Hotels and restaurants
Tourist information
Museums and monuments
At night

EMERGENCY NUMBERS
112 Military Police (Carabinieri)
113 State Police (Polizia)
115 Fire Department
116 Road Assistance
117 Financial police
118 Medical Emergencies
1515 Fire Watch
1530 Coast guard

159

ALGHERO

ℹ️ Ufficio del Turismo
Via Columbano 6,
tel. 079997521
www.comune.alghero.ss.it

Hotels

Calabona *⁑* ★
Calabona, tel. 079975728
www.hotelcalabona.it

110 rooms. Restaurant, parking, air conditioned, swimming pool, sauna

Credit cards: American Express, Diners Club, Visa, Mastercard

In a splendid position, white Mediterranean style building with comfortable rooms; two swimming pools, one with hydromassage jets, and a large terrace for sunbathing.

Club Rina Hotel *⁑*
Via delle Baleari 34,
tel. 079984240
www.bluhotels.it

80 rooms. Restaurant, parking, air conditioned, swimming pool, tennis

Credit cards: American Express, Diners Club, Visa, Mastercard

Recently built, 100 meters from the sea with good facilities for holidays, meetings and conferences. Accommodation is also available in apartments housed in the annex of the same name. Special arrangement with nearby beach

Continental ***
Via F.lli Kennedy 66,
tel. 079975250
www.hotelcontinetalalghero.it
Open June-September

32 rooms. Parking.

Credit cards: American Express, Diners Club, Visa

Close to the old town center, a small block built in the sixties with a garden; guests may use the swimming pool at the Hotel Calabona, which belongs to the same management.

Dei Pini *⁑*
Le Bombarde, tel. 079930157
www.hoteldeipini.it
Open April-October

98 rooms. Restaurant, parking, air conditioned, tennis

Credit cards: American Express, Visa, Mastercard

Overlooking the beach, Spanish style architecture; elegant rooms and a pleasant dining room with a great view of the sea.

Florida ***
Via Lido 15, tel. 079950500
www.hotelfloridaalghero.it

76 rooms. Restaurant, parking, air conditioned, swimming pool, gym

Credit cards: American Express, Diners Club, Visa, Mastercard

Modern, in a good position on the Lido beach and a few minutes from the old town center. Well-appointed, refurbished rooms; buffet breakfast and restaurant with a great view.

Punta Negra *⁑*
Punta Negra, tel. 079930222
www.hotelpuntanegra.it
Open April-October

93 rooms. Restaurant, parking, air conditioned, swimming pool, tennis

Credit cards: American Express, Visa, Mastercard

In the heart of a pinewood. A pleasant Mediterranean style building which has good leisure and sports facilities. Buffet breakfast, restaurant for hotel guests only.

Riviera ***
Lido San Giovanni, Via F.lli Cervi 6, tel. 079951230
www.hotelriviera-alghero.com
Open March-October

55 rooms. Restaurant, air conditioned, swimming pool

Credit cards: Diners Club, Visa, Mastercard

Built in the late sixties, close to the beach. Good facilities in communal areas. Restaurant for hotel guests only.

Villa Las Tronas *⁑* ★
Lungomare Valencia 1,
tel. 079981818
www.hvlt.com

25 rooms. Restaurant, parking, air conditioned, swimming pool, gym

Credit cards: American Express, Diners Club, Visa, Mastercard

Located in a beautiful park, this is an elegant building dating from the late 19th century with art nouveau design. Very comfortable rooms and pleasant reception rooms providing internet access. Bicycles are available for guests to use.

Rural Lodgings

Cuccureddu
Santa Maria la Palma, regione Guardia Grande, podere 84
tel. 079919111
www.agricuccureddu.com
Restaurant, bicycles available

In the splendid bay of Porto Conte, this family run rural lodging has a veranda and a large garden. Inside there are four comfortable apartments and a restaurant where you can try traditional Sardinian cuisine

prepared with ingredients supplied by the same family.

Granja Rosa
Santa Maria la Palma, podere 60, tel. 079999227
www.granjarosa.it
Restaurant

Simple, inviting hotel surrounded by a large garden. Accommodation consists of four double rooms and a bungalow which sleeps four people. The restaurant serves Sardinian and Catalan specialties.

La Valle del Mirto
Santa Maria la Palma, regione Zirra 38, tel. 079533115
www.terranostra.sardegna.it
Restaurant

This rural lodging provides excellent cuisine and fine wines and liqueurs (especially *mirto* and *limoncello*) to accompany their food cooked to time-honored recipes. You may visit the necropolis of Anghelu Ruju, various nuraghi and the Caves of Neptune.

Le Tre Grazie
Santa Maria la Palma 74,
tel. 079999093
www.letregrazie.it
Restaurant

Holidays on a renovated farm with handy facilities. An ideal base for exploring the island.

Pesci in Faccia
Malai, strada 2 Mari km 1,8,
tel. 079951844
Restaurant

New owners now offer fishing holidays. Here you can try the day's catch cooked in a variety of ways based on Sardinian recipes.

Restaurants

Al Tuguri ⅠⅠ
Via Maiorca 113, tel. 079976772
www.altuguri.it
Closed Sunday
Cuisine: Sardinian and Catalan
Credit cards: Visa

In an ancient Catalan house; reservations are recommended if you wish to dine here as there is a limited number of place settings. Good menu includes fresh fish. Fitting choice of Sardinian wines.
The management hold themed evenings dedicated to sea urchins, lobster, mushrooms and artichokes.

Andreini ⅠⅠⅠ &
Via Arduino 45, tel. 079982098
Closed Monday
Cuisine: Revisited Sardinian
Credit cards: American Express, Diners Club, Visa, Mastercard

Restaurant run by a tight-knit family of two bothers: the menu principally consists of tasty Sardinian dishes.
Good choice of cheese, oils and cold meats

La Lepanto ¶¶¶ ★
Via Carlo Alberto 135,
tel. 079979116
Closed Sunday in winter
Cuisine: Sardinian and classic
Credit cards: American Express, Diners Club, Visa, Mastercard
Large, comfortable restaurant with a veranda and beautiful views from the windows. Carefully prepared dishes based on classic and ever popular local ingredients. Good cellar stocking Sardinian wines, quality oils, large assortment of cheeses.

Pavone ¶¶¶
Piazza Sulis 3/4, tel. 079979584
Closed Sunday midday in summer and Sunday evening in winter
Cuisine: fish
Credit cards: American Express, Diners Club, Visa
A summer terrace overlooking the sea of the Riviera del Corallo and a fish menu with inventive flourishes combined with a judicious selection of wines.

Pietro ¶¶ &
Via Machin 20, tel. 079979645
Closed Wednesday (except in summer)
Cuisine: Sardinian
Credit cards: Diners Club, Visa, Mastercard
Near the ancient church of S. Francesco, a traditional, cozy restaurant serving mainly fish. Do not miss the typical island desserts.

Rafel ¶¶
Via Lido 20, tel. 079950385
Closed Thursday
Cuisine: Sardinian
Credit cards: American Express, Diners Club, Visa, Mastercard
Right on the beach, with every ingredient provided by the sea; good view of the bastions and Capo Caccia. The garlic and vinegar sauce, spaghetti à la muscardine, lobster and crema catalana desserts deserve a special mention.

Sa Mandra ¶
Santa Maria la Palma, strada Aeroporto Civile 21/A
tel. 079990150
www.aziendasamandra.it
Open evenings only (weekends only in winter)
Closed Monday

Cuisine: local
Credit cards: American Express, Visa, Mastercard
Rustic ambience, run by two brothers who both cook and wait on tables. Cuisine is mainly based on local tradition, principally using farm produce, although fish is always on the menu. You begin with cream cheese with thyme, followed by seven herb ravioli with saffron and fresh cherry tomatoes. Oil, cheese and cold meats all come from the farm owned by the same family.

At night

Colonial Cafè
Via Carbia 13, tel. 079977353
You will find a great ambience in this venue which is also open in winter and which is both a disco and disco pub. You may also try typical Sardinian dishes and good pizzas in the restaurant

L'Arca
Lungomare Dante 6,
tel. 079977972
Night club open until dawn and closed on Monday. As well as a disco and disco pub it has 2 bars and 62 tables outside, with an ice-cream parlor and coffee shop.

La Siesta
Strada per Villanova Monteleone al km 6, tel. 079980137
www.siestadisco.com
This disco has two outdoors dance floors and holds themed evenings with Latin American and pop music.

Poco Loco
Via Gramsci 8, tel. 0799731034
www.pocolocoalghero.it
A multifunctional venue with an internet café, bowling alley and music workshop. Plays various types of music: from jazz to blues and from rock to world music.

Museums

Aquarium di Alghero
Via XX September 1,
tel. 079978333
www.aquariumalghero.it
Opening times: June, 1st-15th October:Monday-Sunday 10.00-13.00, 16.00-21.00.July,September: Monday-Sunday 10.00-13.00, 17.00-23.00. August: Monday-Sunday 10.00-13.30, 17.00-00.30. 16 October-March: Saturday, Sunday and public holidays: 15.00-20.00 April-May:Monday-Sunday 10.00-13.00, 15.00-20.00.

Collezione Mineralogica
Maristella, tel. 079942082
Opening times: visits by arrangement.

Museo Diocesano d'Arte Sacra ★
Piazza Duomo 1,
tel. 0799733041
www.algheromuseo.it
Opening times: spring and autumn: Monday-Sunday 10.00-12.30, 17.00-20.00.Summer:Monday-Sunday 10.00-12.30, 18.00-21.00 (August 19.00-23.00).Christmas period: Monday-Sunday 16.00-20.00.Group visits by arrangement: November, January and February.

ÀRBATAX

ℹ Pro Loco
Via Lungomare 21,
tel. 0782667690

Hotels

Arbatasar ★★★
Via Porto Frailis 11,
tel. 0782651800
www.arbatasar.it
45 rooms. Restaurant, parking, air conditioned, swimming pool
Credit cards: American Express, Diners Club, Visa, Mastercard
Centrally located, a modern three-story villa, suitable for business guests. Provides comfy rooms and some suites, swimming pool in the garden, restaurant open to non hotel guests serving regional and classic cuisine. Buffet breakfast with homemade sweets and fresh pastries.

La Bitta ★★★ & ★
Porto Frailis, tel. 0782667080
www.arbataxhotels.com
55 rooms. Restaurant, parking, air conditioned, swimming pool
Credit cards: American Express, Visa, Mastercard
Situated in a small cove with a beach equipped with loungers and sun umbrellas, this comfortable hotel has pleasant rooms, an elegant country-style restaurant serving traditional and international cuisine, a freshwater swimming pool and jacuzzi, various sports and leisure activities, new beauty center.

La Perla ★★★
Viale Europa 15, tel. 0782667800
10 rooms. Parking, air conditioned
Credit cards: American Express, Diners Club, Visa, Mastercard
For the last 40 years the Murgia family have warmly welcomed their guests in this villa near the sea; in the tranquillity of the veranda or garden you can breathe in the warm island fragrances. Buffet breakfast with home baking.

Relais Monte Turri *⁑*
Via Bellavista 1, tel. 0782667500
www.mobygest.it
Open mid May-September
42 rooms. Restaurant, air conditioned, swimming pool, sauna
In a secure position at the top of Parco Bellavista, surrounded by a lush garden, this is the ideal place for a relaxing holiday. You will enter the main building, La Torre, which houses the lobby, the restaurant with a patio providing great views and a swimming pool on a terrace ideal for sunbathing.
There are also some rooms, furnished in the distinctive Sardinian style. Other rooms have been created in little stone dwellings which recall a traditional village in the heart of the countryside.
Guests have access to a small sandy cove and some rocks, reached by a glass elevator.

Villaggio Saraceno ***
San Gemiliano, tel. 0782667318
www.arbataxhotels.com
Open May-October
129 rooms. Restaurant, parking, air conditioned, swimming pool, tennis
Credit cards: Visa, Mastercard
Resort consisting of wooden and stone bungalows, surrounded by vegetation, with a restaurant for resort guests only, sports facilities, kids' club and a jetty.

ARITZO
Hotels
Sa Muvara *⁑* &
Via Funtana Rubia, tel. 0784629336
www.samuvarahotel.com
Open April-mid November
65 rooms. Restaurant, parking, air conditioned, swimming pool, sauna, tennis, gym
Credit cards: American Express, Visa, Mastercard
In a context steeped in tradition, a comfortable tourist resort with a large park, buffet breakfast and traditional restaurant (the chef uses organic ingredients): numerous sports (canoeing, kayaking, swimming, fishing etc.) and excursions.

Rural Lodgings
Aradoni
Aradoni, tel. 3334315027
Restaurant, mountain bike hire
A beautifully kept and original rural lodging surrounded by lush vegetation. You stay in "Pinnette", hut dwellings typical

of Gennargentu, covered in cork or twigs, with wooden furnishings.

Museums
Ecomuseo della Montagna Sarda
Via G. Marconi, tel. 0784629801
Opening times: Tuesday-Sunday 10.00-13.00, 16.00-19.00.

ARZACHENA

> 🄸 **Ufficio Turismo**
> *Via Firenze 2, tel. 0789849388*
> *www.comunearzachena.it*

Hotels
Airone *⁑* &
Strada per Baia Sardinia, tel. 0789933021
www.hotel-airone.com
70 rooms. Restaurant, parking, air conditioned, swimming pool, tennis
Credit cards: American Express, Diners Club, Visa, Mastercard
A few hundred meters from the sea, a low Mediterranean style building with a large swimming pool and poolside bar.
The rooms are furnished with distinctive handmade Sardinian furniture and fabrics; traditional and international cuisine.
Sports and conference facilities are available.

Citti ** & ★
Viale Costa Smeralda 197, tel. 078982662
www.hotelcitti.com
50 rooms. Parking, air conditioned, swimming pool
Credit cards: American Express, Diners Club, Visa, Mastercard
Renovated, family run Bed & Breakfast located at the entrance to the town, also a no-frills place to stay for out of season travelers.

Club Hotel Laconia ***
Laconia, tel. 078986007
Open April-mid October
165 rooms. Restaurant, parking, swimming pool
Credit cards: American Express, Diners Club, Visa
On the sea; numerous suites and a shuttle service to the beach; activities day and night for adults and children.

Meliá Poltu Quatu *⁑* & ★
Poltu Quatu, tel. 0789956200
www.solmelia.com
Open April-October
142 rooms. Restaurant, swimming pool, sauna, gym
Credit cards: American Express, Diners Club, Visa, Mastercard

Overlooking the exclusive harbor, it enjoys a magnificent view of the islands belonging to the Maddalena archipelago. Guests are accommodated in rooms decorated Mediterranean style.
There are many facilities for guests: a beauty center, sauna, gym, lobby bar and three dining rooms. You may also hire rowing boats and smart yachts.

Rocce Sarde ***
San Pantaleo di Olbia, tel. 078965265
www.roccesarde.it
Open April-October
80 rooms. Restaurant, parking, air conditioned, swimming pool, tennis, gym
Credit cards: American Express, Diners Club, Visa, Mastercard
In a picturesque location, a Mediterranean style, functional structure with a lovely garden and spaces allocated to sports activities. Swimming pool set among rocks and shuttle service to the beach; buffet breakfast, piano bar in the evenings, restaurant serving Sardinian and inventive cuisine

Sant'Andrea ***
San Pantaleo di Olbia, via Zara 36/44, tel. 078965205
www.giagonigroup.com
Open mid April-mid October
15 rooms. Restaurant, parking, air conditioned, swimming pool
Credit cards: American Express, Diners Club, Visa, Mastercard
Centrally located, recently built cottage in the traditional Sardinian style with a few well-appointed, cozy rooms. Buffet breakfast with home baking.

Rural Lodgings
Ca' la Somara
Sarra Balestra, tel. 078998969
www.wel.it/lasomara
Restaurant, swimming pool
Rural hospitality a short distance inland from Costa Smeralda: under the large marquee lit at night by lanterns you can try treatments for energy and relaxation.
As well as the beautiful Sardinian beaches there are many sports activities and other forms of entertainment on offer.

Cudacciolu
Cudacciolu, tel. 078981207
www.agriturismocudacciolu.it
Restaurant
A pleasant rural lodging just a short distance from the beaches of Costa Smeralda. In the main part of the building there is a small dining room with cheerful wall paintings

⁑⁑⁑ ⁑⁑ *⁑* *** ** * Hotels 🍴🍴🍴🍴 🍴🍴🍴 🍴🍴 🍴 ⑂ Restaurants & Disabled ★ Special TCI Rates

and a veranda for eating out in the summer: the two adjacent buildings, which also have small verandas, house the rooms.

La Mesenda
Malchiddu, tel. 078981950
www.lamesenda.it
Hospitality in an old stable transformed into a country residence in the distinctive style of the farmhouses of these parts, with farming utensils and tools hanging on the walls. You will be given a warm and cordial welcome.
Leisure activities include trekking and guided visits to the archeological sites or nature reserves in the surrounding area.

Rena
Rena, tel. 078982532
Restaurant
Located in the hills just 6 km from the sea, framed by granite rocks, a large building dating from 1882 with original features and furnishings. In the communal areas and rooms you can breathe tradition: bare stone walls, wooden beams and a granite fireplace.
Large veranda with tables for dining on traditional Gallura cooking.

Restaurants

Giagoni ▓▓▓▓
San Pantaleo di Olbia,
via Zara 36/44
tel. 078965205
www.giagonigroup.com
Open mid April-mid October
Closed Monday in low season
Cuisine: creative
Credit cards: American Express, Diners Club, Visa, Mastercard
This restaurant is a cross between rustic and elegant. The carefully planned menu, based on whatever ingredients are in season, is the main attraction of this restaurant, which serves balanced and tasty meals of mainly fish from the coast.

La Bahia ▓▓▓ ★
Poltu Quatu, tel. 0789956200
www.solmelia.com
Open April-October
Cuisine: Sardinian and Spanish
A long vaulted gallery, drapery and furniture made by local craftsmen, tablecloths in shades of fawn and chocolate, steel tablemats, flower arrangements used as lamps. Good choice of local and Italian wines.

Lu Branu ▓ ♿
SS Arzachena-Palau,
tel. 078983075
www.lubranu.it

Open evenings only, May-September
Cuisine: Sardinian
Credit cards: American Express, Diners Club, Visa, Mastercard
Here, in a corner of the Sardinian countryside, you can try out the local cuisine, starting with cold meats and cheeses, produced by the family firm, all accompanied with local red or white wine and traditional liqueurs.

Lu Stazzu ▓▓ ♿ ★
Turning for Baia Sardinia, S.P. Porto Cervo-Arzachena
tel. 078982711
www.lustazzu.com
Open April-mid October
Cuisine: Sardinian
Credit cards: American Express, Diners Club, Visa, Mastercard
In the shelter of a copse of juniper trees and centuries-old olive trees, two large dining rooms with big exposed beams and arched windows from which you can admire Maddalena island. *Porcetto* and wild boar are cooked on a grill on the terrace in front of the guests: kitchen open until midnight.

At night

El Peyote
Santa Teresina Mirialveda, tel. 078998698
One of the most popular new venues on the Costa Smeralda. Excellent Mexican cuisine. Themed parties and Latin American music.

ATZARA

Rural Lodgings

Zeminariu
Zeminariu, tel. 078465235
Open by arrangement
Restaurant
On the western slopes of Gennargentu, surrounded by almond trees and woods; close to the village; a private house with communal areas separate from the stables and storerooms.

Museums

Pinacoteca d'Arte Moderna e Contemporanea «Antonio Ortiz Echagüe»
Piazza A. Ortiz Echague 1, tel. 078465508
web.tiscali.it/balero
Opening times: Summer: Tuesday and Friday-Sunday 10.00-13.00, 16.00-19.00; Wednesday and Thursday 16.00-19.00. Winter: Tuesday-Sunday 10.00-13.00, 16.00-19.00.

BAIA SARDINIA

Hotels

Club Hotel *▮*
Tel. 078999006, www.bajahotels.it
Open April-mid October
82 rooms. Restaurant, parking, air conditioned
Credit cards: American Express, Diners Club, Visa, Mastercard
Built in a lovely Mediterranean style with an elegant feel; terraces overlooking the sea and buffet breakfast.

Cormorano *▮*
Strada di Pini, tel. 078999020
www.hotelcormorano.it
Open April-September
75 rooms. Restaurant, parking, air conditioned, swimming pool, tennis
Credit cards: American Express, Diners Club, Visa, Mastercard
In the peace and quiet of an enchanting cove, a pleasant hotel with finely furnished, comfortable rooms and a small terrace overlooking the sea; good facilities for meetings and small conferences.

Gran Relais dei Nuraghi *▮*
Via Tremonti, tel. 078999501
www.hotelinuraghi.it
Open April-October
34 rooms. Restaurant, parking, air conditioned, swimming pool, tennis
Credit cards: American Express, Diners Club, Visa, Mastercard
Surrounded by vegetation, elegant post house inspired by the ancient nuraghic villages. Accommodation in some suites and numerous bungalows, many of which have terraces, gardens or private swimming pools. Buffet breakfast in the large dining room in the heart of the village, which metamorphoses into an American bar in the evenings.

La Bisaccia *▮*
Tel. 078999002
www.hotellabisaccia.it
Open mid May-mid October
109 rooms. Restaurant, parking, air conditioned, swimming pool
Credit cards: American Express, Diners Club, Visa, Mastercard
By the sea, a friendly hotel which has basic rooms with balconies and some suites with Jacuzzis. Buffet breakfast and restaurant serving classic and Sardinian specialties.

Mon Repos-Hermitage *▮*
Via Tre Monti, tel. 078999011
www.hotelmonrepos.it
Open mid April-mid October

60 rooms. Restaurant, parking, air conditioned, swimming pool, gym
Credit cards: Visa, Mastercard
Overlooking the sea, a typical Mediterranean style structure with different room types, all of which are air conditioned and well-appointed; spacious communal areas; restaurant "Conchiglia" serves classic and Sardinian cuisine.

Restaurants

Baia Blu ¶¶
Piazzetta Centrale,
tel. 078999085
Open Easter-mid October
Cuisine: fish
Credit cards: Visa
Pretty restaurant in the main square serving excellent fish and farm produce. Seafood starters, pasta with locally caught lobster and crayfish displayed in a tank in the restaurant. Cellar stocks regional labels only.

Casablanca ¶¶¶
Tel. 078999006
www.bajahotels.it
Open mid May-mid September, only in the evenings
Cuisine: Mediterranean
Credit cards: American Express, Diners Club, Visa, Mastercard
The terrace overlooking the sea and piano bar in the evenings make this restaurant something special; a combination of the day's catch and a careful selection of local ingredients topped with superb service. There are two menus which are both fish based. Excellent wine cellar.

Grazia Deledda ¶¶¶
Tilzitta, road to Baja Sardinia,
tel. 078998990
www.hotelristorantegraziadeledda.it
Open April-October
Cuisine: Sardinian and experimental
Credit cards: American Express, Diners Club, Visa, Mastercard
A restaurant famous for its cuisine which draws on the most deeply rooted local traditions; extensive wine list and great atmosphere. Do not miss the fresh pasta, mushrooms (when in season) and mountain ham.

At night

Ritual
La Crucitta, tel. 078999032
www.ritualtheoriginalclub.it
A picturesque venue built into rock which can cater for over 200 people.
Disco and disco pub.

Mamma Orsa
Baia Sardinia, tel. 078999462
One of the most famous venues in the Costa Smeralda, situated in a splendid position with a view of the harbor.
Elegant furnishings, themed parties and live music.

BARÙMINI
Restaurants

Sa Lolla ¶ ⅗
Via Cavour 49, tel. 0709368419
Closed Monday
Cuisine: Sardinian
Credit cards: American Express, Diners Club, Visa, Mastercard
An old, renovated, private house, this is a cozy restaurant with bare stone walls, wood and terracotta floors.
Dishes are typical of the island's interior: mutton with wild thistles, snails and almond sweets.

Su Nuraxi ¶¶ ⅗ ★
Strada Provinciale,
tel. 0709368305
www.hotelsunuraxi.it
Closed Tuesday, except between June and September
Cuisine: Sardinian
Credit cards: Visa, Mastercard
Spacious restaurant which takes its name from the nearby nuraghic settlement. Serves traditional cuisine and a few vegetarian dishes, combined with island wines; they produce their own oil.

BOSA

> ℹ️ **Centro Informazioni Turistiche**
> *Via Colombo 10,*
> *tel. 0785377108*
> *www.comune.bosa.nu.it*

Hotels

Al Gabbiano ★★★ ★
Bosa Marina, viale Mediterraneo, tel. 0785374123
www.bosa.it/gabbianohotel
30 rooms. Restaurant, parking, air conditioned
Credit cards: American Express, Diners Club, Visa, Mastercard
Close to the sea, a well-appointed modern building; lively restaurant specializing in Sardinian cuisine which, in summer, moves out beneath a large gazebo in the garden.

Mannu ★★★
Viale Alghero, tel. 0785375307
28 rooms. Restaurant, parking, air conditioned

Credit cards: American Express, Visa
Out of the way hotel, at the start of the coastal road to Alghero.
Busy restaurant "Giancarlo e Rita", provides rooms and handy facilities.

Sa Pischedda ★★★
Via Roma 8, tel. 0785373065
www.hotelsapischedda.it
18 rooms. Restaurant, parking, air conditioned
Founded in 1896, in the charming old center of this ancient mediaeval town, it provides cozy rooms with small balconies or verandas, some with a view of the river Temo, others split level. You may take a trip on the galleon which belongs to the owner.

Restaurants

Borgo Sant'Ignazio ¶¶
Via S. Ignazio 33,
tel. 0785374662
Closed Tuesday (in winter)
Cuisine: local, Barbagia
Credit cards: American Express, Diners Club, Visa, Mastercard
The restaurant is in an old, beautifully restored house in the mediaeval town.
Serves traditional dishes made into something special with a dash of sophistication; tasty almond sweets.

Sa Pischedda ¶¶ ⅗ ★
Via Roma 8, tel. 0785373065
www.hotelsapischedda.it
Closed Tuesday
Cuisine: Sardinian
Credit cards: Visa, Mastercard
Late 19th century building now used as an hotel. The restaurant-pizzeria is something special due to the freshness of its fish, the main item on the menu.

CABRAS
Hotels

Sinis Vacanze Sa Pedrera ★★★
San Salvatore,
S.P. Cabras-S. Giovanni Sinis,
km 5,5
tel. 0783370018
www.sapedrera.it
14 rooms. Restaurant, parking, air conditioned, tennis
Credit cards: American Express, Diners Club, Visa, Mastercard
Located on the Sinis peninsular, a cozy family atmosphere, ideal if you are interested in outdoor sports: busy restaurant "Sa Pedrera" serves regional and Italian cuisine.

⋕⋕⋕ ⋓⋓⋓ ⁕⋕⁕ ★★★ ★★ ★ Hotels ¶¶¶¶¶ ¶¶¶¶ ¶¶¶ ¶¶ ¶ Restaurants ⅗ Disabled ★ Special TCI Rates

Villa Canu ★★★ ♿
Via Firenze 9, tel. 0783290155
www.villacanu.com
23 rooms. Parking, air
conditioned
Credit cards: American Express,
Diners Club, Visa, Mastercard
In the center of the village,
a simple, no-frills hotel
providing accommodation
in an inner courtyard dwarfed
by an ancient stone millstone.
Well-kept communal areas
and large, bright rooms.
Buffet breakfast.

Restaurants

Dune 🍴 ♿
*San Giovanni di Sinis, borgata
Marina, tel. 0783370089*
*Closed Sunday evening and
Monday in low season*
Cuisine: Sardinian
Credit cards: American Express,
Diners Club, Visa, Mastercard
Two dining rooms, one with
a veranda, plus a pleasant area
for dining outside; dishes
are prepared with the best
ingredients the sea and the
ponds of Cabras have to offer.

Il Caminetto 🍴
Via C. Battisti 8, tel. 0783391139
www.villacanu.com
*Closed Monday
(except in August)*
Cuisine: Sardinian
Credit cards: American Express,
Diners Club, Visa, Mastercard
Centrally located, a modern
restaurant serving traditional
cuisine, mainly fish.

Sa Funtà 🍴
Via Garibaldi 25, tel. 0783290685
Closed Sunday
Cuisine: Sardinian and creative
Here you can try time-honored
or innovative recipes and finish
off with traditional sweet
delicacies from the island.
Do not miss the house brews.

At night

Caramella Bar
Vai Roma 2, tel. 3487946322
www.caramellabar.it
Youthful ambience a short
distance from the sea. Excellent
music program with live music
and house evenings with DJs
and karaoke.

Museums

Museo Civico di Cabras
*Via Tharros 121,
tel. 0783290636-0783370019*
www.penisoladelsinis.it
*Opening times: Summer:
Monday-Sunday 9.00-13.00,
16.00-20.00. Winter: Monday-
Sunday 9.00-13.00, 15.00-19.00.*

CAGLIARI

🛈 **Assessorato al Turismo**
*Via Sonnino,
tel. 0706778472*
www.comune.cagliari.it

Hotels

Caesar's Hotel ★★★
Via Darwin 2/4, tel. 070340750
www.caesarshotel.it
48 rooms. Restaurant, parking,
air conditioned
Credit cards: American Express,
Diners Club, Visa, Mastercard
Small, elegant hotel providing
well-appointed rooms and
suites; conference center,
banquet and reception rooms.
Buffet breakfast; a warm and
inviting atmosphere can also
be found in the restaurant
"Da Cesare" serving Sardinian
cuisine.

Italia ★★★ ★
Via Sardegna 31, tel. 070660410
108 rooms. Air conditioned
Credit cards: American Express,
Diners Club, Visa
In a good position near the
harbor, this renovated building
has large, comfortable rooms.
The stairs leading to the upper
floors have a lovely banister
dating from the early 20th
century.

Jolly Hotel ★★★ ★
*Circonvallazione Nuova 626,
tel. 070521373*
www.jollyhotels.it
129 rooms. Restaurant, parking,
air conditioned
Credit cards: American Express,
Visa, Mastercard
Situated at the junction
on the SS 131, a traditional
atmosphere appreciated
by tourists in transit and
businessmen; facilities suitable
for business meetings.
Restaurant "Bell'Italia" has
a rustic feel.

Mediterraneo ★★★
*Lungomare Colombo 46,
tel. 070342361*
www.hotelmediterraneo.net
140 rooms. Restaurant, parking,
air conditioned
Credit cards: American Express,
Diners Club, Visa, Mastercard
Situated in the heart
of the city, attention to detail
and a comfortable stay
are guaranteed by a highly
professional management team:
cozy rooms, large communal
areas embellished with marble
of many hues; American bar
and summer garden.
The well-appointed conference
center makes it a suitable venue

for conferences and business
meetings.

Panorama ★★★ ♿ ★
Viale Diaz 231, tel. 070307691
www.hotelpanorama.it
90 rooms. Restauarant, air
conditioned, swimming pool
Credit cards: American Express,
Diners Club, Visa, Mastercard
Near the trade fair, a well-
appointed structure with
modern furnishings. Provides a
good level of hospitality due to
its numerous suites and the
busy restaurant "Belvedere";
bar for light snacks, ice cream
parlor and cafeteria with pool
service. A terrace for sunbathing
overlooks the pool.

Regina Margherita ★★★ ★
*Viale Regina Margherita 44,
tel. 070670342*
www.hotelreginamargherita.com
99 rooms. Air conditioned
Credit cards: American Express,
Diners Club, Visa, Mastercard
In the old town center, a
prestigious hotel which meets
international standards, ideal for
business guests and visiting
tourists; comfortable and
spacious rooms, elegant
communal areas, American bar
with tables on the terrace.

Sardegna ★★★ ♿
Via Lunigiana 50, tel. 070286245
www.shg.it
90 rooms. Restaurant, parking,
air conditioned
Credit cards: American Express,
Diners Club, Visa, Mastercard
Quiet, with an elegant
atmosphere, air conditioned,
well-appointed rooms, used
mainly by business people;
buffet breakfast, restaurant
"La Scala" serves regional and
traditional cuisine.

Ulivi e Palme ★★★ ★
Via P. Bembo 25, tel. 070485861
www.uliviepalme.it
23 rooms. Restaurant, parking,
air conditioned, swimming pool,
tennis, gym
Credit cards: American Express,
Diners Club, Visa, Mastercard
In a residential area, "hotel"
formula with accommodation
in large rooms and breakfast
or "residence" formula in the
over one hundred self-catering
apartments (not forgetting the
restaurant " Severino a
Cagliari", which has a lovely
view and is part of the
complex).

Restaurants

Al Porto 🍴
Via Sardegna 44, tel. 070663131
Closed Monday

Cuisine: Sardinian
Credit cards: American Express,
Diners Club, Visa, Mastercard
Elegant atmosphere, focussing
mainly on fresh seasonal
produce and fish specialties
with some inventive flourishes.
Interesting wine list proposed
by the sommelier-owner; good
selection of oils, cold meats and
cheeses.

Antica Hostaria ¶¶
Via Cavour 60, tel. 070665870
Closed Sunday
Cuisine: Sardinian
Credit cards: American Express,
Diners Club, Visa, Mastercard
Small, elegant restaurant
serving regional cuisine with
some curious innovations.

Crackers ¶¶ &
Corso Vittorio Emanuele 195,
tel. 070653912
Closed Wednesday
Cuisine: Piedmontese and
classic
Credit card: American Express,
Diners Club, Visa, Mastercard
A corner of Piedmont in Sardinia
sums up this restaurant with
a homely atmosphere.
The menu includes variously
inspired dishes but mainly
risotto and boiled meats
accompanied by judiciously
chosen wines.

Dal Corsaro ¶¶¶ ★
Viale Regina Margherita 28,
tel. 070664318
www.dalcorsaro.com
Closed Sunday
Cuisine: Sardinian
Credit cards: American Express,
Diners Club, Visa, Mastercard
This restaurant, with its
traditional, cozy feel has
distinguished itself for years
due to its courteous service
and the culinary standard
of the food served; fish
specialties, good wine list,
tasty almond sweets.

Dal Corsaro ¶¶¶¶
Poetto, tel. 070370295
Closed midday Monday in
summer, Monday in winter
Cuisine: Mediterranean
Credit cards: American Express,
Diners Club, Visa, Mastercard
In a charming position on the
harbor, three elegant dining
rooms and a lovely terrace
overlooking the sea.
The traditional, dishes are
all made to a high standard
using regional produce and
vary according to the day's
catch. Good wine list includes
the very best of the island's
wines.

Flora ¶¶ &
Via Sassari 47, tel. 070664735
Closed Sunday
Cuisine: Sardinian and classic
Credit cards: American Express,
Diners Club, Visa, Mastercard
Charming trattoria with antique
furniture and ornaments.
The menu includes traditional
dishes made with regional farm
produce and fish.

S'Apposentu ¶¶ &
Via S. Alenixedda,
tel. 0704082315
www.sapposentu.it
Closed Monday and Sunday
Cuisine: creative regional
Credit cards: American Express,
Diners Club, Visa, Mastercard
Inside the Teatro Lirico this
minimalist restaurant serves
food that bears the hallmark
of its creative and professional
young chef.

Trattoria Lillicu ¶
Via Sardegna 78, tel. 070652970
Closed Sunday
Cuisine: fish
Credit cards: American Express,
Diners Club, Visa, Mastercard
Pleasant ambience where you
can enjoy Cagliari cooking, eating
off solid marble tables. The menu
consists almost entirely of fresh
fish, prepared in different ways
depending on the season. There
is no written menu, the waiter
will tell you what there is and,
apart from some classic dishes,
the menu changes frequently
at the whim of the chef.

Trilogy Club ¶¶ &
Via Sassari 11/13, tel. 070656060
Closed Sunday
Cuisine: Sardinian and classic
Credit cards: American Express,
Visa, Mastercard
Flawless service is guaranteed
in this elegant, centrally located
restaurant with modern, tasteful
furnishings and sophisticated
prepared dishes typical of
classic and Sardinian cuisine.
Regional wines only.

At night

Abbey Road
Via Dolcetta 4, tel. 070275555
This venue winks at typical
London clubs. Extremely
pleasant ambience and excellent
program of musical events.
Restaurant is self-service
at lunchtimes.

Antico Caffè
Piazza Costituzione 12,
tel. 070650943
Historical venue protected by
the Ministry of Cultural Heritage.
Its unique atmosphere hasn't
changed since 1855.

Beergarden
Via Angioy 49, tel. 070667449
Pub decorated in various styles
where you can drink excellent
Austrian beer.

New Open Gate
Via Venturi 18, tel. 070498196
This historical Cagliari disco has
been operating for twenty years.
Music for all tastes depending
on the evening.

Trigamus
Via Newton 10, tel. 070485381
Here you can listen to live sixties
and Latin-American music.
They also serve good pizzas.

Museums

Galleria Comunale d'Arte
Giardini Pubblici, largo G. Dessì,
tel. 070490727
www.collezioneingrao.it
Opening times: Summer:
Wednesday-Monday 9.00-13.00,
17.00-21.00. Winter: Wednesday-
Monday 9.00-13.00, 15.30-19.30.

Museo Archeologico Nazionale
Cittadella dei Musei, piazza
Arsenale, tel. 070655911
www.crs4.it/OLD/RUGGIERO/MUS
EO/mus_ind.html
Opening times: Tuesday-Sunday
9.00-20.00.

Museo d'Arte Siamese
«Stefano Cardu»
Cittadella dei Musei, piazza
Arsenale, tel. 070651888
Opening times: Summer:
Tuesday-Sunday 9.00-13.00,
16.00-20.00. Winter: Tuesday-
Sunday 9.00-13.00, 15.30-19.30.

Museo del Santuario di Nostra
Signora di Bonaria
Piazza Bonaria, tel. 070301747
www.nsdibonaria.it
Opening times: Monday-Sunday
9.30-11.30, 17.00-19.30. Closed
Saturday morning. Opening
times may vary.

Museo del Tesoro e Area
Archeologica di Sant'Eulalia -
MUTSEU
Vico del Collegio 2, tel. 070663724
web.tiscali.it/mutseu
Opening times: Tuesday-Sunday
10.00-13.00, 17.00-20.00. Longer
opening times in summer.

Museo di Mineralogia
«L. De Prunner - Museo Sardo
di Geologia e Paleontologia
«D. Lovisato»
Via Trentino 51,
tel. 0706757712-0706757736
www.unica.it/dister
Opening times: Visits by
arrangement

Museo Diocesano
Via Fossario, tel. 070652498-
070554220

www.museoduomodicagliari.it
Opening times: Tuesday-Sunday
10.00-13.00, 16.30-19.30. Visits
also by arrangement

Orto Botanico - Dipartimento di Scienze Botaniche
Via S. Ignazio da Laconi 11,
tel. 0706753501-0706753522
digilander.libero.it/emcalvino/ort
o_botanico/
Opening times: April-October:
Monday-Sunday 8.00-13.00,
15.00-19.00. Closed 1st January,
Easter, 1st May (morning only),
15th August, 25th December.

Pinacoteca Nazionale
Cittadella dei Musei, piazza
Arsenale, tel. 070674054
Opening times: Tuesday-Sunday
9.00-20.00.

Raccolta delle Cere Anatomiche di Clemente Susini
Cittadella dei Musei, piazza
Arsenale 1,
tel. 0706757627-0706754001
medicina.unica.it/cere
Opening times: Tuesday-Sunday
9.00-13.00, 16.00-19.00.

CALA GONONE

> 🔲 **Ufficio Informazioni**
> tel. 078493696

Hotels

Cala Luna ★★ ♿
Lungomare Palmasera 6,
tel. 078493133
www.hotelcalaluna.com
Open April-November
26 rooms. Restaurant, air
conditioned
Credit cards: American Express,
Diners Club, Visa, Mastercard
On the seafront; an elegant
Mediterranean style building.
Well-appointed rooms, most
with balconies and sea views.
The romantic restaurant
overlooking the sea serves
traditional dishes and fish
specialties.

Costa Dorada ★↕★
Lungomare Palmasera 45,
tel. 078493332
www.hotelcostadorada.it
Open Easter-mid October
28 rooms. Restaurant, air
conditioned
Credit cards: American Express,
Visa, Mastercard
Right on the sandy and pebbly
beach, an elegant structure with
rooms in Sardinian-Spanish
style and some suites with
Jacuzzis. Large terrace with sun
loungers and umbrellas and a
view of the gulf of Orosei; buffet
breakfast and well-kept
restaurant.

Miramare ★★★
Piazza Giardini 12, tel. 078493140
www.htlmiramare.it
Open Easter-October
35 rooms. Restaurant, parking,
air conditioned
Credit cards: American Express,
Diners Club, Visa, Mastercard
A renovated fifties house in
a central location just a short
distance from the sea; rooms
with terraces and a garden-
restaurant with a great view.

Pop ★★★ ★
Via Marco Polo 2, tel. 078493185
www.hotelpop.com
16 rooms. Restaurant, parking,
air conditioned
Credit cards: American Express,
Diners Club, Visa, Mastercard
This modern hotel has
comfortable rooms with small
balconies furnished in the
Sardinian style. Managed by the
owners who will give you a
cordial welcome.

Restaurants

Al Porto ⁈♿ ★
Piazza del Porto 2,
tel. 078493185
www.hotelpop.com
Cuisine: Sardinian and fish
Credit cards: American Express,
Diners Club, Visa, Mastercard
Near the harbor, serves the most
classic regional dishes; in summer
you may dine until late on the
terrace. Barbagia oil and cheeses.

CALASETTA

> 🔲 **Pro Loco**
> Lungomare Colombo 1,
> tel. 078188534
> www.prolococalasetta.it

Hotels

Cala di Seta ★★★ ♿
Via Regina Margherita 61,
tel. 078188304
www.hotelcaladiseta.it
21 rooms. Restaurant, air
conditioned
Credit cards: American Express,
Visa, Mastercard
In the old town center, a
Mediterranean style building
with two lovely terraces and
rooms with sea views. The
restaurant serves Sardinian
and classic cuisine (homemade
pasta and red wine produced
by the owners).

Fjby ★★
Via Solferino 83, tel. 078188444
20 rooms. Restaurant, air
conditioned
Credit cards: American Express,
Diners Club, Visa

Near the harbor, simple and
basic, busy restaurant serves
fish cooked to Sardinian recipes.

Luci del Faro ★★★ ♿
Mangiabarche, tel. 0781810089
www.hotelucidelfaro.com
38 rooms. Restaurant, parking,
air conditioned, swimming pool,
tennis
Credit cards: American Express,
Diners Club, Visa, Mastercard
A short distance from the sea,
this hotel is built in
Mediterranean style around
a large swimming pool.
Functional, bright rooms, some
with sea views; restaurant with
a wonderful view serves
Sardinian cuisine; shuttle
service to the principal beaches
in the area.

Stella del Sud ★★★ ★
Spiaggia Grande, tel. 0781810188
www.hotelstelladelsud.com
50 rooms. Restaurant, parking
air conditioned, swimming pool,
tennis
Credit cards: American Express,
Diners Club, Visa, Mastercard
Right on the beach, a low, well-
kept building in an oasis
of maquis for relaxing stays;
long-established family
management; accommodation
in large rooms and a garden
with garden furniture.

Rural Lodgings

Tupei
Vigna Grande, tel. 0781810025
www.agriturismotupei.com
Open by arrangement
Restaurant
On the furthest tip
of Sant'Antìoco island, a patio
and inner courtyard provide
access to the main part of
the building with the dining
room and rooms. Ideal above
all for horse lovers, who may
take riding lessons or go
on excursions on horseback
to explore the island's
treasures.

CARBONIA
Restaurants

Bovo-Da Tonino ⁈
Via Costituente 18,
tel. 078162217
Closed Sunday
Cuisine: classic
Credit cards: American Express,
Diners Club, Visa, Mastercard
An expert family team mainly
offers fresh fish served in the
garden in the summer.
The menu includes: tuna à la
Cannonau, spaghetti with sea
urchins, mixed grill.

At night

Poppy's Pub
Via G.M. Angioj 32,
tel. 078162944
www.poppyspub.com
Large venue, one of its kind, with beerhouse, pizzeria and restaurant. In the pub there is a collection of English antiques. Friendly and relaxing atmosphere.

Museums

Civico Museo Archeologico «Villa Sulcis» Carbonia
Via Napoli, tel. 0781691131
www.sardinia.net/carbonia
Opening times: Summer: Tuesday-Sunday 9.00-13.00, 16.00-20.00. Winter: Tuesday-Sunday 9.00-13.00, 15.00-19.00.

Museo Civico di Paleontologia e Speleologia «E. A. Martel» Carbonia
Via Campania 61b,
tel. 0781691006
www.sardinia.net/carbonia
Opening times: Summer: Tuesday-Sunday 9.00-13.00, 16.00-20.00. Winter: Tuesday-Sunday 9.00-13.00, 15.00-19.00.

CARLOFORTE

> ⓘ **Pro Loco**
> Corso Tagliafico 2,
> tel. 0781854009
> www.prolococarloforte.it

Hotels

Hieracon ★★★
Corso Cavour 62,
tel. 0781854028
web.tiscali.it/hotelhieracon
24 rooms. Restaurant, air conditioned
Credit cards: Visa, Mastercard
Comfortable, early 20th century building, centrally located and close to the jetty; small apartments, elegant rooms and a busy restaurant serving fish specialties; large inner garden.

Paola ★★★
Tacca Rossa
S.P. Punta Tonnare,
tel. 0781850098
Open Easter-October
21 rooms. Restaurant, air conditioned
Credit cards: American Express, Diners Club, Visa, Mastercard
Simple hotel providing all the basics for peaceful holidays surrounded by nature; newly built gazebo for pleasantly idling away the hours.

Restaurants

Al Tonno di Corsa ⫟⫟
Via Marconi 47, tel. 0781855106
www.tonnodicorsa.it
Closed Monday (in winter)
Cuisine: Sardinian
Credit cards: American Express, Diners Club, Visa, Mastercard
The name of the restaurant, located in the old town center, recalls a fishing tradition which belongs to this ancient island town. The chef faithfully reproduces time-honored and modern traditional recipes.

Da Nicolò ⫟⫟ ♿
Corso Cavour 32, tel. 0781854048
www.danicolo.com
Open Easter-mid November
Closed Monday (except between mid June and mid August)
Cuisine: Sardinian and Ligurian revisited
Credit cards: American Express, Diners Club, Visa, Mastercard
Historical restaurant divided into inside dining rooms and a summer veranda with two distinct types of cuisine (traditional and inventive) both highly recommended thanks to the talent of the young chef who served a tough apprenticeship in famous restaurants. Excellent choice of wines.

Dau Bobba ⫟⫟ ♿
Segni, strada delle Saline,
tel. 0781854037
www.carloforte.net/daubobba
Closed Tuesday in low season
Cuisine: fish
Credit cards: Diners Club, Visa, Mastercard
Restaurant in what was a tuna canning factory in the forties. The chef, and owner, offers an inventive fish menu which combines tradition and innovation, using extremely fresh ingredients and fresh pasta. Excellent choice of wines and liqueurs.

Da Vittorio ⫟⫟
Corso Battellieri 11,
tel. 0781855200
www.ristorantedavittorio.carloforte.it
Closed Monday and Tuesday
Cuisine: regional
Credit cards: American Express, Diners Club, Visa, Mastercard
Its nearness to the sea and its food distinguish this typical stone restaurant with a rustic feel, where tradition is wedded to the imagination of Vittorio "the whizz of Carloforte cuisine"; you may dine all year round under a lovely art nouveau gazebo.

Galman ⫟⫟
Bellavista, tel. 0781852088
www.carloforte.it/hotelgalman
Open March-October,
evenings only
Cuisine: regional
Credit cards: American Express, Diners Club, Visa, Mastercard
Informal but elegant ambience with menus personally devised by the owner, inspired by fish and especially tuna recipes. Do not miss the vegetable couscous and homemade lemon sorbet.

At night

Guardi Mori
Guardia Mori
Original and exclusive open air disco in an ancient redoubt. Music for all tastes, above all soul and jazz.

CASTELSARDO

Hotels

Costa Doria ★★★
Lu Bagnu, corso Italia 73,
tel. 079474043
www.hotelcostadoria.it
68 rooms. Restaurant, air conditioned
Credit cards: American Express, Diners Club, Visa, Mastercard
Small modern building about 100 meters from the beach. Provides a good standard of accommodation despite being fairly basic. Restaurant "Da Bore" serves regional cuisine and mainly fish specialties.

Nadir ★★★ ♿
Via Colle di Frigiano 1,
tel. 079470297
www.hotelnadir.com
32 rooms. Restaurant, air conditioned
Credit cards: American Express, Diners Club, Visa, Mastercard
Situated in a lovely position with a great view of the gulf of Asinara this is a recently built hotel with air conditioning and all mod cons; the restaurant, with a terrace overlooking the sea, serves fish cuisine and traditional Sardinian dishes.

Riviera ★★★
Lungomare Anglona 1,
tel. 079470143
www.hotelriviera.net
34 rooms. Restaurant, parking, air conditioned
Credit cards: American Express, Diners Club, Visa, Mastercard
Completely renovated, in a lovely location between the walls of the castle and the beach, this hotel guarantees pleasant stays in simple, fresh and pretty rooms, some of which have sea views. Large terrace with great view of the gulf of Asinara; meeting rooms.

Restaurants

Fofò ¶¶ ♿
Lungomare Anglona 1,
tel. 079470143
www.hotelriviera.net
Closed Wednesday
Cuisine: Sardinian
Credit cards: American Express,
Diners Club, Visa, Mastercard
Restaurant with a classic feel,
run by the same family since
1960. Among the specialties
served in the dining room
or on the lovely terrace with
a sea view are: risotto with
cuttlefish ink and spaghetti
à la spider-crab.

Sa Ferula ¶¶ ♿ ★
Lu Bagnu, corso Italia 1/B,
tel. 079474049
Closed Thursday (in low season)
Cuisine: Sardinian
Credit cards: American Express,
Diners Club, Visa, Mastercard
A lovely terrace with a sea view
where you can eat roast meat
as well as fish until midnight.
The management prides itself
on its attention to detail.

DORGALI

> ℹ️ **Assessorato al Turismo**
> Viale Umberto 37, tel.
> 0784927236, www.dorgali.it
> ℹ️ **Pro Loco Associazione
> Turistica**
> Via Lamarmora 108,
> tel. 078496243

Hotels

Ispinigoli ★★★ ♿ ★
Ispinigoli, tel. 078495268
www.hotelispinigoli.com
Open March-November
24 rooms. Restaurant, parking,
air conditioned
Credit cards: American Express,
Visa, Mastercard
Family run hotel: large terraces
overlook the surrounding
countryside, the grotto of the
same name and the ancient
thermal pool in the environs;
the sea is a few kilometers
away and the beaches are not
crowded. The rooms are large
with verandas and country-style
furnishings. Play park for
children.

Monteviore ★★★
Monteviore, tel. 078496293
www.hotelmonteviore.it
Open April-October
19 rooms. Restaurant, swimming
pool
Credit cards: Diners Club, Visa,
Mastercard
A few meters from the sea

at Cala Gonone, this is a small,
romantic structure surrounded
by unique nature: the rooms,
each with a terrace, overlook
Gorroppu gorge and Tiscali
mountain; you will find basic
comforts and a cordial welcome.

Rural Lodgings

Biriddo
Biriddo, tel. 0783411660
www.sardegnaturismo.net
Restaurant
The farm is in the heart of the
countryside and surrounded
by olive trees. There are a few
wooden bungalows with large
rooms and verandas. Some of
the specialties of the restaurant
are the typical potato bread,
bread stuffed with fresh cheese
and mint, cold meats and short-
crust pastries filled with jam.

Restaurants

Ispinigoli ¶¶
Ispinigoli, tel. 078495268
www.hotelispinigoli.com
Open March-November
Cuisine: Sardinian and fish
Credit cards: American Express,
Diners Club, Visa, Mastercard
Run by the same family
for a quarter of a century;
interesting cuisine made with
excellent ingredients supplied
by the family firm; the menu
includes meat, fish
and vegetarian dishes.
Children's menu.

Museums

**Mostra Permanente Salvatore
Fancello**
Viale Umberto 37,
tel. 078494945-0784929240
www.dorgali.it
Opening times: Summer:
Monday-Sunday 9.00-12.00,
18.00-21.00.

Museo Archeologico
Via La Marmora, tel. 078496243
www.ghivine.com
Opeing times: Winter: Monday-
Sunday 9.00-13.00, 14.00-16.30.
Summer: Monday-Sunday 16.00-
19.00.

FLUMINIMAGGIORE

Hotels

Sardus Pater ★★★ ♿
Portixeddu, tel. 078154949
www.hotelsarduspater.it
14 rooms. Restaurant, air
conditioned
Credit cards: American Express,
Diners Club, Visa, Mastercard
On the slopes of Monte Su
Guardianu, 400 meters from the
sea, it has an unparalleled view
of the coast. The rooms, with
independent verandas and

entrances, are in a typically
low building with country-style
furnishings. The restaurant
serves traditional Sardinian
and classic cuisine.

Museums

Museo Archeologico
Via Asquer, tel. 0781580840
Opening times: Temporarily
closed.

Museo Paleontologico
Via Vittorio Emanuele,
tel. 0781580165
Opening times: Visits by
arrangement.

GAVOI

Hotels

Gusana ★★★
Gusana, tel. 078453000
35 rooms. Restaurant, parking,
air conditioned, swimming pool,
tennis
Credit cards: American Express,
Diners Club, Visa
On the shores of the lake of
Gusana, a peaceful and relaxing
hotel, run by a family for over
thirty years: ideal for families
with children for whom there
is a special menu (up to the age
of six).

Taloro ★★★ ♿
Lago di Gusana, tel. 078453033
90 rooms. Restaurant, parking,
air conditioned, swimming pool,
tennis
Credit cards: American Express,
Diners Club, Visa, Mastercard
Surrounded by nature, with
a view of the lake, equipped
with a wellness center,
it provides guests with the
opportunity to go horse-riding
at a nearby stables.

Rural Lodgings

Antichi Sapori
Via Cagliari 192, tel. 078452021
www.terranostra.sardegna.it
Open by arrangement
Restaurant
We are north of Gennargentu,
near the lake of Gusana.
The farm is in a traditional
village of stone houses built
in a semi-circle around a dell;
there are many activities on
offer including sports and crafts
(also lessons in basket-
weaving).

Fuego
Lago di Gusana, tel. 078452052
Restaurant
In an area that has many
centuries-old trees, this
is a simple, rustic structure,
especially suitable for horse-
riding and fishing. In the
restaurant, open to non-guests,

you will find local cuisine. Nearby there are public swimming pools and, in winter, you can go trekking in the mountains.

Restaurants

Santa Rughe ¶¶
Via Carlo Felice 2, tel. 078453774
www.santarughe.it
Closed Wednesday (except August)
Cuisine: Sardinian
Credit cards: American Express, Diners Club, Visa, Mastercard
The name is a homage to the nearby piazza of Santa Croce, in local dialect "Santa Rughe". The restaurant is picturesque, with bare stone walls and lovely touches. It serves excellent regional cuisine, using the finest local ingredients.

GHILARZA

Hotels

Su Cantaru ★★
Via Mons. Zucca 2, tel. 078554523
23 rooms. Tennis
Credit cards: Visa
At the end of the village, near the SS 131 bis Losa/Nùoro, heading towards Nùoro, this is a simple, no-frills hotel.

Museums

Casa Museo di Antonio Gramsci - Centro di Documentazione, Ricerca e Attività Museale
Corso Umberto 57, tel. 078554164
www.casagramscighilarza.org
Opening times: Monday-Sunday 10.00-13.00, 16.30-19.30. Closed Tuesday.

IGLESIAS

ℹ **Associazione Pro Loco Iglesias**
Via Roma 10, tel. 078131170
www.proloiglesias.it

Restaurants

Gazebo Medioevale ¶¶ &
Via Musio 21, tel. 078130871
www.gazebomedioevale.it
Closed Sunday
Cuisine: Sardinian and creative
In one of the most ancient buildings in the old town center, two dining rooms with high ceilings and wooden beams which echo the architectural motifs of the mediaeval age. Fish cuisine based on a judicious choice of ingredients, depending on the season and the market; on the menu you will find starters, pasta and rice

dishes, main courses (including tuna fillet with soy sauce and balsamic vinegar) and excellent homemade cold desserts

Pan di Zucchero ¶
Nebida, via Centrale 365, tel. 078147114
Closed Monday (except in summer)
Cuisine: Sardinian and classic
Credit cards: Diners Club, Visa, Mastercard
Pleasant family run restaurant which takes its name from the nearby stack which towers over the gulf: fish specialties and, in season, the must-try porceddu.

Museums

Museo dell'Arte Mineraria
Via Roma 47, tel. 0781350037
www.museoartemineraria.it
Opeing times: April-June: Saturday and Sunday 18.00-20.00. July-September: Friday, Saturday and Sunday 19.00-21.00. Visits by arrangement in other periods.

LA MADDALENA

ℹ **Ufficio Turistico**
tel. 0789790633, www.lamaddalena.it

Hotels

Cala Lunga ★☆★
Porto Massimo, tel. 0789793000
www.ventaglio.com
Open June-September
70 rooms. Restaurant, parking, air conditioned, swimming pool
Credit cards: American Express, Diners Club, Visa, Mastercard
Overlooking a lovely bay, a renovated Mediterranean style building, with fine facilities; also suitable for families with children. Week long stays.

Garibaldi ★★★
Via Lamarmora, tel. 0789737314
www.hotelgaribaldi.info
Open mid March-mid October
19 rooms. Air conditioned
Credit cards: American Express, Diners Club, Visa, Mastercard
In a quiet spot, 150 meters from the harbor of Cala Gavetta and the old town center, a Bed and Breakfast with a classic feel dating from the eighties; buffet breakfast.

Nido d'Aquila ★★★ ★
Nido d'Aquila, tel. 0789722130
www.hotelnidodaquila.it
Open April-October
44 rooms. Parking, air conditioned
Credit cards: American Express, Diners Club, Visa

Just 20 meters from the sea, in the cool and quiet of a lovely garden, a modern, family run hotel; six self-catering apartments and a jetty for small boats. Meals can be taken in the restaurant located just beyond the inner courtyard.

Museums

Museo Archeologico Navale «Nino Lamboglia»
Mongiardino, tel. 0789790660
Opening times: Temporarily closed.

Museo Garibaldino Nazionale di Caprera
Isola di Caprera, tel. 0789727162
Opening times: Tuesday-Saturday 9.00-13.30, 14.00-18.30; Sunday 9.00-13.30.

NÙORO

ℹ **Punto Informa Nùoro**
Corso Garibaldi 155, tel. 078438777

Hotels

Grillo ★★★ &
Via Mons. Melas 14, tel. 078438678
www.grillohotel.it
46 rooms. Restaurant, air conditioned
Credit cards: American Express, Diners Club, Visa, Mastercard
Centrally located, renovated sixties building; provides comfortable and functional rooms, some with Jacuzzis or showers with hydomassage jets, buffet breakfast, Sardinian cuisine using local ingredients.

Paradiso ★★★
Via Aosta 44, tel. 078435585
42 rooms. Restaurant, parking, air conditioned
Credit cards: American Express, Diners Club, Visa, Mastercard
Near the stadium, a staid and pristine hotel with refurbished rooms; also suitable for business meetings.

Rural Lodgings

Costiolu
Costiolu, SS 389, km 90, tel. 0784260088
www.agriturismocostiolu.com
Open by arrangement
Restaurant
The sweeping views are of the rugged countryside, granite and holm-oaks and cork trees of the highlands north of Nùoro: the livestock farm breeds sheep, goats, horses, cows and pigs; other animals, such as wild boar are glimpsed on the road to the nuraghic villages of Su Costiolu and Noddule, which can be

reached by trekking or excursions on horseback. You stay on the upper story of a farmhouse built around a farmyard which has various barns, a cellar and a large dining room.

Testone &

Via Verdi, tel. 0784230539
www.agriturismotestone.com
Restaurant, mountain bike hire
An exceptional location, to say the least: the farm is situated on high land with wonderful scenery.
A variety of farming activities are carried out. The owners also offer traditional cooking , needless to say using organic ingredients. Their salvaging of the old stone hamlet and commitment to educating people in farming lore is admirable.

Restaurants

Canne al Vento ⫴

Via Biasi 123, tel. 0784201762
Closed Sunday
Cuisine: Barbagia
Credit cards: American Express, Diners Club, Visa, Mastercard
Extremely lively and friendly environment; the cook uses mainly farm produce to produce dishes such as roast *porcetto* and stewed mutton, as well as fish.

Ciusa ⫴ &

Viale Ciusa 55, tel. 0784257052
www.restaurantciusa.com
Closed Tuesday
Cuisine: Sardinian revisited
Credit cards: American Express, Diners Club, Visa, Mastercard
Outside the small town heading towards Monte Ortobene you will find this small, simple and well-kept modern restaurant. The chef proposes inventive dishes using unusual combinations of ingredients; the menu varies depending on what is in season.

At night

El Barrito Latino
Via Catte
Brand new venue on two floors with a diary crammed with musical events and initiatives. Eighties and live music. Open on Sunday afternoons for the younger crowd.

Grillo
Via Mons. Giuseppe Melas 14, tel. 078432005
Disco and disco pub with a pleasant ambience; you may dine in the excellent restaurant.

La Boca Chica
Via Mughina 94, tel. 3293120010
New venue with restaurant,

pizzeria, pub and, on Thursday evenings, disco pub with live music shows.

Museums

Museo Archeologico Nazionale
Piazza Asproni, via Mannu, tel. 078431688-078438053
Opening times: Tuesday-Saturday 9.00-13.00; Tuesday and Thursday also 15.00-17.30.

Museo Deleddiano - Casa Natale di Grazia Deledda
Via Deledda 42, tel. 0784258088-0784242900
www.museodeleddiano.it
Opening times: 15th June-September: Monday-Sunday 9.00-20.00. October-14th June: 9.00-13.00, 15.00-19.00.

Museo dell'Arte della Provincia di Nùoro - M.A.N. ★
Via Satta 15, tel. 0784252110-0784252189
Opening times: Tuesday-Sunday 10.00-13.00, 16.30-20.30.

Museo della Vita e delle Tradizioni Popolari Sarde
Via Mereu 56, tel. 0784257035
Opening times: 15th June-30th September: Monday-Sunday 9.00-20.00. October-14th June: Monday-Sunday 9.00-13.00, 15.00-19.00.

OLBIA

🛈 **Consorzio Turistico Olbia Gallura**
Via Regina Elena 52, tel. 078926673, www.ctog.it

Hotels

Cavour ★★★ &
Via Cavour 22, tel. 0789204033
www.cavourhotel.it
21 rooms. Parking, air conditioned
Credit cards: American Express, Diners Club, Visa, Mastercard
In the heart of the old city center, ten minutes from the harbor and the railway station and two kilometers from the airport, a hotel built in 1999 with comfortable, well-furnished rooms; buffet breakfast.

Centrale ★★★ ★
Corso Umberto 83/85, tel. 078923017
www.hotelcentraleolbia.it
21 rooms. Air conditioned
Credit cards: American Express, Diners Club, Visa, Mastercard
Centrally located, a recently renovated mid 18th century building with much improved accommodation. Modern and quietly elegant rooms and bathrooms; buffet breakfast. Shortly to be awarded 4 stars.

Daniel ★★★
Murta Maria, via Maltineddu, tel. 0789379030
www.hotel-daniel.it
18 rooms. Parking, air conditioned, tennis
Credit cards: American Express, Diners Club, Visa, Mastercard
The country village where it is located is just a few kilometers from the most well-known beaches in the area: the beach of Murta Maria is perfect for windsurfing and sailing enthusiasts. The hotel is a Bed and Breakfast, with large, well-appointed rooms; buffet breakfast.

ITI Colonna Palace Hotel Mediterraneo ★★★ ★
Via Montello 3, tel. 078924173
70 rooms. Restaurant, parking, air conditioned
Credit cards: American Express, Diners Club, Visa, Mastercard
Located in the city center, a short distance from the harbor and the airport, it has well-appointed rooms furnished in Sardinian style. Some have terraces with views. American bar and small rooms for business meetings complement the whole.

Li Cuncheddi ★★★
Capo Ceraso, tel. 078936126
www.hotellicuncheddi.com
Open mid April-mid October
80 rooms. Restaurant, parking, air conditioned, swimming pool, tennis
Credit cards: American Express, Diners Club, Visa, Mastercard
Overlooking a small bay with a dazzling white sandy beach, this is a modern and elegant complex with interiors designed in an innovative and unusual style; well-appointed, air conditioned rooms and some suites, most of which have sea views. Plenty of equipment is available for leisure activities and, from June to September, there is entertainment, a kids' club and a diving center.

Luna Lughente ★★★ &
Pittulongu, tel. 078957521
www.shg.it
58 rooms. Restaurant, parking, air conditioned, swimming pool, tennis
Credit cards: American Express, Diners Club, Visa, Mastercard
Out of the center, this hotel has rooms and some suites equipped with technologically advanced equipment, especially suitable for those who, for business or leisure purposes, seek modernity and comfort.

Martini *⁑* & ★
Via G. D'Annunzio,
tel. 078926066
www.hotelmartiniolbia.com
66 rooms. Parking, air
conditioned
Credit cards: American Express,
Diners Club, Visa, Mastercard
Inaugurated in 1994, it offers
a good standard of
accommodation, comfortable,
sound-proof rooms and a multi-
purpose room equipped for
conferences and meetings.

Meliá Olbia *⁑* & ★
Circonvallazione Nord direzione
Golfo Aranci, tel. 0789554000
www.solmelia.com
219 rooms. Restaurant, parking,
air conditioned, swimming pool,
tennis, gym
Credit Cards: American Express,
Diners Club, Visa, Mastercard
In a picturesque location, it has
rooms in the main block and
in the annex "Borgo Italiano" on
the hill. Facilities include a large
conference center with rooms
which can hold up to 800
people, a tennis center, Olympic
swimming pool, shops and
many free time courses.

Stefania *⁑*
Lido di Pittulongu, strada
Panoramica al km 4,8
tel. 078939027
www.stefaniahotel.it
38 rooms. Restaurant, parking,
air conditioned, swimming pool,
tennis
Credit cards: American Express,
Diners Club, Visa, Mastercard
Small hotel with typical Arabic-
Moorish style architecture.
Rooms and a couple of suites as
well as spacious reception
rooms. Lovely swimming pool
with a view of Tavolara island
and, 100 meters away, a beach
for hotel guests only.

Stella 2000 *** &
Viale Aldo Moro 70,
tel. 078951456
www.hotelstella2000.com
32 rooms. Restaurant, parking,
air conditioned
Credit cards: American Express,
Diners Club, Visa, Mastercard
Renovated building with
spacious, soundproof, air
conditioned rooms and finely
furnished reception rooms.
Restaurant for hotel guests
only, serving mainly fish
specialties.

Tavolara ***
Pittulongu, via Monte Ruiu 30,
tel. 0789398042
www.hoteltavolara.com
16 roooms. Parking,
air conditioned

Credit cards: American Express,
Visa, Mastercard
Country house surrounded
by a large garden of maquis:
provides a few rooms and
two suites, all furnished with
handmade wooden furniture in
rustic Sardinian style, some with
an independent entrance. Large
terrace with a great view of the
gulf of Olbia and the island of
Tavolara.

Rural Lodgings

Sa Crestja Ezza
Berchiddeddu-Sa Castanza,
tel. 078941771
Restaurant
Surrounded by Mediterranean
vegetation, a simple farm
providing accommodation in
small independent converted
sheep pens or in the farmhouse.
In the communal areas,
furnished in a rustic style, there
are farming tools and
implements. Terrace looks down
the hill.

Restaurants

Gallura ⅢⅢ
Corso Umberto 145,
tel. 078924648
Closed Monday
Cuisine: fish
Credit cards: American Express,
Diners Club, Visa
A well-kept and pretty
restaurant where the owner
and chef contributes with his
cooking to make your stay
pleasant: proof of the pudding
are the customers who come
from all over the world to try
fish delicacies and, in winter,
heartier country fare.

Gambero ⅰ
Via Lamarmora 6, tel. 078923874
Closed Monday
(except in summer)
Cuisine: fish
Credit cards: American Express,
Diners Club, Visa, Mastercard
Based on time-honored
tradition, a small restaurant with
a few tables arranged around
the fire which crackles
pleasantly in the winter.
Excellent fish and seafood.

Molara ⅱ ★
Circonvallazione Nord direzione
Golfo Aranci, tel. 0789554000
www.solmelia.com
Cuisine: Spanish and
Mediterranean
Credit cards: American Express,
Diners Club, Visa, Mastercard
Restaurant with elegant
interiors, serves sophisticated
dishes with unusual
combinations of ingredients
wedding Sardinian and Spanish
fragrances and flavors.

Nino's ⅢⅢ
Lido di Pittulongu, strada
Panoramica al km 4,8
tel. 078939027
www.stefaniahotel.it
Open March-October
Closed Wednesday (in low
season)
Cuisine: Sardinian
Credit cards: American Express,
Diners Club, Visa, Mastercard
Sea view with terrace and
garden for summer evenings;
Moorish style ambience similar
to the hotel which houses it.
Cuisine draws on the best of
local traditions, mainly fish.

At night

Capricorno Club
Via Catello Piro 2, tel. 078924700
Friendly, youthful and fun venue,
one of the most fashionable in
Olbia. Music varies depending
on the evening.

Garage
Via Barbagia, tel. 078921033
Youthful and informal night club
which holds themed evenings
and original happenings such as
body painting, graffiti and wall
painting

OLIENA
Hotels

Su Gologone *⁑*
Su Gologone, tel. 0784287512
www.sugologone.it
Open mid March-October
and Christmas period
65 rooms. Restaurant, parking,
air conditioned, swimming pool,
tennis, gym
Credit cards: American Express,
Diners Club, Visa, Mastercard
Charming building in a peaceful
location. Has a fitness center
and gives guests the
opportunity to consult books,
papers and maps of Sardinia.
Guests sleep in comfortable
rooms, embellished with
Sardinian handcrafted
furnishings.

Rural Lodgings

Camisadu
Logheri, tel. 3683479502
Restaurant
Accommodation in a modern
structure in a valley lush with
broom, myrtle, cork and holm
oaks. The farm has a small
ethnographic museum and
offers guided tours.

Guthiddai
Guthiddai, tel. 0784286017
www.agriturismoguthiddai.com
Open March-October
Restaurant
In a splendid valley of vineyards

⁑⁑⁑ ⁑⁑⁑ *⁑* *** ** * Hotels ⅢⅢⅢ ⅢⅢ ⅢⅢ ⅱ ⅰ Restaurants & Disabled ★ Special TCI Rates

and olive groves, near the springs of Su Gologone.
The sea is 15 km away, but the farm is, above all, an ideal base for exploring nature.

Restaurants

Cikappa ⁙
Via Martin Luther King 2/4, tel. 0784288024
www.cikappa.com
Cuisine: Sardinian
Credit cards: American Express, Diners Club, Visa, Mastercard
Pretty restaurant which serves traditional regional cuisine using basic ingredients with strong flavors. Homemade pasta, good choice of local cheeses. Pizzas too.

Su Gologone ⁙
Su Gologone, tel. 0784287512
www.sugologone.it
Open mid March-October and the Christmas period
Cuisine: Barbagia
Credit cards: American Express, Diners Club, Visa, Mastercard
In one of the most picturesque parts of the island, a typical restaurant which serves food cooked with meat and vegetables, faithful to the Sardinian gastronomic tradition.

ORISTANO

[i] **Assessorato al Turismo**
tel. 0783791312,
www.comune.oristano.it
[i] **Pro Loco**
Via Vittorio Emanuele 8,
tel. 078370621

Hotels

I.S.A. ★★★
Piazza Marino 50,
tel. 0783360101
49 rooms. Restaurant, air conditioned
Credit cards: American Express, Diners Club, Visa, Mastercard
In the city center, a hotel with efficient facilities and large rooms with marble floors and period furnishings; able to cater for both tourists and businessmen.

Mistral ★★★
Via Martiri di Belfiore, tel. 0783212505
48 rooms. Restaurant, parking, air conditioned
Credit cards: American Express, Diners Club, Visa, Mastercard
Comfortable and modern, soberly elegant. Provides large, bright rooms, conference rooms or rooms for small business meetings; sweet buffet breakfast.

Mistral 2 ★★★
Via XX Settembre, tel. 0783210389
www.shg.it/mistral2/
132 rooms. Restaurant, parking, air conditioned, swimming pool
Credit cards: American Express, Diners Club, Visa, Mastercard
Modern, functional and quiet hotel providing multi-purpose rooms for conferences and meetings; terrace for sitting outdoors, small ornamental garden, busy restaurant.

Rural Lodgings

Il Giglio
Massama, tel. 3491447955, www.agriturismoilgiglio.com
Restaurant
In the valley of Tirso, a small farming hamlet guarantees peaceful stays a short distance from archeological sites and the sea. The farm boasts a great deal of experience in growing and processing cereals and corn and in breeding livestock. Accommodation is in a renovated private house. Cooking lessons, walks and activities for schoolchildren.

Restaurants

Antica Trattoria del Teatro ⁙
Via Parpaglia 11, tel. 078371672
Closed Wednesday and Sunday (except the summer)
Cuisine: Sardinian and revisited
Credit cards: American Express, Diners Club, Visa, Mastercard
Small and cozy, reservations are recommended. Dishes are carefully prepared to regional and international recipes with the chef and owner's inventive flair. Fish, homemade pasta; excellent choice of good quality oils, trolley with 40 kinds of Sardinian cheeses.

Da Gino ⁙
Via Tirso 13, tel. 078371428
Closed Sunday
Cuisine: Sardinian
Credit cards: Visa, Mastercard
In the old town center, a friendly trattoria serving mainly fish: there is always fresh fish and seafood on the menu; the renowned lobster "à la Gino" is the restaurant's pièce de résistance.

Faro ⁙⁙
Via Bellini 25, tel. 078370002
www.ristoranteilfaro.net
Closed Sunday
Cuisine: Sardinian
Credit cards: American Express, Diners Club, Visa, Mastercard
Inviting restaurant where you can sample the flavors and thrills of time-honored Sardinian recipes;

in season entire menus are variations on the theme of snails and cèpe mushrooms. Extensive wine list and good selection of Sardinian oils and cheeses.

Museums

Antiquarium Arborense - Museo Archeologico «G. Pau»
Piazzetta Corrias,
tel. 0783791262
Opening times: Monday-Sunday 9.00-14.00, 15.00-20.00.

OROSEI

[i] **Pro Loco**
Piazza del Popolo 12,
tel. 0784998367
www.proloco-orosei.com

Hotels

Cala Ginepro ★★★
Cala Ginepro, viale Cala Ginepro 76, tel. 078491047
www.hotelcalaginepro.com
136 rooms. Restaurant, air conditioned, swimming pool, tennis
Credit cards: American Express, Diners Club, Visa
Renovated, in a strategic position in the center of one of the most beautiful bays in the gulf of Orosei. The entire complex, divided into two blocks, provides quiet and refined accommodation.

Club Hotel Torre Moresca ★★★
Cala Ginepro, tel. 078491230, www.itihotels.it
Open May-September
210 rooms. Restaurant, parking, air conditioned, swimming pool, tennis, gym
Credit cards: American Express, Diners Club, Visa, Mastercard
Between the sea and a pinewood, a recently built structure on different levels, with a small central piazza for evening entertainment; a fitness center and internet point were added not long ago.

I Giardini di Cala Ginepro ★★★
Cala Ginepro, viale Cala Ginepro 97, tel. 078491160
www.hotelgiardinicalaginepro.com
Open April-October
171 rooms. Restaurant, parking, air conditioned, swimming pool, sauna, tennis, gym
Credit cards: American Express, Diners Club, Visa
In the splendid gulf of Orosei, on the edges of a dense pinewood. This elegant and comfortable hotel is made up of two elongated blocks with well-appointed rooms and a restaurant for hotel guests only.

If you want to get back into shape there is a nature trail, swimming pool with hydromassage jets, sauna and Turkish bath.

Maria Rosaria *‡* ★
Via G. Deledda 13, tel.
078498657, www.itihotels.it
64 rooms. Restaurant, parking, air conditioned, swimming pool
Credit cards: American Express, Diners Club, Visa, Mastercard
Traditional hospitality in a comfortable and modern, family run hotel; shuttle service to the beach at a small charge.

Su Barchile ★★★
Via Mannu 5, tel. 078498879,
www.subarchile.it
10 rooms. Restaurant, parking, air conditioned
Credit cards: American Express, Diners Club, Visa, Mastercard
In the old town center, a simple hotel with comfortable rooms and rustic furnishings; traditional cuisine is served in a country-style dining room and at tables outdoors in the summer; you may hire bicycles and take boat trips around the gulf.

Restaurants

Su Barchile ｜｜｜
Via Mannu 5, tel. 078498879
www.subarchile.it
Cuisine: Sardinian and fish
Credit cards: American Express, Diners Club, Visa, Mastercard
In the heart of the town, this restaurant is a genuine example of Sardinian tradition, from the dining room to the kitchen. Meat and fresh fish purchased from the same fisherman for thirty years.

Museums

Museo "Giovanni Guiso"
Via Musio, tel. 0784997084-
0784998367
Opening times: June-September: Tuesday-Sunday 9.30-12.30, 17-22. October-May: Saturday-Sunday 9.30-12.30, 17-22.

PALAU

🛈 **Ufficio per il Turismo**
Piazza Popoli d'Europa 1,
tel. 0789770813
www.palau.it

Hotels

Capo d'Orso *‡* ★
Cala Capra, tel. 0789702000
www.delphina.it
Open mid May-September
75 rooms. Restaurant, air conditioned, swimming pool, tennis

Credit cards: American Express, Visa, Mastercard
A beautifully kept hotel, consisting of a group of small stone buildings set deep in the heart of a peaceful, centuries-old olive grove, overlooking the sea.

La Roccia ★★★
Via dei Mille 15, tel. 0789709528
www.hotellaroccia.com
22 rooms. Parking, air conditioned
Credit cards: American Express, Diners Club, Visa, Mastercard
About a hundred meters from the harbor, a classic Bed and Breakfast, whose name derives from the mass of granite which towers over the garden and takes up part of the entrance hall; large communal spaces, modern furnishings and buffet breakfast.

Palau Hotel *‡* ★
Via Baragge, tel. 0789708468
www.palauhotel.it
Open April-October
95 rooms. Restaurant, parking, air conditioned, swimming pool
Credit cards: American Express, Visa, Mastercard
Modern building located in the high part of Palau with a view of the islands which make up the Maddalena archipelago; well-appointed rooms and comfortable suites, almost every one with a sea view; well-equipped conference center, piano bar and disco, patio, terrace for sunbathing and garden with garden furniture.

Piccada ★★★ ♿
Via degli Asfodeli 6,
tel. 0789709344
www.hotelpiccada.com
61 rooms. Parking, air conditioned, sauna, gym
Credit cards: American Express, Diners Club, Visa, Mastercard
Above the small tourist harbor, a seventies building which has been entirely renovated and furnished with locally handcrafted furniture; comfortable rooms, most of which have independent entrances and terraces for sunbathing. Buffet breakfast; connected to the restaurant "Zio Nicola" under a different management.

Restaurants

Da Franco ｜｜｜｜
Via Capo d'Orso 1,
tel. 0789709558
www.ristorantedafranco.it
Closed Monday (in low season)
Cuisine: Sardinian
Credit cards: American Express, Diners Club, Visa, Mastercard

For many years this has been an elegant landmark for fish cuisine; a fine cellar and excellent choice of extra virgin olive oils.

Gritta ｜｜｜ ★
Porto Faro, tel. 0789708045
Open mid March-mid October
Closed Wednesday (except in summer)
Cuisine: Sardinian and classic
Credit cards: American Express, Diners Club, Visa, Mastercard
A splendid view of the islands of Maddalena and Caprera can be enjoyed from this pretty restaurant. Dishes are prepared according to tradition using local ingredients: excellent list of liqueurs.

Sotto le Stelle ｜｜ ★
Via Capo d'Orso 90,
tel. 0789709619
Cuisine: Sardinian and classic
Credit cards: American Express, Diners Club, Visa, Mastercard
Near the tourist harbor, a simple restaurant with a veranda where you can dine until midnight. Serves fish and other dishes but also good pizzas, accompanied by a selection of mainly local wines. Piano bar or background music.

PORTO CERVO

Hotels

Balocco *‡* ★
Liscia di Vacca, tel. 078991555
www.hotelbalocco.it
Open April-October
40 rooms. Parking, air conditioned, swimming pool
Credit cards: American Express, Diners Club, Visa, Mastercard
Elegant and romantic Mediterranean style building with a view of the harbor; suites and rooms with all mod cons and period furnishings, cheerful and cozy communal areas; buffet breakfast.

Cala di Volpe ‡‡‡
Cala di Volpe, tel. 0789976111
www.luxurycollection.com/caladi volpe
Open April-October
125 rooms. Restaurant, parking, air conditioned, swimming pool, sauna, tennis, gym
Credit cards: American Express, Diners Club, Visa, Mastercard
Large complex which resembles an ancient island village. Elegant environment in rustic Sardinian style with wi-fi Internet access; extremely spacious rooms and suites; one of the most exclusive hotels on the Costa Smeralda.

Capriccioli ★★★ ♿
Capriccioli, tel. 078996004
www.hotelcapriccioli.it
Open April-September
46 rooms. Restaurant, parking, air conditioned, swimming pool, tennis
Credit cards: American Express, Visa, Mastercard
Low building that fits beautifully into the surrounding nature with a seawater swimming pool and small play park in a well-tended garden; its forte is the restaurant "Il Pirata" which overlooks the beach.

Cervo Hotel Costa Smeralda Resort ★★★
tel. 0789931111
www.sheraton.com/cervo
108 rooms. Restaurant, air conditioned, swimming pool, sauna, tennis, gym
Credit cards: American Express, Diners Club, Visa, Mastercard
Elegant and refined complex, which caters for both the demanding tourist and the businessman. The low buildings are arranged around a patio and have beautifully kept rooms and excellent sports and conference facilities.

ITI Relais Colonna
Porto Cervo ★★★ ★
Porto Cervo, tel. 078992627
www.itihotels.it
Open April-September
20 rooms. Restaurant, air conditioned, swimming pool
In the heart of the town, a small villa built in the typical architectural style of the Costa Smeralda. The interiors are bright and attention has been paid to every detail, rooms and communal areas are furnished simply and elegantly.

Le Ginestre ★★★
tel. 078992030,
www.leginestrehotel.com
Open April-October
80 rooms. Restaurant, parking, air conditioned, swimming pool, tennis
Credit cards: American Express, Diners Club, Visa
Deep in the heart of a nature reserve, this complex consists of low buildings which fit beautifully into the environment and are connected to the beach by a footpath. A modern multi-purpose conference room and restaurant serving Sardinian and international cuisine (in a dining room separate from the hotel, which has a terrace with a great view) complement the whole.

Luci di la Muntagna ★★★
Via Sa Conca, tel. 078992051

www.altamarea.it
Open mid April-October
65 rooms. Restaurant, air conditioned, swimming pool
Credit cards: American Express, Diners Club, Visa
Overlooking the sea with architecture reminiscent of the Moorish style; well-appointed rooms.

Nibaru ★★★
Cala di Volpe, tel. 078996038
www.hotelnibaru.it
Open mid April-mid October
45 rooms. Parking, air conditioned, swimming pool
Credit cards: American Express, Diners Club, Visa, Mastercard
Mediterranean style structure with large arches leading to the freshwater swimming pool. Comfortable rooms and a kids' club; buffet breakfast. Close to Pevero Golf Club.

Pitrizza ★★★
Liscia di Vacca, tel. 0789930111
www.luxurycollection.com/hotelpitrizza
Open May-September
55 rooms. Restaurant, parking, air conditioned, swimming pool, sauna, gym
Credit cards: American Express, Diners Club, Visa, Mastercard
On the bay of Liscia di Vacca, a structure consisting of traditionally built villas, hidden between the maquis and the rocks. Large rooms with terraces and typical Sardinian furnishings; swimming pool dug into the rock with the beach a short distance away.

Romazzino ★★★
Romazzino, tel. 0789977111
www.luxurycollection.com/romazzino
Open April-October
94 rooms. Restaurant, parking, air conditioned, swimming pool, tennis, gym
Credit cards: American Express, Diners Club, Visa, Mastercard
Exclusive, traditional island construction in the setting of a garden which slopes to the beach; excellent standard of rooms, sports and leisure facilities

Selis ★★★ ★
Azzacultedda, tel. 078998630
www.selishotel.com
18 rooms. Restaurant, parking, air conditioned, swimming pool
Credit cards: American Express, Visa, Mastercard
Its lovely location distinguishes this rustic, inviting and comfortable hotel with well-appointed rooms; restaurant

"Gambero Rosso" serves regional cuisine, well-tended garden for lazing in.

Valdiola ★★★ ★
Cala di Volpe, tel. 078996215
www.wel.it
Open March-October
33 rooms. Restaurant, parking, air conditioned, swimming pool
Credit cards: American Express, Diners Club, Visa, Mastercard
Built in Mediterranean style with a garden, near a golf course and tennis courts. Rooms with balconies; reception rooms which have a cozy feel, due to their bamboo furnishings and handcrafted Sardinian embroidery; restaurant with fireplace and country-style furnishings.

Restaurants

Gianni Pedrinelli ₸₸₸ ♿
At the turning for Pevero, tel. 078992436
www.giannipedrinelli.it
Open March-October (from June to September, evenings only)
Cuisine: Sardinian and classic
Credit cards: American Express, Diners Club, Visa, Mastercard
Romantic location with a garden. Serves a classic repertoire of local recipes: fish and seafood are in very much in evidence but you will also find porcetto cooked on the spit; a variety of good cheeses from Sardinia and other parts of Italy, judicious choice of wines and oils.

Grill ₸₸₸
Piazzetta Cervo, tel. 0789931111
www.sheraton.com/cervo
Open March-November
Cuisine: Mediterranean
Credit cards: American Express, Diners Club, Visa, Mastercard
An international flavor; mainly fish cuisine; you may dine until late at night. Good choice of wines, oils, cheeses and cold meats.

Spinnaker ₸₸₸ ♿
Liscia di Vacca, tel. 078991226
Open April-September
Closed Wednesdays in May
Cuisine: Emilian and classic
Credit cards: American Express, Diners Club, Visa, Mastercard
The name already gives you an idea of the nautical theme which continues through to the kitchen where you will also see signs of the Emilian influence combining fresh homemade pasta with vegetables and meat.

At night

Aqua
Porto Cervo, Marina Nuova
Brand new venue located on the

first floor of the Yacht Club Costa Smeralda. As well as a bar and restaurant there is also a disco and disco pub.

Billionaire
Porto Cervo, Golfo Pevero, tel. 078994192
www.billionaireclub.it
In an ancient villa; one of the most exclusive clubs in Europe. On the terrace you may try international cuisine while downstairs you may dance in one of the most beautiful discos on the island.

Blues Cafè
Liscia di Vacca, Baja Ruja, Porto Cervo, tel. 078991682
Only open in the summer and occasionally in the spring, this place is ideal for those who love nightlife and having fun. Interiors are in tune with the philosophy of the place; excellent cocktails.

Caffè du Port
Porto Vecchio, tel. 078992348
One of the most characteristic cafés in Porto Cervo, wonderful choice of cocktails and excellent breakfasts in the morning.

Pepero Club
Piccolo Pevero, tel. 078994434
Historic and extremely fashionable, elegant and luxurious venue. Only open in the summer, it holds themed parties and live music evenings and caters for private dinners.

Sottovento Club
Condominio Sottovento, Porto Cervo, tel. 078992443
www.sottoventoclub.com
Exclusive club with a disco and restaurant; popular with a select clientele. Excellent ambience and music.

PORTO CONTE
Hotels

Baia di Conte ★☆★
Via Imbenia, tel. 079949000
Open June-September
290 rooms. Restaurant, parking, air conditioned, swimming pool, sauna, tennis, gym
Credit cards: American Express, Diners Club, Visa, Mastercard
Modern and well-appointed hotel with leisure and sports facilities; organization is reminiscent of a holiday resort.

El Faro ★☆★ &
tel. 079942010
www.elfarohotel.it
Open mid April-mid October
92 rooms. Restaurant, parking, air conditioned, swimming pool, sauna, tennis
Credit cards: American Express,

Diners Club, Visa, Mastercard
Large hotel which fits beautifully into the surrounding nature; a variety of rooms, a cozy and inviting restaurant with terraces overlooking the headland, well-appointed conference rooms and wellness center. There are also recreational activities for keeping fit, leisure and fun.

Porto Conte ★★★ ★
tel. 079942036
www.hotelportoconte.com
Open mid April-mid October
144 rooms. Restaurant, parking, air conditioned, swimming pool, tennis
Credit cards: American Express, Diners Club, Visa, Mastercard
Situated between the pinewood and the sea; kids' club, private beach and jetty; well-appointed suites; restaurant serves fish and farm produce cooked to Italian and Sardinian recipes.

PORTO ROTONDO
Hotels

Domina Palumbalza Sporting ★★★ &
In the gulf of Marinella, tel. 078932005
www.dominapalumbalza.it
Open May-mid October
81 rooms. Restaurant, parking, air conditioned, swimming pool, tennis, gym
Credit cards: American Express, Diners Club, Visa, Mastercard
Located in an enchanting natural inlet with a small private harbor in a large, privately owned park. Rooms are well-appointed with independent entrances and balconies and terraces which overlook the sea or a garden; facilities for small conferences and internet access.

ITI Colonna San Marco ★★★ ★
Piazza S. Marco, tel. 078934110
www.itihotels.it
Open April-September
34 rooms. Restaurant, air conditioned, swimming pool
Credit cards: American Express, Diners Club, Visa, Mastercard
Mediterranean style building with elegant and well-furnished interiors. Provides accommodation in large, bright rooms and two comfortable suites; buffet breakfast and restaurant serves classic cuisine.

Sporting ★★★
Via Clelia Donà dalle Rose 16, tel. 078934005
www.sportingportorotondo.it
Open May-October
27 rooms. Restaurant, parking, air conditioned, swimming pool

Credit cards: American Express, Diners Club, Visa, Mastercard
In an enchanting bay, an elegant complex surrounded by nature and made special by its traditional Mediterranean architecture. Air conditioned rooms with private terraces and beach access. To complement the whole there is a restaurant renowned for its regional cooking, a piano bar and the opportunity to do water sports.

Restaurants
Da Giovannino ⋔⋔⋔
Piazza Quadrata, tel. 078935280
Open February-October
Closed Sunday evening and Monday (in winter)
Cuisine: Sardinian
Credit cards: American Express, Diners Club, Visa, Mastercard
On one of the most exclusive stretches of the coast, an extremely popular and renowned address with an elegant and inviting feel and a lovely garden. The menu mainly consists of impressively presented and flavorsome fish dishes; excellent cellar; some accommodation available.

Palumbalza ⋔⋔
Sul golfo di Marinella, tel. 078932005
www.dominapalumbalza.it
Open May-mid October
Cuisine: Sardinian and classic
Credit cards: American Express, Diners Club, Visa
In a splendid location with a covered terrace overlooking the small private harbor and the sea; serves fish and farm produce; also offers a "light" menu.

At night
Country Club
Villaggio Rugiada, tel. 078934294
Picturesque structure built into the rocks with restaurant, piano bar and disco. Soft atmosphere.

Rha
Via della Cava del Tom
Cheerful and very young ambience; extremely crowded in summer, excellent cocktails. Mainly open in summer.

PORTOSCUSO

☑ **Ufficio Informazioni**
Via G. Galilei 1, tel. 0781510015

Hotels
La Ghinghetta ★★★
Via Cavour 28, tel. 0781508143
Open April-October
8 rooms. Restaurant, parking, air conditioned

Credit cards: American Express,
Diners Club, Visa

Small and elegant hotel, built
in a Mediterranean style in an
enchanting setting.
Provides rooms with sea views;
run by the same family for over
thirty years.

Panorama ★★★ ★
Via G. Cesare 40, tel. 0781508077
www.panoramahotel.ca
36 rooms. Air conditioned
Credit cards: American Express,
Diners Club, Visa, Mastercard
Bed and Breakfast with very
pleasant reception rooms and
simple rooms which enjoy a
lovely view of the small
pleasure boat harbor; buffet
breakfast; facilities for small
conferences.

Restaurants
La Ghinghetta Ⅲ
Via Cavour 26, tel. 0781508143
Open April-October, evenings only
Closed Sunday
Cuisine: experimental Sardinian
Credit cards: American Express,
Diners Club, Visa, Mastercard
In a small seaside village, a little,
romantic inn which has only
seven tables. Beautifully cooked
and presented fish dishes.
Judicious choice of wines and
small selection of Sardinian oils.

PORTO TORRES

> ☑ **Pro Loco Associazione**
> **Turistica**
> *Piazza Garibaldi 15,*
> *tel. 079515000*

Hotels
Libyssonis ★★★ ♿
Serra dei Pozzi, tel. 079501613
36 rooms. Restaurant, parking,
air conditioned, swimming pool
Credit cards: American Express,
Diners Club, Visa, Mastercard
Well-appointed hotel a little
way out of the center; buffet
breakfast; Sardinian and classic
cuisine. Work in progress will
eventually provide a fitness
center and covered swimming
pool.

Torres ★★★
Via Sassari 75, tel. 079501604
70 rooms. Restaurant, parking,
air conditioned
Credit cards: American Express,
Diners Club, Visa, Mastercard
In the center, a large, well-run
hotel; rooms with balconies and
country-style furnishings, art-
nouveau restaurant serving
Sardinian cuisine and cuisine
from other regions of Italy.

Restaurants
Li Lioni ⅡⅠ
Li Lioni, SS 131, tel. 079502286
www.lilioni.it
Closed Wednesday
(Monday midday and
Wednesday in August)
Cuisine: Sardinian
Credit cards: American Express,
Diners Club, Visa, Mastercard
Country-style restaurant which
also caters for coeliac sufferers;
in summer you can dine out
on the large veranda which
overlooks the garden.

Museums
Antiquarium Turritano
Via Ponte Romano 92,
tel. 079514433
Opening times: Tuesday-Sunday
9.00-20.00.

PULA

> ☑ **Pro Loco**
> *Piazza del Popolo,*
> *tel. 0709245250*

Hotels
Abamar ★★★
Santa Margherita, viale Zeus,
tel. 070921555
www.abamarhotel.it
Open mid May-September
82 rooms. Restaurant, parking,
air conditioned, swimming pool,
tennis
Credit cards: Diners Club, Visa,
Mastercard
In a lovely location, equipped
for small conferences and
meetings as well as for families
with children and seaside
holidays in general; beautiful
garden.

Baia di Nora ★★★ ♿
Su Guventeddu, SS 195,
tel. 0709245551
www.hotelbaiadinora.com
Open April-October
121 rooms. Restaurant, parking,
air conditioned, swimming pool,
tennis, gym
Credit cards: American Express,
Diners Club, Visa, Mastercard
Seafront hotel consisting of low
buildings overlooking a square
with a garden. Provides a wide
range of facilities for sports and
conferences; spacious rooms
have balconies or space to sit
outside.
Restaurant close to the beach.

Castello ★★★
Santa Margherita, SS 195,
km 39,6, tel. 070921516
www.fortevillageresort.com
Open Easter-October
181 rooms. Restaurant, parking,

air conditioned, swimming pool,
sauna, tennis, gym
Credit cards: American Express,
Diners Club, Visa, Mastercard
Surrounded by pine trees,
in a quiet corner of Fort Village
Resort, a comfortable hotel with
well-appointed, air conditioned
rooms, junior suites and suites;
sports equipment is available,
beauty center, wellness center
and spa treatments. Restaurant
"Cavalieri".

Costa dei Fiori Hotel ★★★
Santa Margherita, SS 195,
km 33, tel. 0709245333
www.costadeifiori.it
Open April-mid October
86 rooms. Restaurant, air
conditioned, swimming pool,
sauna, tennis
Credit cards: American Express,
Diners Club, Visa, Mastercard
In a park, hotel built around
a large central swimming pool;
rooms furnished with handmade
Sardinian style furniture,
refurbished restaurant "Piazza
Gabriele" for hotel guests only.

Flamingo ★★★
Santa Margherita, SS 195,
km 33,8, tel. 0709208361
www.hotelflamingo.it
Open mid April-mid October
188 rooms. Restaurant, parking,
air conditioned, swimming pool,
tennis
Credit cards: American Express
Large Mediterranean style hotel
with a beach, ideal for family
holidays. Spacious rooms and
a restaurant with tables which
spill out onto the patio around
the swimming pool.

Is Molas Golf Hotel ★★★
Is Mòlas, tel. 0709241006
www.ismolas.it
84 rooms. Restaurant, parking,
air conditioned, swimming pool,
tennis
Credit cards: American Express,
Diners Club, Visa, Mastercard
Elegant hotel with facilities for
recreation and leisure.
Comfortable, renovated rooms;
busy restaurant "Le Mole" and
shuttle service to the beach.
Sports facilities and splendid 27
hole golf course.

Is Morus Relais ★★★
Santa Margherita, SS 195,
km 37,4, tel. 070921171
www.ismorus.it
Open Easter- mid October
85 rooms. Restaurant, parking,
air conditioned, swimming pool,
tennis
Credit cards: American Express,
Diners Club, Visa, Mastercard
Pleasant structure with well-
appointed rooms and suites,

divided into a central block and small villas of various typologies in a pinewood which slopes down to the beach.

Lantana Hotel & Residence *⁑* ♿ ★
Viale Nora, tel. 070924411
www.lantanahotel.com
Open May-October
45 rooms. Restaurant, parking, air conditioned, swimming pool
Credit cards: American Express, Visa, Mastercard
Accommodation in a park in two and three room apartments and in rooms with patios on the ground floor and terraces with garden furniture on the first floor; shuttle service to Nora beach. New Mediterranean style à la carte restaurant serves Sardinian and international specialties.
Only open in the evenings between June and September.

Mare e Pineta ★★★
Santa Margherita, SS 195, km 33,8, tel. 0709208361
Open May-mid October
60 rooms. Restaurant, parking, air conditioned, swimming pool, tennis
Credit cards: American Express
A cool pinewood is the setting for this hotel, composed of small buildings arranged in a semicircle around a central block. Rooms are of average size, with bamboo or country-style furnishings. Pleasant communal areas, some overlooking the pinewood.

Nora Club *⁑* ♿
Nora, viale Nora, tel. 070924422
www.noraclubhotel.it
25 rooms. Parking, air conditioned, swimming pool,
Credit cards: American Express, Diners Club, Visa, Mastercard
The small stone buildings of this hotel make it almost a small Mediterranean village, set deep in the heart of a large garden. The sea is about 800 meters away, but guests may borrow bicycles to get to the beach; buffet breakfast.

Villa del Parco *⁂*
Santa Margherita, SS 195, km 39,6, tel. 070921516
www.fortevillageresort.com
Open Easter-October
47 rooms. Restaurant, parking, air conditioned, swimming pool, sauna, tennis, gym
Credit cards: American Express, Diners Club, Visa, Mastercard
Surrounded by nature, a well-maintained and exclusive structure in the grounds of the Forte Village Resort. Extremely

comfortable rooms and communal areas with a pleasant ambience. Guests may use a wellness and beauty center as well as sports and leisure facilities. Restaurant "Belvedere" with great views and elegant à la carte menu.

Restaurants

Murales ⑪ ♿
Via Caprera 6, tel. 0709246029
Closed Tuesday except in summer
Cuisine: Sardinian
Credit cards: American Express, Diners Club, Visa, Mastercard
A small entrance hall leads into an inner courtyard, with palm trees and flowerbeds, before reaching the large dining room and veranda, which can be uncovered. Traditional food, grilled meat and fish.

Su Gunventeddu ⑪ ★
Nora, tel. 0709209092
www.sugunventeddu.com
Closed Tuesday
Cuisine: Sardinian and classic
Credit cards: American Express, Diners Club, Visa, Mastercard
Pleasant atmosphere, with a terrace and garden for dining outside in summer, where the quality of the food, principally fish from the day's catch, is always excellent. Good list of local wines.

QUARTU SANT'ELENA

> 🄳 *Centro Informazioni Turistiche*
> *Via Melibodes, tel. 070835177*

Hotels

Califfo *⁑* ♿
Via Leonardo da Vinci 118, tel. 070890131
www.hotelcaliffo.com
130 rooms. Restaurant, air conditioned, swimming pool, tennis
Credit cards: American Express, Diners Club, Visa, Mastercard
In a picturesque location at the end of Poetto beach, this hotel provides accommodation in comfortable rooms. Well-equipped conference center with rooms that can hold up to 400 people, large restaurant also open to non hotel guests.

Italia ★★★ ♿ ★
Via Panzini on the corner of viale Colombo, tel. 070827070
www.bestwestern.it/italia-ca
83 rooms. Parking, air conditioned

Credit cards: American Express, Diners Club, Visa
Comfortable rooms and small, functional self-catering apartments make this modern hotel a landmark for both business guests and holiday-makers: restaurant service by request only.

Setar *⁑* ♿
S'Oru de Mari, via Leonardo da Vinci 1, tel. 07086021
www.hotelsetar.it
152 rooms. Restaurant, air conditioned, swimming pool, tennis, gym
Credit cards: American Express, Diners Club, Visa
Efficiently run hotel with well-appointed rooms, gym and beauty center; restaurant "Sa Pingiada" with terrace overlooking a swimming pool and "Kontiki" with pizzas and barbecue.

Restaurants

Hibiscus ⑪ ★
Via Dante 81, tel. 070881373
www.antoniofigus.it
Open evenings only
Closed Sunday
Cuisine: experimental Sardinian
Credit cards: American Express, Diners Club, Visa, Mastercard
In a lovely private house, with a garden for dining outside in the summer, an inviting and tastefully decorated restaurant. Serves fish and farm produce cooked to clever and inventive recipes; beautifully prepared and presented food.

Su Meriàgu ⑪ ♿
Sant'Andrea, via L. da Vinci 140, tel. 070890842
www.sardegnasud.it
Closed Tuesday (in winter)
Cuisine: Sardinian
Credit cards: American Express, Visa, Mastercard
Roast *porcetto* and fish from the gulf as well as homemade pastries and sweets in this restaurant close to the sea with tables on the patio; you can also eat pizza in the small square outside.

At night

F.B.I.
Via Brigata Sassari 68, tel. 070885678
Disco and pub, live music evenings and cabaret, as well as dance music.

Museums

Museo Etnografico «Il Ciclo della Vita»
Via Eligio Porcu 271, tel. 070812462

⁑⁑⁑ ⁂ *⁑* ★★★ ★★ ★ Hotels ⑪⑪⑪⑪⑪ ⑪⑪⑪⑪ ⑪⑪⑪ ⑪ ⑰ Restaurants ♿ Disabled ★ Special TCI Rates

*Opening times: May-October:
Monday-Sunday 9.00-13.00, 17.00-22.30. November-April: Monday-Sunday 9.00-13.00, 16.00-20.00.Visits by arrangement.*

SANLURI

ⓘ **Pro Loco**
*Via Mazzini 74,
tel. 0709370505
www.prolocosanluri.it*

Museums

Castello di Sanluri
*Via Generale Nino Villa Santa 1,
tel. 0709307184
www.sabattalla.it*

Opening times: 1st July-20th September: Sunday 9.30-13.00, 16.30-21.00; Monday, Wednesday and Friday 16.30-21.00. 21st September-30th June: Sunday and holidays 9.45-13.00, 16.00-19.30. Also group visits by arrangement.

SANTA GIUSTA

Restaurants

Abarossa ⌁
*Via Giovanni XXIII 4,
tel. 0783357189
Closed Wednesday*

Cuisine: Sardinian and classic

Credit cards: American Express, Diners Club, Visa, Mastercard

Two large, modernly furnished dining rooms with a chaste ambience; regional cuisine ranging from fish to meat.

SANTA MARIA NAVARRESE

Hotels

Agugliastra ★★★ ♿
*Piazza Principessa di Navarra 27, tel. 0782615005
www.hotelagugliastra.it*

19 rooms. Restaurant, air conditioned

Credit cards: American Express, Diners Club, Visa, Mastercard

In the old town center, a small building with well-appointed rooms and cozy communal areas; busy restaurant serves traditional Sardinian and classic dishes.

Mediterraneo ★★ ♿
*Via Lungomare, tel. 0782615380
www.albergomediterraneo.it
Open April-October*

32 rooms. Restaurant, parking, air conditioned

Credit cards: Visa, Mastercard

With direct beach access, this is a landmark for nature-lovers. Accommodation in comfortable

rooms; restaurant serving typical dishes and fish specialties; lovely inner garden with a beautiful view.

Santa Maria ★★★
*Via Plammas 30, tel. 0782615315
www.albergosantamaria.it
Open April-October*

35 rooms. Restaurant, parking, air conditioned

Credit cards: American Express, Visa, Mastercard

Centrally located, proven family management, with great facilities such as internet access. Popular with families who have children, an ideal solution for holidays combining the sea and the hills and as a base for excursions: also has a boat for trips around the gulf of Orosei and a minibus for walks in the mountains or in the interior.

SANT'ANTÌOCO

ⓘ **Pro Loco**
*Piazza Repubblica 41,
tel. 078182031*

Hotels

L'Eden ★★★ ♿
*Piazza Parrocchia 15,
tel. 0781840768
www.albergoleden.com*

26 rooms. Restaurant, parking, air conditioned

Credit cards: American Express, Diners Club, Visa, Mastercard

Centrally-located, this hotel contains some interesting catacombs dating from the 5th-6th century B.C. Also has modernly furnished rooms, quiet tearoom, cozy, country-style restaurant and two conference rooms also suitable for banquets.

Moderno ★★
*Via Nazionale 82, tel. 078183105
web.tiscali.it/albergomoderno*

10 rooms. Restaurant

Credit cards: American Express, Diners Club, Visa, Mastercard

Small hotel built on simple lines; nice restaurant where you can dine outside in a pleasant terrace-garden. Rooms with terracotta floors, built-in wardrobes.

Museums

Mostra Archeologica di Sant'Antioco
*Via Regina Margherita 113,
tel. 078183590-0781841089
www.archeotur.it*

Opening times: Summer: Monday-Saturday 9.00-19.00; Sunday 9.00-13.00, 15.30-

19.00.Winter: Monday-Sunday 9.00-13.00, 15.30-18.00. Closed 1st January, Easter, 8th and 25th-26th December.

Museo Etnografico
*Via Necropoli 24/d,
tel. 0781841089
www.archeotur.it*

Opening times: April-September: Monday-Saturday 9.00-20.00; Sunday 9.00-13.00, 15.30-20.00. October-March: Monday-Sunday 9.30-13.00, 15.00-18.00. Closed 1st January, Easter, 8th, 25th-26th December.

SANTA TERESA DI GALLURA

ⓘ **Pro Loco**
tel. 0789754127

Hotels

Da Cecco ★★★
*Via Po 3, tel. 0789754220
www.hoteldacecco.com
Open mid March-mid November*

32 rooms. Parking, air conditioned

One of the first hotels in the city, located a short distance from the sea; provides accommodation in refurbished rooms, each of which has a balcony or terrace. Buffet breakfast.

G.H. Corallaro ★⁑ ♿
*Rena Bianca, tel. 0789755475
www.hotelcorallaro.it
Open mid April-October*

81 rooms. Restaurant, parking, air conditioned, swimming pool, sauna, gym

Credit cards: American Express, Diners Club, Visa, Mastercard

Located 100 meters from the beach and the same distance form the principal town square, a modern hotel built in Mediterranean style; ideal for relaxing and fun holidays; large rooms with balconies or sea views and communal areas with a pleasant atmosphere.

ITI G.H.Colonna Capo Testa ★⁑ ♿ ★
*Capo Testa, tel. 0789754950
www.itihotels.it
Open May-September*

140 rooms. Restaurant, air conditioned, swimming pool, gym

Credit cards: American Express, Diners Club, Visa, Mastercard

This recently built hotel has favored Mediterranean style architecture, embellished with hand-carved stone and granite. The rooms, furnished with wooden furniture and

typical Sardinian fabrics,
are large and bright, some
with sea views; there is also
a park with garden furniture,
a private beach, a gym and
a shuttle service to Santa Teresa
di Gallura.

Marinaro ★★★
Via Angioy 48,
tel. 0789754112
www.hotelmarinaro.it
27 rooms. Restaurant,
air conditioned
Credit cards: American Express,
Visa, Mastercard
Located in the town center,
but not far from the sea, this
hotel provides functional
and modern rooms, and
a restaurant, the feather
in its cap, serving beautifully
prepared and unpretentious fish
dishes.

Miramare ★★★
Piazza della Libertà 6,
tel. 0789754103
Open mid May-mid October
14 rooms.
Credit cards: American Express,
Diners Club, Visa, Mastercard
By the sea and in the old town
center, this is a plain, white
building from which you can
see as far as Corsica. Simple,
homely accommodation.
Buffet breakfast.

Shardana ★★★ ♿
Santa Reparata, tel. 0789754031
www.hotelshardana.com
Open May-September
75 rooms. Restaurant, parking,
air conditioned, swimming pool
Credit cards: American Express,
Diners Club, Visa, Mastercard
An enchanting landscape of sea
and rocks; you can enjoy
a great deal of privacy
in the small renovated dwellings
which match the setting
perfectly. Buffet breakfast
and restaurant serving classic
cuisine; ideal for relaxing stays.

Restaurants

S'Andira ⑪
Santa Reparata,
via Orsa Minore 1,
tel. 0789754273
www.sandira.it
Open May-September
Cuisine: classic
Credit cards: American Express,
Diners Club, Visa, Mastercard
Friendly, with a lovely veranda
and gazebo for dining out
in summer. Serves mainly fish
with particular attention given
to the choice of ingredients;
good selection of typical
Sardinian cheeses, special
menus for food allergies.

SAN TEODORO

☑ **Ufficio Turistico**
Piazza Mediterraneo 1,
tel. 0784865767
www.santeodoroturismo.com

Hotels

Due Lune ★★★
Punta Aldia, tel. 0784864075
www.duelune.com
Open May-September
65 rooms. Restaurant, parking,
air conditioned, swimming pool,
tennis, gym
Credit cards: American Express,
Diners Club, Visa, Mastercard
Modern and elegant hotel with
sports and leisure facilities
(including a 9 hole golf course),
located in a good position near
the beach; buffet breakfast
and restaurant serving Sardinian
and classic cuisine.

Onda Marina ★★★
Via del Tirreno 24, tel. 0784865788
www.hotelondamarina.it
Open April-October
36 rooms. Restaurant, parking,
air conditioned
Credit cards: American Express, Visa
Three-story building, approximately
100 meters from the beach: simple
comforts, spacious rooms with sea
views and an elegantly furnished
restaurant also open to non guests.

Restaurants

Da Silvio ⑪ ♿ ★
Badualga, tel. 0784865090
Cuisine: Sardinian and fish
Credit cards: American Express,
Diners Club, Visa, Mastercard
Art nouveau style restaurant,
with a garden and terrace; island
specialties, mainly fish (also
vegetarian dishes). Pizzas too.

Lu Impostu ⑪
Lu Impostu, tel. 0784864076
Open mid May-September
Cuisine: fish
Credit cards: American Express,
Diners Club, Visa, Mastercard
This restaurant looks like a
typical Gallura stazzo, in an
excellent postion on Lu Impostu
beach, serving fish only.

SANTU LUSSURGIU

☑ **Comune**
tel. 07835519200
www.comunesantulussurgiu.it

Hotels

Antica Dimora del Gruccione ★★★ ♿
Via Michele Obinu 31,
tel. 0783552035
www.anticadimora.com

8 rooms. Restaurant
Credit cards: American Express,
Diners Club, Visa, Mastercard
18th century stone dwelling with
arches, vaults and exposed
beams. Each room is different,
some furnished with period
furniture, others in a more modern
style; breakfast with homemade
sweets, restaurant serving
traditional Sardinian food. Ideally
placed for excursions along the
coast and into the interior.

Sas Benas ★★★ ♿
Piazza S. Giovanni,
tel. 0783550870
9 rooms. Restaurant
Credit cards: American Express,
Diners Club, Visa, Mastercard
In the old town center, not far
from the sea and the principal
archaeological sites in the area.
Provides accommodation in
seven rooms and two suites
with basic, classic furnishings.

Restaurants

La Bocca del Vulcano ⑦
Via L. Alagon 27,
tel. 0783550974
www.laboccadelvulcano.it
Closed Sunday evening (except
by arrangement)
Cuisine: Sardinian
Credit cards: American Express,
Diners Club, Visa, Mastercard
A modern, family-run restaurant.
Among the outstanding
specialties the following deserve
a mention: gnochetti in a basket,
ravioli with wild boar sauce, wild
boar with cèpe mushrooms; you
must try the seadas with bitter
strawberry honey.

Sas Benas ⑦ ♿
Piazza S. Giovanni,
tel. 0783550870
Cuisine: Sardinian
Credit cards: American Express,
Diners Club, Visa, Mastercard
Friendly restaurant in the center
with a warm, homely atmosphere
and vaults in trachyte (a typical
stone of the area), where you
may try traditional, mainly meat
based, Sardinian specialties.
Their steak with cèpe mushrooms
and grilled meat is also excellent.

SASSARI

☑ **Ufficio Relazioni
con il pubblico**
Viale Dante 48, tel. 800327171
www.comune.sassari.it

Hotels

Carlo Felice ★★★ ♿
Via Carlo Felice 43,
tel. 079271440
www.bestwestern.it

★★★ ★★★ ★★★ ★★★ ★★ ★ Hotels ⑪⑪⑪⑪⑪ ⑪⑪⑪⑪ ⑪⑪⑪ ⑪ ⑦ Restaurants ♿ Disabled ★ Special TCI Rates

60 rooms. Restaurant, parking, air conditioned
Credit cards: American Express, Diners Club, Visa
Renovated building dating from 1964 providing accommodation in well-appointed rooms and new conference facilities, ideal for business people; restaurant serves Sardinian and classic cuisine, also open to non guests.

Frank Hotel ★★★
Via A. Diaz 20, tel. 079276456
www.frankhotel.com
103 rooms. Parking, air conditioned, gym
Credit cards: American Express, Visa, Mastercard
Large, centrally-located hotel with excellent facilities.
A good hotel for business people who may use the conference and meeting room. Buffet breakfast.

Grazia Deledda ★★★
Viale Dante 47, tel. 079271235
www.hotelgraziadeledda.it
127 rooms. Restaurant, parking, air conditioned, gym
Credit cards: American Express, Diners Club, Visa, Mastercard
Comfortable and efficient hotel dating from 1965; provides rooms and some suites for greater comfort; elegant and spacious communal areas, buffet breakfast.

Leonardo da Vinci ★★★ ★
Via Roma 79, tel. 079280744
www.leonardodavincihotel.it
118 rooms. Air conditioned
Credit cards: American Express, Diners Club, Visa, Mastercard
Located near the archaeological museum Sanna, this hotel is housed in a lovely modern building which has preserved its historical facade. Rooms have new furnishings, pleasant communal areas with marbles, sofas and an internet point, as well as good facilities for conferences and meetings, which make it suitable for business guests.

Rural Lodgings

Antichi Sapori
Campanedda, via Campanedda, tel. 079306213
www.antichisaporiagriturismo.it
Restaurant, swimming pool
In the north west part of the island, a simple but well-kept structure, with country-style and modern furnishings. The homely atmosphere, garden with garden furniture and closeness to the beach make it suitable for pleasant stays.
As well as breeding sheep

and pigs, the farm also grows olives, whose harvest is mainly destined for the kitchen.

Dettori
Campanedda, via Macomer 19, tel. 079306054
www.sardegnaturismo.net
Restaurant
This farm is in the country a few minutes by car from the beaches of Alghero, l'Argentiera, Porto Ferro or Stintino.
Signora Maria is skilled at preparing traditional Sardinian food using ingredients grown on the farm where they breed goats, pigs and chickens and grow olives.

Finagliosu
Palmadula, tel. 336777141
web.tiscali.it/finagliosu
Restaurant, mountain bike hire
Credit cards: American Express, Diners Club, Visa, Mastercard
We are in the peaceful countryside among the colors and fragrances of the maquis and grazing animals. Family run; Sardinian food prepared with homegrown ingredients. Nearby attractions include the irresistible sea, the ancient, picturesque mining village of Argentiera and Lake Baratz, the only natural lake in Sardinia, bordered by a splendid pinewood.

L'Agliastru
Campanedda, via Monte Casteddu-Podere 75, tel. 079306070
Restaurant
Equidistant from the beaches of Alghero, Castelsardo and Stintino, this farm, situated on the top of a hill with other similar buildings, offers a valid alternative to the crowding on the coast in the summer months.

Restaurants

Antica Hostaria ⁓⁓
Via Cavour 55, tel. 079200066
Closed Sunday
Cuisine: experimental Sardinian
Credit cards: American Express, Diners Club, Visa, Mastercard
The rooms are now larger and more comfortable while the food hasn't changed. Traditional dishes reworked in a modern key and a determination to use only what is seasonal.
Large cellar and exhaustive selection of oils and cheeses.

Castello ⁓⁓
Piazza Castello 7, tel. 079232041
Closed Wednesday
(except June-mid September)
Cuisine: classic
Credit cards: American Express,

Diners Club, Visa, Mastercard
Efficient and cordial management; cuisine reflects the seasons with an abundance of fish as well as meat dishes; good cellar and judicious selection of oils and cheeses.

Giamaranto ⁓⁓
Via Alghero 69, tel. 079274598
www.giamaranto.it
Closed Sunday
Cuisine: Sardinian and creative
Credit cards: American Express, Diners Club, Visa, Mastercard
Restaurant run with huge professionalism.
The atmosphere is very pleasant, the service cordial and efficient. The numerous dishes on the menu are prepared with local produce to traditional recipes.

Liberty ⁓⁓⁓
Piazza N. Sauro 3, tel. 079236361
Closed Sunday (in summer)
Cuisine: Sardinian
Credit cards: American Express, Diners Club, Visa, Mastercard
In an ancient building renovated in the style of art nouveau, an inviting restaurant which serves good regional cooking, mainly fish, outdoors and late in the evening in summer,.
Large assortment of oils, cold meats and cheeses, judicious selection of wines.

Senato ⁓⁓ ⅋
Via Alghero 36, tel. 079277788
Closed Sunday
Cuisine: Sardinian
Credit cards: American Express, Diners Club, Visa, Mastercard
Good regional cooking with a predominance of seafood and mushrooms when they are in season; do not miss the excellent Sardinian wines. This elegant restaurant is located in the business district of the city.

Museums

Museo Archeologico-Etnografico «Giovanni Antonio Sanna»
Via Roma 64, tel. 079272203
Opening times: Tuesday-Sunday 9.00-20.00.

Museo Diocesano del Tesoro del Duomo
Piazza Duomo, tel. 079232067-079233166
www.diocesi.sassari.it
Opening times: Tuesday, Friday, Saturday 10.00-12.00, 16.00-18.00.

Museo Geo-Mineralogico «Aurelio Serra»
via De Nicola 9, tel. 079229264-079229350
Opening times: Monday-Friday

9.00-13.00; Tuesday, Thursday also 15.30-17.30.

Museo Storico della Brigata Sassari
Piazza Castello 9, tel. 079233177
www.assonazbrigatasassari.difesa.it
Opening times: Monday-Friday 8.00-16.30; Saturday 8.00-13.00.

SENORBÌ

Hotels

Sporting Hotel Trexenta ★★★ &
Via Piemonte, tel. 0709809383
www.sht.it

32 rooms. Restaurant, parking, air conditioned, swimming pool, sauna, gym

Credit cards: American Express, Diners Club, Visa, Mastercard

Small art nouveau style hotel which opened in 1992, with well-appointed rooms and some comfortable suites; first class leisure and sports facilities; restaurant "Da Severino 2" serves Sardinian cuisine, also open to non guests.

Restaurants

Severino ⅋⅋
Via Piemonte 3, tel. 0709808181
Closed Monday
Cuisine: Sardinian
Credit cards: American Express, Visa, Mastercard

Its large seating capacity does not jeopardize the high standard of preparation of mainly fish dishes cooked to Sardinian and international recipes; do not miss the typical almond sweets.

SINISCOLA

Hotels

L'Aragosta ★★★
La Caletta, via Ciusa 11, tel. 0784810046
www.laragostahotel.com

27 rooms. Restaurant, parking, air conditioned, swimming pool

Credit cards: American Express, Diners Club, Visa, Mastercard

In a peaceful position, a stark, modern villa with many verandas and terraces; proven family management. Restaurant serves regional and classic cuisine, tables outdoors.

STINTINO

> ℹ️ **Pro Loco**
> *Piazza dei 45, tel. 079520081*
> *www.infostintino.com*

Hotels

Cala Rosa ★☆★
Ovile del Mercante, tel. 079520005

www.calarosa.it
Open April-October
120 rooms. Restaurant, parking, air conditioned, swimming pool, tennis

Credit cards: American Express, Diners Club, Visa, Mastercard

Close to Pelosa beach, this is a recently built hotel with elegantly furnished rooms and good leisure facilities.

Rural Lodgings

Cala Scoglietti
Pedro Nieddu, tel. 0783411660
www.sardegnaturismo.net

This is a famous spot for beach holidays. The farm is a little remote, in tranquil countryside; the coast may also be explored with horses from the nearby stables.

Depalmas Pietro
Preddu Niedu, tel. 079523129
Restaurant

2 km from the sea, this cereal-growing farm provides accommodation in six simple rooms with a modern feel. Natural, relaxing environment with Parco dell'Asinara, shooting and horse-riding nearby. Restaurant serves Sardinian dishes and home cooking, reservations are required.

Restaurants

Silvestrino ⅋⅋
Via Sassari 12, tel. 079523007
www.silvestrino.it
Closed Thursday (in low season)
Cuisine: Sardinian
Credit cards: American Express, Visa, Mastercard

In a picturesque location, with dining outside in the summer and an exhaustive choice of traditional fish and other dishes; typical Sardinian sweets for dessert.

Museums

Museo della Tonnara «Il Ricordo della Memoria» ★
Porto Stintino Mannu, tel. 079523357
Opening times: June-September: Monday-Sunday 17.00-20.00. Visits by arrangement in other periods

TEMPIO PAUSANIA

> ℹ️ **Pro Loco**
> *Piazza Gallura 2, tel. 079631273*

Hotels

Delle Sorgenti ★★★
Viale delle Fonti 6, tel. 079630033
27 rooms. Restaurant, parking
Credit cards: American Express, Visa

Its closeness to the Rinaggiu springs means that, as well as a relaxing holiday, you can also try spa treatments

Pausania Inn ★★★ &
SS 133 Tempio Pausania-Palau, km 1, tel. 079634037
www.hotelpausania.com

53 rooms. Restaurant, parking, air conditioned, swimming pool, tennis

Credit cards: American Express, Diners Club, Visa, Mastercard

Close to the town center, on the road which goes down to the sea, this hotel has been open since 1998, with well-kept, comfortable rooms, large communal areas and a terrace with a view and patio; restaurant serves typical Sardinian specialties.

Petit Hotel ★★★ & ★
Piazza A. De Gasperi 9, tel. 079631134
www.petit-hotel.it

59 rooms. Restaurant, air conditioned

Credit cards: American Express, Diners Club, Visa, Mastercard

Its central location and well-appointed rooms make this modern house a perfect example of local hospitality, thanks too to its management which places an emphasis on quality. Bright, well-furnished restaurant serves Sardinian and classic cuisine.

Rural Lodgings

Stazzo La Cerra & ★
Puchianna, tel. 079670972
www.agriturismolacerra.it
Restaurant

A breathtaking view of the Gallura interior; as for the sea, it is close to the Costa Smeralda and Parco Nazionale dell'Arcipelago della Maddalena. Organic farming workshops are held; a short distance away there is a farm restaurant serving local specialties and vegetarian dishes.

Museums

Museo Bernardo De Muro
Parco della Rimembranza, tel. 0796390080-079679952
Opening times: Summer: Monday-Friday 8.00-14.00, 16.30-19.30. Winter: Monday-Friday 8.00-14.00, 15.30-19.30.

TERME AURORA

Hotels

Aurora Terme ★★★ & ★
San Saturnino, tel. 079796871
www.termeaurora.it
Open June-November

★★☆ ★★★ ★★★ ★★ ★ Hotels ⅋⅋⅋⅋⅋ ⅋⅋⅋⅋ ⅋⅋⅋ ⅋⅋ ⅋ Restaurants & Disabled ★ Special TCI Rates

66 rooms. Restaurant, parking, air conditioned, swimming pool, tennis, gym

Credit cards: American Express, Diners Club, Visa, Mastercard

Modern, efficient complex, surrounded by a large park; recently refurbished rooms. Spa treatments with sulfuric waters containing sodium chloride, bromide and iodide; thermal swimming pool with hydromassage.

TERME DI SARDARA

Hotels

Antiche Terme di Sardara ★★★
Santa Maria, tel. 0709387025
www.termedisardara.it

100 rooms. Restaurant, parking, air conditioned, swimming pool, sauna, tennis, gym

Credit cards: American Express, Visa, Mastercard

A renovated, end of the 19th century hotel in a lovely park. Offers a relaxing atmosphere and a high standard of facilities, including a well-appointed beauty and wellness center (which are an integral feature of the hotel); regional and classic cuisine.

Eucalipti Terme ★★★ ♿
Santa Maria de is Acquas, tel. 0709385044
www.termesardegna.it

51 rooms. Restaurant, parking, air conditioned, swimming pool, tennis, gym

Credit cards: Visa, Mastercard

Low building in the heart of the countryside at the foot of the castle of Monreale; well-appointed and modernized, comfortable rooms; restaurant serves traditional cuisine; bar overlooks one of two thermal swimming pools; beauty center for face and body treatments.

TEULADA

| ℹ️ Pro Loco
Piazza Mazzini 8,
tel. 0709270032

Rural Lodgings

Coop. Agrituristica Matteu ★
Matteu, tel. 0709270003
Open by arrangement
Restaurant, bicycle hire
Credit cards: American Express, Diners Club, Visa, Mastercard

Rural lodging in green hills; pretty rooms with country-style furnishings overlooking an inner terrace with a gazebo and arbor, where you can try unpretentious cooking. Nearby there are the beaches and rocks of the picturesque Costa del Sud and, in the grounds, a nuragh.

Costa del Sud
Sa Tuerra, tel. 3493602181
www.terranostra.sardegna.it
Mountain bike hire

Near the pleasure boat harbor and the beaches of Chia, a pretty whitewashed building with light blue shutters. Pretty rooms with terracotta floors and wooden furnishings; lovely patio with tables and sun loungers and tables for simply lazing.

Is Truiscus
Su Mendulau, SS 195, tel. 0709271256
Restaurant, mountain bike hire
For lovers of the country and simplicity, accommodation in three large rooms furnished with handmade furniture and a lovely patio overlooking a large well-kept garden. You may take part in wild boar hunts.

Sa Tiria
SS 195, km 67,5, tel. 0709283704
digilander.iol.it/sa_tiria
Restaurant

Sa Tiria is the name, in Sardinian, of the broom which grows wild and tinges the countryside around this farm, lying halfway between the sea and the mountains, with yellow. Accommodation in rooms in a farm outhouse with disabled facilities. You may feast on traditional local cuisine prepared with farm produce.

Restaurants

Da Gianni ❙❙ ♿
Porto Budello, tel. 0709283015
Closed Monday
Cuisine: Sardinian
Credit cards: American Express, Diners Club, Visa, Mastercard

Trattoria housed in a remote farmhouse, whose furnishings reflect the country style and the informal nature of the environment. Traditional Sardinian fish cuisine based on the day's catch; small selection of regional wines.

TORTOLÌ

| ℹ️ Pro Loco
Via Mazzini 7,
tel. 0782622824

Hotels

Victoria ★★★ ♿
Via Mons. Virgilio 72, tel. 0782623457
www.hotel-victoria.it

60 rooms. Restaurant, parking, air conditioned, swimming pool

Credit cards: American Express, Diners Club, Visa, Mastercard

A perfect solution for business people, in the center and on the main street; provides a conference center, wi-fi internet access in the communal areas, swimming pool with solarium, American bar; buffet breakfast on the top floor with a terrace with a great view. Large restaurant under a different management.

Restaurants

Da Lenin ❙
Via S. Gemiliano 19, tel. 0782624422
Closed Sunday
Cuisine: fish
Credit cards: American Express, Diners Club, Visa, Mastercard

Regional cuisine, specialized in preparing rice and pasta dishes with seafood and fish from the sea; run with care and professionalism; specialties vary depending on what's available from the market.

VILLACIDRO

Museums

Museo di Santa Barbara
Piazza S. Barbara, tel. 070932018
Opening times: Saturday and Sunday 9.00-12.00, 16.00-20.00; Thursday 9.00-12.00. Visits by arrangement on other days.

VILLANOVAFORRU

Hotels

Funtana Noa ★★★ ♿
Via Vittorio Emanuele III 66/68, tel. 0709331019
www.residencefuntananoa.it

30 rooms. Restaurant, parking, air conditioned

Credit cards: American Express, Diners Club, Visa, Mastercard

On a slope surrounded by olive and almond trees, this recent building echoes local rural architecture, with an inner courtyard and fountain. Large, comfortable rooms, communal areas for socializing, reading room and restaurant serving traditional Sardinian cuisine.

Le Colline ★★★ ★
Funtana Jannus, tel. 0709300123

20 rooms. Restaurant, parking, air conditioned

Credit cards: American Express, Diners Club, Visa, Mastercard

This already comfortable hotel is now having a new extension built which will contain forty comfortable rooms; busy restaurant serves traditional, local and international cuisine.

Museums

Museo Archeologico Genna Maria
Piazza Costituzione,
tel. 0709300050-0709300048
www.provincia.cagliari.it
Opening times: Summer: Tuesday-Sunday 9.30-13.00, 15.30-19.00. Winter: Tuesday-Sunday 9.30-13.00, 15.30-18.00.

VILLASIMIUS

> ☑ **Ufficio Turistico**
> Piazza Giovanni XXIII,
> tel. 0707928017

Hotels

Atahotel Tanka Village Resort
★★★ ᠔ ★
Tanca Elmas, tel. 0707951
www.atahotels.it
Open May-September
903 rooms. Restaurant, parking, air conditioned, swimming pool, sauna, tennis, gym
Credit cards: American Express, Visa
On flat groundsurrounded by lush maquis, accommodation in comfortable apartments and bungalows (linked by a little train); five restaurants, one reserved for children; entertainment and many sports and leisure facilities. Various meeting rooms for business people plus an open air amphitheater with 450 seats

Cala Caterina ★★
Cala Caterina, via Lago Maggiore 32, tel. 070797410
www.mobygest.it
Open April-September
48 rooms. Restaurant, air conditioned, swimming pool
In one of the most picturesque corners of the south-east coast, in a secluded spot, a typical Mediterranean style building with well-appointed rooms. Facilities include a swimming pool, beauty center and restaurant serving Sardinian and classic cuisine. Lovely little sandy beach, just a short distance away, surrounded by the vegetati on which is unique to the island.

Cormoran-Le Residenze del Cormorano ★★★ ᠔
Campus, tel. 07079340
www.hotel-cormoran.com
Open mid May-mid October

120 rooms. Restaurant, parking, swimming pool, tennis
Credit cards: American Express, Diners Club, Visa, Mastercard
Made up of a circular building and a series of small villas, it offers hotel and residential accommodation.
On some evenings entertainment is provided in the garden; sunbathing and swimming from the adjacent beach; ideal for water sports enthusiasts but also for families with children.

Dell'Ancora ★★★ ᠔
Via del Mare 132, tel. 070791272
www.hoteldellancora.it
30 rooms. Restaurant, parking, air conditioned
Credit cards: American Express, Diners Club, Visa, Mastercard
The white and light blue hues and the use of stone and wood distinguish this hotel built in traditional Sardinian style, a few meters from the sea. Simple, cozy rooms with balconies, garden with tables for dining and live music entertainment; restaurant serving Sardinian and classic cuisine.

Le Zagare ★★★
Campus, S.P. to Villasimius, km 49, tel. 070791581
www.altamarea.it
Open May-September
54 rooms. Restaurant, parking, air conditioned, swimming pool, sauna
Credit cards: American Express, Diners Club, Visa, Mastercard
Deep in the heart of an orange grove, next to a residence providing various types of accommodation; the Mediterranean colors and a magnificent sea guarantee a tranquil ambience and an invigorating stay.

Simius Playa ★★★ ᠔
Via del Mare, tel. 07079311
www.simiusplaya.com
Open May-October
39 rooms. Restaurant, parking, air conditioned, swimming pool, tennis
Credit cards: American Express, Diners Club, Visa, Mastercard
Opposite an enchanting bay and a few meters from the sea; brand new decor; atmosphere comparable to a private residence; spacious and well-appointed rooms. Buffet breakfast, restaurant

serving Sardinian and classic cuisine.

Sofitel Thalassa Timi Ama
★★★ ᠔ ★
Notteri, tel. 07079791
www.sofitel.com
Open May-October
275 rooms. Restaurant, parking, air conditioned, swimming pool, sauna, tennis, gym
Credit cards: American Express, Diners Club, Visa, Mastercard
Near the pool of Notteri (famous for its pink flamingoes) this is a new construction with every imaginable facility, including conference, sports and leisure facilities; some suites, large rooms, two restaurants, one of which is on the beach and has fish barbecues. Entertainment and kids' club, new beauty center "Thalassa".

Stella Maris ★★★ ᠔
Campulongu, tel. 070797100
www.stella-maris.com
Open Pasqua-Epifania
53 rooms. Restaurant, parking, air conditioned, swimming pool, tennis
Credit cards: American Express, Visa, Mastercard
In the middle of Campulongu bay, a recently built, well-appointed Mediterranean style hotel with sports and leisure facilities. Buffet breakfast; restaurant serves classic and Sardinian cuisine.

Restaurants

Il Moro ¶¶
Villaggio dei Mandorli,
tel. 070798180
Closed Tuesday (except in summer)
Cuisine: Sardinian
Credit cards: American Express, Visa, Mastercard
Pristine environment with a large garden for dining outside in the summer; traditional flavors and fragrances with grilled meats and mixed roasts very much in evidence.

Museums

Museo Archeologico
Via Frau 5, tel. 070790023
www.villasimiusweb.com
Opening times: 15th June-15th September: Tuesday-Sunday 10.00-13.00, 21.00-24.00. 16th September-14th June: Tuesday-Thursday 10.00-13.00; Friday-Sunday 10.00-13.00, 17.00-19.00. Visits also by arrangement

METRIC CONVERTIONS

DISTANCE

Kilometres/Miles

km to mi	mi to km
1 = 0.62	1 = 1.6
2 = 1.2	2 = 3.2
3 = 1.9	3 = 4.8
4 = 2.5	4 = 6.4
5 = 3.1	5 = 8.1
6 = 3.7	6 = 9.7
7 = 4.3	7 = 11.3
8 = 5.0	8 = 12.9

Meters/Feet

m to ft	ft to m
1 = 3.3	1 = 0.30
2 = 6.6	2 = 0.61
3 = 9.8	3 = 0.91
4 = 13.1	4 = 1.2
5 = 16.4	5 = 1.5
6 = 19.7	6 = 1.8
7 = 23.0	7 = 2.1
8 = 26.2	8 = 2.4

WEIGHT

Kilograms/Pounds

kg to lb	lb to kg
1 = 2.2	1 = 0.45
2 = 4.4	2 = 0.91
3 = 6.6	3 = 1.4
4 = 8.8	4 = 1.8
5 = 11.0	5 = 2.3
6 = 13.2	6 = 2.7
7 = 15.4	7 = 3.2
8 = 17.6	8 = 3.6

Grams/Ounces

g to oz	oz to g
1 = 0.04	1 = 28
2 = 0.07	2 = 57
3 = 0.11	3 = 85
4 = 0.14	4 = 114
5 = 0.18	5 = 142
6 = 0.21	6 = 170
7 = 0.25	7 = 199
8 = 0.28	8 = 227

TEMPERATURE

Fahrenheit/Celsius

F	C
0	-17.8
5	-15.0
10	-12.2
15	-9.4
20	-6.7
25	-3.9
30	-1.1
32	0
35	1.7
40	4.4
45	7.2
50	10.0
55	12.8
60	15.5
65	18.3
70	21.1
75	23.9
80	26.7
85	29.4
90	32.2
95	35.0
100	37.8

LIQUID VOLUME

Liters/U.S. Gallons

L to gal	gal to L
1 = 0.26	1 = 3.8
2 = 0.53	2 = 7.6
3 = 0.79	3 = 11.4
4 = 1.1	4 = 15.1

Liters/U.S. Gallons

L to gal	gal to L
5 = 1.3	5 = 18.9
6 = 1.6	6 = 22.7
7 = 1.8	7 = 26.5
8 = 2.1	8 = 30.3

GENERAL INDEX

GLOSSARY

Acropolis
Fortified high city area or citadel of an ancient city

Ambo
Raised platform in an early Christian church from which parts of the service were conducted

Amphitheater
Oval or round building with tiers or seats around a central arena, used in ancient Roman times for gladiatorial contests and shows

Anticella
Ante-chamber, or space before the cella (the principal chamber or enclosed part of a classical temple)

Apse
Part of a church at the end of the nave; generally semi-cylindrical in shape, with a semi-spherical roof.

Architrave
Horizontal support or beam above a door or opening.

Ashlar
Type of external wall covering, made of protruding, roughly-hewn stones

Atrium
Forecourt of an early Christian church, flanked or surrounded by porticoes.
Also an open-air central court around which a house is built.

Basilica
Rectangular-shaped building, used in Roman times for the administration of justice. In early Christian times, used for worship, and generally having a central nave and side aisles, possibly with apse.

Bastion
Projecting part of a fortification, in the form of an irregular pentagon.

Capital
Part which links a column to the structure above. In classical architecture, capitals were Doric, Ionian or Corinthian

Cavea
Spectator seating of a theater or amphitheater, usually divided into sections which were assigned to different social classes.

Cella
Principal chamber or enclosed part of a classical temple where the cult image was kept

Choir
Area for choir members, either in front of or behind the main altar in the church presbytery

Counter-facade
Internal wall of the facade of a building

Curtain (wall)
Masonry fortifications, walls and towers, built around castle

Cusp
Cone- or pyramid-shaped ornamental decoration, and relief work; typical of Gothic period

Domus de janas
Neolithic Sardinian tombs cut out of the rock; the words mean "houses of the fairies"

Drum
Part of a cupola, with vertical walls, which the dome extends from

Edicule
Small, classical-style structure, containing a sacred image, either inside a church or building or standing on its own

Ex-voto
Object given in thanks for grace received from a saint or the Virgin; generally a painting, or wood or silver object, related in some way to the grace received

Greek cross
Cross with arms of equal length

Hypogeum
Subterranean excavation for burial of the dead

Latin Cross
Cross with a longer vertical arm than horizontal arm

Loculus, pl. loculi
Place of burial, rectangular in shape and built into a wall, or found in walls of catacombs.

Lunette
Semi-circular space on a wall, vault or ceiling, often decorated with a painting or relief

Necropolis
Pre-Christian tombs grouped in or over a particular area, or the area itself

Oratory
Place of worship or church, reserved for certain people or communities

Portal
Doorway, gate or entrance, especially an imposing one

Predella
Small painting, usually in sections, attached below a large altar piece

Presbytery
Part of the church where the main altar is situated; generally raised or separated from the rest of the nave by a balustrade or such like

Pronaos
Front part or entrance area to a building, with columns

Retablo
Large wooden structures, placed behind the church altar, and made by assembling various component parts

in wood (panels, frames); from the Latin retro tabula, meaning "behind the altar"

Sacellum
In ancient times, a small roofless temple consecrated to a deity; later, a chapel in a church

Sacristy
Part of church where furnishing and vestments are kept, and where clergy prepare for services

Simulacrum
Sacred image or statue, sometimes central to a procession

Tetrastyle
Describing a building or temple with a portico of three columns at one end

Tophet
Sanctuary, or holy area, for Phoenician and Carthaginian divinities

Transept
Area perpendicular to the nave, often extending out at the sides and giving the building a cross-shaped ground-plan

Truss
Projection from the face of a wall, often serving to support a cornice.

Uraeus
Representation of the sacred snake, as an emblem of supreme power; worn by Egyptian divinities and sovereigns

Vestibule
Ante-chamber, entrance hall or lobby

PICTURE CREDITS

Notes